RED MEXICO

Francis McCULLAH

RED

MEXICO

Foreword by
Bishop Martín DÁVILA GÁNDARA

Historical appendix by
María Concepción MÁRQUEZ SANDOVAL, Ph.D.

Reconquista Press

Originally published in 1928 by Brentano's Ltd.,
London

Front cover: Capitain Alcantar (courtesy of the Museo Cristero /
Centro de Estudios Cristeros Alfredo Hernández Quezada of
Encarnación de Díaz in Jalisco).

ISBN 978-1-912853-10-6

CONTENTS

Part IV
MEXICO AND AMERICA

FOREWORD

NINETY years after Francis McCullagh first published *Red Mexico*, Reconquista Press has had the excellent idea of reprinting this important book, a transcendent work making clear the truth about the historical causes of the first armed revolution in the last century. As such, it is full of interesting experiences of the author, as well as a very good documentation of the time.

After nine decades since the first edition of this work, I see it necessary through this foreword, to consider and focus on the points that could better clarify the data and information given by the author.

"He who loves his life will lose it. He who hates his life in this world will keep it to eternal life" (John XII, 25).

The socialist revolution in Mexico, misnamed the "Mexican Revolution," had wreaked havoc, and it was not so long after, a time plagued by misfortunes for the country and the Catholic Church, that the anti-Christian Constitution was promulgated in 1917.

This legal instrument unleashed terrible persecutions against the Catholics, for its measures were alien to the feelings of the Mexican population, which was mainly Catholic (97%), and which suffered from the conspiracy of a minority in the service of the Masonic Grand Lodges of the Scottish, York, and National Mexican rites.

This anti-Mexican conflict would not have occurred if President Plutarco Elías Calles had acted as a fair and neutral governor respecting the Mexican and Catholic people. But the instruction of the Masonic Lodges in the United States was firstly to foster a socialist revolution in our country, and then impose *ejidos* or common land division similar to the *kolkhoz* of the Soviet Union.

Religious persecution and an evil desire to eliminate religion through the shedding of blood has been the constant feature of all Masonic revolutions; first the French, then the Mexican, the Spanish, the Cuban and the Russian. With the gender ideology of a few decades ago, the World Revolution has changed tactics, they have learned that spilling blood and murdering Christians cannot eradicate the Catholic religion. In Mexico, from the communist Álvaro Obregón, then Lázaro Cárdenas, and through atheist Marxist teachings, sexual education in schools began to have better results for that ominous cause.

The Cristero War can be called a true and authentic counter-revolution, as it opposed the main aims of the Communist revolution, which emanated from and was sponsored by the financiers of a "capitalist" country, controlled behind the scenes by the power of Freemasonry.

The Mexican Communist Revolution had mainly to do with the imposition of "directive 6" of the New Orleans lodges, which consisted in dividing the Mexican agricultural field into *ejidos* (Soviet *kolkhozes*). The purpose of this was not the better productive use of the land, nor the just and fair distribution of the countryside, but the economic ruin and political control of the peasants to whom the government lent the land, this is how the famous "*agraristas*" were born.

The same thing that happened in the countryside was done in the cities, with the unions controlled by the socialist government, having tied the workers with the exclusion clause if they were not docile to the policies and desires of the rulers. These *agraristas* and unionized workers, controlled by the government, were later used by Elías Calles in the struggle against the Cristeros. The armed struggle of 1910 began because neither Porfirio Díaz, nor Francisco I. Madero, nor much less Victoriano Huerta, accepted the directive 6 that the Grand Orient wanted to impose on them. Carranza was favored because he accepted part of the directive 6, and also persecuted the Church in part and instituted the famous Constitution of 1917, whose articles against the Church were written in the secret lodges.

In the case of President Victoriano Huerta, neither Villistas nor Zapatistas together, armed by the lodges, could overthrow his government; that is why the Yankee army intervened to impose Masonic laws. This is how the invasion and disembarkation of troops in Veracruz occurred again to defeat Huerta and install a dynasty of pro-marxist rulers.

The Cristeros arose in 1926, and if they had won the war as was expected in mid-1929, the armed freemasonry would have intervened to re-establish the Masonic government of Calles as they had already planned, and as they had previously done against Huerta. This was not necessary because the Cristeros were first infiltrated by false Catholics, and betrayed by a conspiracy between the designated bishops, the US ambassador and the Vatican Secretary of State, the denounced Mason Pietro Gasparri; who, according to the wise Marquis de La Franquerie, betrayed the confidence of Pope Pius XI.

According to La Franquerie, Gasparri was formed in the Masonic circle of the communist cardinal Mariano Rampolla del Tindaro (*Chiesa Viva*, Magazine No. 51, March 1976).

Gasparri directed everything from Rome, sending altered messages to the Cristeros and the bishops, negotiating in secret with Morrow, the United States ambassador, with the Masonic government, and directing the liberal bishops, who concluded the treacherous arrangements for the Church and the Cristeros along with the anti-religious, freemason and liberal government of Portes Gil, a puppet of Calles.

Likewise, the betrayal of the Cristeros was carried out by General Jesús Degollado Guízar (nephew of Bishops Antonio and Rafael Guízar and cousin of the pederast Marcial Maciel Degollado-Guízar, founder of the Legionaries of Christ), who handed over the Cristero General Enrique Gorostieta and thousands of fighters with the false promise of an armistice.

Degollado Guízar came out well after the arrangements, unlike the other Cristero leaders who were deported or arrested and killed after handing over their weapons.

The years from 1926 to 1929 were lavish in martyrs who, faithful to Christ, preferred to die rather than deny Him. Our country was soaked with the blood of brothers; federalists, *agraristas* and Cristeros—all Catholics—facing a tremendous struggle against the imposition of anti-Christian ideologies on the Mexican people, a struggle that would cost thousands of lives.

The anti-Christian government intended to pull the Cross of Christ out of Mexico, but a whole population told with their blood that they preferred to die rather than to change their King; a whole population with their blood, legitimized the reign of Christ in our homeland. The essence of the diabolical struggle against God and the Holy Catholic Church continues, thus the importance of this work by Francis McCullagh, whose stories revive the anguish of people suffering the betrayal of their rulers in favor of the anti-Mexican interests.

Today, just like a century ago, we ask God and the Blessed Virgin of Guadalupe, our Blessed Mother, to protect us.

Mons. Martín Dávila Gándara.
A Catholic Bishop on missions.

PREFACE

THE political and economic position of Mexico at the present moment is very critical; and, despite a vast amount of bluster on the part of President Calles, that truculent gentleman has sunk into what is practically a condition of dependence on the United States which, without having recourse to military measures, can bring him to heel any time it likes by financial pressure or by the manipulation of the Arms Embargo.

Up till 1914, a Mexican President could sometimes play off Europe against the Northern Colossus, but Calles cannot do so now, and no ruler of Mexico can ever do so again, for Europe has carried out a diplomatic evacuation of Latin America.

There is something pathetic, therefore, in the mad floundering of the large, uneducated man who is at present the Dictator of Mexico. Towards the end of the year 1926, he plunged about wildly, like a whale that had been harpooned; but he only succeeded in entangling himself more and more. By his foolish persecution of the Mexican Church, he has overcome all the deep repugnance of the Episcopate, the clergy, and the landowners for the *Gringo*, who would now be welcomed as a deliverer.

In his speeches he strikes a strong nationalistic note, but by his acts he weakens Mexican Nationalism, and increases the number of Mexicans who speak English, and are more familiar with the north side of the Rio Grande than the south side. These results he obtains, in spite of himself, (1) by his banishment of religion from the schools, a measure which has made many Mexican parents send their children to Catholic schools in the

United States; (2) by his expulsion of political opponents who bring their families with them to San Antonio, El Paso or Los Angeles; (3) by his confiscatory Agrarian laws which have driven north so many Mexican ranchers and *hacendados*, and (4) by his persecution of the clergy which has driven large numbers of them into the United States where the younger ones, at all events, will have to learn English and may probably become more or less Americanized. I do not mean that it would be bad for them to become Americanized: I only cite their case to show how Calles, despite his furious nationalism, is breaking Mexican nationalism to pieces.

By the economic difficulties which he has provoked, Calles has caused 15 per cent of the working population of Mexico, comprising the best Mexican peons and artisans to cross the frontier into Texas, New Mexico, Arizona, and California, where there are now about three million Mexicans who have learned English and become accustomed to American institutions. Even if many of these emigrants return to their native land, they will only come to prepare the way for the American advance. In 1928 the population of Mexico was two and a half millions less than it had been in 1914. On 21st June, 1927, the *Excelsior* newspaper of Mexico City estimated that the Mexicans were leaving Mexico at the rate of 5,000 per day and said that their places were being taken by Chinese and Japanese. It pointed out that in some places, Mexicali for example, there are now more Chinese than Mexicans. General López, the Governor of Guerrero, was so alarmed at the exodus that he suggested gifts of land to intending emigrants, but the *Excelsior* pointed out that the workmen and peons preferred the United States, not because they could get land there but because they could go to church, have their children taught religion, and feel that their little savings would not be arbitrarily confiscated by the Police.

Thus, Plutarco Elías Calles, this bewildered and half-savage Dictator who hates the United States and detests the English language, is doing more than any Mexican President ever did to throw his country under the feet of the United States, and to make his people speak English.

The New York papers sometimes flatter him, describe him as a man of iron, and praise his Napoleonic energy; but his political conduct is that of a madman. Mexico, with its fifteen million inhabitants in a country nearly four times as large as France, is dangerously under-populated, and its population is dwindling instead of increasing. A strong dictator who was at the same time wise would concentrate on the encouragement of immigration, especially from Italy whose immigrants have been worth their weight in gold to Argentina and who are practically shut out of the United States. But Calles not only fails to get European emigrants; as we have just seen, he is losing even his Mexicans; and the Chinese who are replacing them are a poor substitute.

He got into difficulties simultaneously with the Church, the Mexican landowners, the foreign landowners and the Oil men. Two years ago he foolishly tried his hand at foreign politics, and attempted to organise a Central American League against the Yankee, but by March, 1928, he had calmed down considerably, owing no doubt to the soothing assurances of Mr. Dwight W. Morrow, the American Ambassador, and was apparently without any foreign policy at all.

He may break out again before he leaves office in July, 1928; or he may persuade his fellow dictator, Obregón, to break out; and in any case the absorption of Mexico can hardly be expected to be painless and uneventful.

But that Mexico will eventually fall under some sort of American Protectorate seems fairly certain. The great increase of American interests in the Caribbean, and in Central America, and her determination to dig another trans-Oceanic Canal, this time through Nicaragua; all these facts will lead gradually and almost imperceptibly to Mexico being caught in the same silken toils as Cuba. In ten years' time we shall probably see America intervening in Mexico as a matter of course and in accordance with treaty, whenever a revolution breaks out in that country, exactly as she intervenes to-day in Cuba and Haiti. The United States will never feel sure of her two canals till she has acquired a definite protectorate over all the countries lying between them and the Rio Grande.

I must admit that all the Americans whom I met during a long journey in the United States last year were strongly opposed to armed intervention in Mexico, but in all probability there will be no armed intervention. Through the mistakes of her rulers, and the inexorable force of circumstances, and the tremendous power of American finance and industry, Mexico will drift imperceptibly into the American orbit as some of the native States of Central India drifted into the English orbit.

Even after one crosses the frontier into Mexico at Laredo or El Paso or Nogales, one still seems to feel the throbbing of that colossal machine in the north; and one easily realises on such occasions how damaging the very vibrations of such a machine run be to an old building which is unprotected against them.

And Mexico is entirely defenceless now. Calles has rendered her so by the acute divisions he has created among the people, by the foolish expectations lie has aroused among the peasants and artizans, by the lawlessness he has let loose all over the Republic. She was not always defenceless. Only fourteen years ago, she was still perfectly safe under the strong Conservative administration of General Victoriano Huerta, and she would have not only remained safe but increased in prosperity and in strength if merely allowed to grow normally in her own way and at her own slow rate.

Unfortunately she was disturbed by the hysterical interference of President Wilson who wanted, forsooth, to give every peon a vote, though his charity might better have begun at home with the negroes of his own South who all have a vote but are never allowed to use it.

In race, religion, history, education, and development, the Mexicans differ profoundly from their neighbours in the North. Out of a population of fifteen millions, there are only about one million White men; and, though the pure-blooded Indians do not number more than three or four millions, the Mestizos or half-castes are practically Indian. The little white blood in their veins has been absorbed, with the result that Mexico cannot be called a White country. And not being a White country, it cannot at present be treated as one; hence the futility of President Wilson's panacea of votes and democratic government.

No race can be branded with the stigma of eternal inferiority; and in due course the Mexican race might have been fit for manhood suffrage; but, by trying to force a democratic system of Government on the Mexicans before they were prepared for it, President Wilson only succeeded in throwing Mexico into the hands of a small gang of unprincipled men filled with crude Bolshevik theories and mad with anti-clericalism. Calles is one of these men; and though he will probably have left office by the time this book appears, his successor will carry on his work, and he himself will be close at hand in case of emergencies. What I say of Calles, therefore, is equally applicable to the next President if the Sonora gang still remains in power; and at the time of writing (March, 1928) there is not the slightest prospect of it being driven from power.

President Wilson's action was not due to the adoption of a new policy at the White House: on the contrary it was due to a policy a hundred years old. As I shall show in the course of this book, the Government of the United States has always favoured those Mexicans who leant towards Socialism and anti-clericalism; and this support has been fatal to Mexico which required a long period of Conservative oligarchic rule or of dictatorship *à la* Porfirio Díaz or *à la* Mussolini.

In one word, America's interference with Mexico ruined Mexico; and it is a noteworthy fact that most of the Latin-American countries, north of the Equator, have been similarly injured, more or less, by the same cause, I mean the Central American Republics, the West Indian Islands, Venezuela, Colombia and Ecuador. The further one gets away from the United States in the direction of the South Pole, the stronger and healthier is the growth of the Latin civilisation. The strongest and most successful growths of all are to be found in Argentina and Chile, which could not get further away from Uncle Sam unless they fell into the Polar Sea.

At first sight, this seems to be a case of almost superhuman craft, the work of super-Machiavellis, but of course Uncle Sam only blundered into this position. To a suspicious Latin-American, however, the whole business would look very black; and I may say that no Sinn Feiner was ever so suspicious of England as Latin-Americans are of *El Coloso del Norte*. Let us see how the position would look to such a Latin-American. Instead of allowing Mexico to develop slowly but surely in its own way, Uncle Sam interfered constantly for seventy long years, always on the side of the Socialistic, disruptive, anti-Catholic party. He asserted loudly, every time he interfered, that his only object was to help the cause of liberty, education, true religion, and good government, but somehow or other he managed to annex a substantial slice of Mexican territory after every one of these philanthropic crusades. In 1819 he bagged Florida; in 1845 Texas and New Mexico; in 1853 Arizona. Incidentally he also got more or less of a hold of Cuba, Panama, Haiti, Puerto Rico, Honduras and Santo Domingo.

With regard to Mexico, he has done worse to that unfortunate country than deprive her of half her territory; he has forced on her a Socialistic and anti-religious gang which could never have got into power without American assistance, and which will keep her forever weak, divided and undeveloped.

But the masterstroke of Machiavellianism is still to come. When urged to help the decent people of Mexico to get rid of this illegal and incompetent Government, Uncle Sam turns up the whites of his eyes and declares that never, never will he intervene in the affairs of another nation. President Wilson actually used words to this effect in a speech he made to a Mexican delegation in Washington on the 9th of May, 1919, *after* he had bombarded Vera Cruz and landed troops there, with the object of driving out the Conservative Huerta and installing as President the anti-clerical Carranza.

President Coolidge had nothing to do with the victory of Carranza, but he is well aware that by refusing to intervene or even to use economic or financial pressure or the Arms Embargo in order to help the Mexican Conservatives to get a better Government, he is taking a course which will lead to the disruption of his southern neighbour, whereas, by helping the Catholics into power, he would offend the Methodists, the Baptists, the Pacifists, and the Morgans, and might be instrumental in creating, south of the Rio Grande, a strong, Conservative Government which might in future neutralise American influence in its territories by giving valuable concessions to Englishmen and other Europeans and introducing large numbers of European immigrants. As a matter of fact, what incensed President Wilson more than anything else against President Victoriano Huerta was the fact that Huerta was favourable to Lord Cowdray and other British concessionaires.

I have dwelt at considerable length on this point because it is the key to this book. The theory underlying all of the following pages is that America is largely responsible for the sad plight in which Mexico finds herself to-day. In 1914 President Wilson helped into the saddle a very disreputable gang of Mexicans, who are in the saddle still, riding roughshod over everything the Mexican esteems, his religion, his law, his system of education, his family life. I dwell at particular length on the religious question because it seems to me the most important of all.

Some sensitive reviewers of this book may object to the horrible details of executions which I give in Part III, but my answer to them is that I give those details deliberately in order to arouse the conscience of the public to what is happening in Mexico. The newspapers for which these reviewers write have adopted a policy of silence, but this policy has led, in my opinion, to the perpetration of more murders by Calles and his gang. A contrary policy, namely, the fullest publicity with regard to Mexico, would have frightened the Mexican Dictators as it frightened the Russian Dictators in 1923 when they murdered Monsignor Budkiewicz. The outburst of indignation in Europe and America prevented the slaughter from going further on that occasion, and, in the opinion of great authorities on Russia, like Sir Bernard Pares, saved the lives of Archbishop Cieplak and Patriarch Tikhon.

When the murders in Mexico began, early in 1927, a similar outburst of indignation would have saved many innocent lives, but when Calles perceived that the outer world maintained complete silence, he piled murder on murder, and became more and more careless about even the appearance of legality, until, finally, the culmination was reached in the four-fold murder of 23rd November, 1928 which I describe in Part III. That atrocity was carried out with such complete and open contempt for every kind of legality that one Protestant Socialist writer, who is as a rule friendly to Calles, was moved to write in the radical *New Republic* of New York that "every constitutional guarantee was violated" in the case of Father Pro and his three companions, that they were given no trial, that no evidence other than mere suspicion was ever advanced against them, that the Press of Mexico City openly professed to believe that the victims were innocent. This writer was Mr. Carleton Beals who was in Mexico City at the time of the murders. He added that Father Pro had been put to death with the direct approval of Calles; and he might have added that on the evening of 22nd November, General Cruz, the Chief of Police, received definite orders from President Calles that this priest was to be executed at once, and that when Cruz was asked what formalities were to be observed in order that some appearance of legality should be given, Calles replied: "*No quiero formas, sino el hecho*" (I don't want formalities, what I want is the fact).

If the reader will turn to the description I give of the Mexican Dictator's character in chapter IV, part II, and to the facts by which I support my statements, he will see that Calles is one of those bullies who are only led into greater excesses by the retreat of their victims. Now, the silence of the world Press has had the same effect on Calles as a retreat: it has made him murder innocent men with an absolute contempt for even the appearance of justice, and it will make him continue doing so until he is stopped by an outburst of indignation or, at all events, by a detailed examination of his proceedings in the great newspapers of America and Europe.

If the publication of the terrible story which I give in Part III leads to such an examination, I shall have attained the object which I had in mind when I began to write this book.

It does not matter to me whether some newspapers take the side of Calles; all I want is that this Mexican question be thoroughly ventilated, and that impartial reporters be sent out to examine it. An examination of the question by some of the Belfast papers might possibly lead them to the conclusion that the Mexican Catholics deserve what they got, but even that antagonism I would regard as healthy and hopeful; it is silent indifference that is unhealthy and hopeless and dead; such indifference is a veritable paralysis of the soul. Besides, what right have the groups of rich men who control most of the English and American newspapers to deprive the poor man of his news? No more right, I say, than the rich Prohibition Party in the United States has to deprive the poor man of his beer. We have no guarantee that this veil of silence may not be dropped over other subjects which newspaper magnates and their powerful friends in finance and in politics may not wish the common herd to discuss. Who is to decide? Best publish "all the news that's fit to print," to use the motto of a New York paper which certainly does not live up to that motto so far as its Mexican news is concerned.

Why have a Press at all, if a taboo can thus be placed on important subjects? A voluntary censorship is just as bad for the public as any other kind of censorship, if it leads to concealment of the truth. If Americans and Englishmen believe in publicity, why do they not give publicity to the Mexican question?

I deal with this matter here, owing to a suspicion that, in books of this kind, reviewers seldom get beyond the preface, but I intend to deal at greater length, towards the end of this work, with the question of the Press. I should like to say here, however, that the principal culprit is the American Press, for Mexico lies in the American journalistic sphere of influence and the only regular foreign journalists in that country are Americans.

When I returned from Russia to London in 1923 with an eye-witness's account of a Soviet trial where I saw two Catholic Prelates condemned to death, the English Press placed no limit to the space which it gave to that subject, and at an indignation meeting presided over by Lord Burnham at King's College, London University, I was supported on the platform by representatives of nearly all the principal religious denominations in England, including Dean Inge, a high officer of the Salvation Army, and the Chief Rabbi.

Now that I bring an equally authentic account, not of two death sentences but of several thousands of death sentences, I find that the newspapers "do not want to touch the subject." Yet the Russian persecution was merely incidental, for the supreme Bolshevik leaders have only a contempt for religion; it was brainless subordinates like Krylenko, "the everlasting student," who staged the Cieplak trial; whereas, on the other hand, the crushing of the Church is the principal item in Calles' programme. This was admitted by Señor Tejeda, Secretary of State in the Calles Administration, in a speech reported in all the newspapers of Mexico City on the 18th of November, 1927. Señor Tejeda's words were as follows: "The most delicate and transcendental problem which confronted General Calles was, without doubt, the religious question, because it affected the future of the country, and for that reason it was carefully thought out beforehand."

In America there is even more reticence. The worthy captains of industry who edit the *Chicago Tribune* point out as an excuse for their silence, that Mexico is a long way off and that not many people can possibly be interested. But the American Press published an enormous amount of matter on the Cieplak trial, though Russia is still further off, and though that trial resulted in only one execution. It may be urged that the corruption which is said to exist among some of the Indian *padres* in Mexico makes people reluctant to support them, but which of us is sinless enough to cast the first stone? These poor men might have had comfort and comparative wealth to-day if they had joined the Schismatic Church which has been founded by "Patriarch" Pérez, under the auspices of Calles, or if they accepted the anti-religious laws, but not a dozen have done so; all the rest prefer to suffer hardship, imprisonment, and sometimes death.

What Church is free from scandal? Not the Russian Church, which the English and American Press so enthusiastically supported even at a time when Rasputin was practically the supreme head of it, and even when, at a later period, some of its bishops and priests had gone over to the Reds.

Much of the information about Mexico which is to be found in the following pages was obtained by me during two trips to that country, one in 1924 at the beginning of the Calles regime, and the other in 1927. I might add that I also spent about a year travelling through Latin America from the Panama Canal to southern Chile.

A final word on the question of the nomenclature employed—an important matter in Latin America, though in London or New York it might seem unworthy of attention.

As the Mexicans also call themselves Americans and consider that they have as much right to do so as the people of the United States, and as Mexico is a Federal Republic made up of united states and situated in North America, there is always some difficulty about nomenclature, especially as one does not like to use the term "Yankee" or *Gringo* and cannot use the Spanish word *Estadunidense*. I have decided however, for the sake of clearness to follow the usual practice, that is to call the natives of Mexico Mexicans, and the people of the United States Americans.

I beg to acknowledge with sincere thanks my indebtedness to Mr. Eber Cole Byam of New Mexico for the historical material which I have used in chapter IV, part I.

London,
July 1, 1928.

WHY MEXICO HAS SUCH A BAD GOVERNMENT

CHAPTER I

MEXICO AND RUSSIA

MEXICO reminds me of Soviet Russia. In both countries a small ruling clique is trying to force on the people a system which the people detest, to de-Christianize them, to change the names of their towns, to cut off all their connection with the past. "We are the men who are out to destroy all tradition in Mexico," said Calles to the delegates of the American Federation of Labour when they paid homage to him in the Chapultepec Palace four years ago; and it is typical of the times we live in that, despite those words, and despite the acts which have followed them the A. F. of L. (a body which contains many pious Catholics, two of them vice-Presidents), persists to this day in believing that there is no religious persecution in Mexico.

This is typical, I say, of the times in which we live. Four hundred years ago Christians disputed about things which had happened and words which were uttered over fifteen centuries earlier, but now they dispute about things which are taking place under their very noses, and about words which are uttered at their very ears. There are cranks who will declare to be white what everyone else sees to be black: in 1918 an English journalist, carried away by his enthusiasm for Lenin, declared the Bolsheviks to be "white as snow," and made this declaration in Moscow itself. It was a case of colour-blindness due to prejudice. Such cases are common in the modern world, and they would make the task of the historian difficult if he were foolish enough to exhaust himself in hopeless arguments with such cranks, and failed to remember that there is a large fair-minded public which will judge any case with impartiality.

"Comrade" Litvinov declared in 1923 that there was "no religious persecution in Russia" though two Catholic Prelates had just been condemned to death under circumstances which proved that there was persecution, and many people in the West took Litvinov's word for it. To-day, President Calles says: "*in Méjico no nay persecución religiosa*"; and there are people who believe him despite the evidence of his own anti-religious laws and of his own acts of repression.

In Russia eighty per cent of the population are opposed to the Soviet Government, so much so that outside the great towns, the life of a Government official is not safe. In Mexico the opposition to the Calles Government is equally strong. But in both countries the ruling clique has dug itself in with such skill, and punishes its enemies with such cruelty that there is no immediate prospect of its being dislodged.

How, then, did that clique come into power? The Bolsheviks seized power in a time of war, revolution and general upheaval. As I have already pointed out in my preface the Mexican Reds were actually helped into the saddle by Mr. Woodrow Wilson, President of the United States. How this came to pass, I shall explain later.

Travelling through Mexico at the present moment, one is reminded at every turn of Soviet Russia. Russia is strewn with confiscated and ruinous factories, monasteries, and country houses. So is Mexico. English and American readers are familiar with the case of poor Rosalie Evans whose hacienda was invaded, illegally, by socialistic rowdies, and who was finally murdered by those rowdies, not one of whom has been punished for the crime. Because he protested to the Mexican Government against this atrocity, Mr. H. A. C. Cummins, the British *Chargé d'Affaires* was denounced by that Government as a *persona non grata*, with the result that Mr. Ramsay MacDonald not only recalled him but severed all diplomatic relations with the gang of murderers who pretend to speak in the name of the Mexican people.

Mrs. Evans's house is now a ruin. Her land is uncultivated, even that portion of it which was taken from her; and, throughout Mexico, there are thousands of country houses and of stolen land in the same condition. The State of Morelos looks as if it had been devastated by an invading army, for not only are the country houses sacked and in ruins but all the sugar refineries are abandoned and gradually falling to pieces. The State of Jalisco is nearly as bad.

The Bolsheviks have changed the name of Petrograd and of many hundreds of their towns as well as many thousands of their streets; and, in making these changes, they have always manifested a strong antipathy for the name of Christ, His holy Mother, and His Saints and a decided preference for the names of criminals who threw bombs and of murderers who were hanged. The present rulers of Mexico have done much the same thing and have been animated by the same motives. The grand old Spanish names which one finds in Mexican streets are being rapidly replaced by the names of obscure and disreputable politicians, and the average inhabitant of the Federal Capital is no more pleased than the average Londoner would be if he awoke one morning to find that a similar change had been made overnight in London by a Socialist Government, that Paternoster Row, for example, had become Rosa Luxemburg Row; St. James's Park, Zinoviev Park; and that Ave Maria Lane was called after Mr. Litvinov instead of after the Mother of God.

Take, for instance, the ancient street of San Francisco in the Federal Capital. It is now called the street of Francis I. Madero, the half-witted politician who succeeded Porfirio Díaz. But this is not a good instance for, after all, Madero was President: in most cases the new name is that of a politician so obscure that not one in a million Mexicans could tell you anything about him without consulting some book of reference, some *Who's Who* of the dead. While putting down the Catholic insurrections which took place in various parts of Mexico during the year 1927, General Joaquín Amaro, the Secretary for War, took it upon himself to change the names of many streets in the manner indicated. But most of the old names are still used, and some of them have not been changed officially. "Isabela la Católica" is still the official as well as the popular designation of a street in Mexico City: it is, of course, the name of the great Queen whose patronage of Christopher Columbus led to the discovery of the New World.

In Mexico as well as in Russia the changes to which I allude are superficial, inasmuch as they do not represent any change of heart or of faith in the people of either country, and as the old names are still used by the people. The name of Lenin may officially replace that of the Madonna as the patron of a Russian city or street, but it does not follow that the Russian people will regard him as they regard the Iversky Virgin; and though "Francisco I. Madero" (I have never been able to ascertain what the "I" stands for) is now the official name of the old Avenida de San Francisco, there is no noticeable decrease in the veneration of the Mexican people for *il poverillo* of Assisi. They still say la Avenida de San Francisco, but they are under no illusions as to which of the two Francises is the saint.

The street called by the short and sweet name of Misericordia is now Mariana Rodriguez del Toro de Lazarín, a lady of whom I know absolutely nothing save that she has got a long-winded name. San Sebastian, whom I know, has been replaced by José Joaquín Herrera, whom I do not know. San Diego has become Cuitlahuac (part of the Indianization programme). Santa Barbara has become Valerio Trujano.

There are new streets, of course, for Mexico City could not help growing even under the Upas-like shade of revolutionary anti-clericalism, but none of these new streets are ever called after Saints: even San Felipe de Jesús, a young Mexican missionary martyred in Japan early in the seventeenth century is not considered worthy of commemoration. Some of these new streets are called after the dates on which some revolution or other occurred—Cinco de Mayo, Cinco de Febrero, Dos de Abril, Diez y Seis de Septiembre. One cannot help speculating on what will happen when all the 365 days of the calendar have been appropriated in this way, and February 29th has been given to some unusually prominent hero, Plutarco Elías Calles or Judas Iscariot.

Some are called after Netzahualcoyotl, Montezuma, Cuauhtemotzín, or the Incas of Peru. Some are called after foreign "comrades" like Garibaldi. One great avenue is called simply "the avenue of the Insurgents," while the words "Reform," "Liberty," "Independence," and the "Constitution" occur frequently in the street directories of the Federal Capital and of the State capitals.

There is a discrepancy, however, between what we see on the surface and what lies beneath; and this discrepancy is symbolical of many things in Mexico—and elsewhere. What we hear shouted at us from every hoarding might be mistaken for the voice of the people, but it is not the voice of the people; as a rule it is the voice of quite a small group of men, who are not in touch with the people at all, save in this sense, that they have their hands in the people's pockets.

It will be difficult for Stalin & Co. to obliterate all traces of Christianity in Russia, for Christianity is part of Russia's very substance, flesh of her flesh and bone of her bone. And, for the same reason, it will be difficult for Calles & Co. to obliterate all traces of Christianity in Mexico. The names of Saints cover half the map. You have towns like San Benito, Santiago, Nombre de Dios, Santa María, San Francisco, Santa Rosalia, Santo Buenaventura, San Bernardo, San Juan de Guadalupe, San Ignacio. Some towns are called after Santa Barbara, who takes care of soldiers and castles; some after San Nicolas, who looks after youths and sailors; some after Santa Catalina de Alejandría, who protects scholars; some after San Jorge, the patron of warriors, knights, and archers; some after San Miguel, the Angel of Death; but by far the most popular patron is, under one or other of her Appellations, *la Purísima, la Santísima Virgen de Guadalupe, Reina de Méjico*. You have rivers like San Lorenzo and San José. You have bays like Vera Cruz. You have islands like Tres Marías, now one of the most terrible Penal Colonies in the world and used illegally by Calles as a place of banishment for Catholics.

Even the mountain ranges bear holy names. The Sierra Madre de Dios guards the east coast and the Sierra Madre Occidental the west. These are the two great ranges that enclose between them the marvellous table-land on which Mexico City stands, and which, uniting again further south, form that long range of Cordilleras which is the backbone of South America.

As for the streets, stand anywhere in the Federal Capital, and repeat aloud the names on the tramcars. It will sound as if you were saying the Litany of the Saints.

During my travels in Mexico last year (1927), I visited the marvellous bay of Mazatlán, and gazed at the Pacific Ocean in front of me and at the shore on either side, broken into lofty, sharp-pointed pinnacles of rock. On the summit of one such pinnacle, Mount Talpita is its name, stands a cross, planted there perhaps by a conquistador.

Those old conquistadores sometimes placed crosses on peaks so inaccessible, on rocky, wave-beaten islets so unapproachable, that the half-caste Turks and Indians who rule Mexico to-day have not the nerve to reach them in order to tear them down. They have to confine themselves to shaking their lists at them from a distance, or to abusing them in the Socialist newspapers and in the grog-shops of the Federal Capital.

Meanwhile, on the summit of pyramid and teocalli and temple of the sun, the Cross still stands triumphant. On top of the great pyramid in the sacred city of Cholula, a pyramid erected in honour of the god Quetzalcoatl, the conquistadores planted not only a cross but a church glittering with a hundred crosses, the great church of Nuestra Señora de los Remedios; and on many other memorials of Mexico's Pagan past, Christianity has left the same indelible mark. Apparently the Conquistadores were not so afraid of the Cross as were the builders of the Ceno-taph in London; and consequently it will take Calles & Co. a long time to obliterate all traces of Christianity from Mexico.

The most remarkable memorials are, of course, the churches, some of which are, from an architectural point of view, better than anything of the same kind that I ever saw in the United States. Indeed it might be said that as the United States is noted for its sky-scrapers, its superb railways stations, and its banks, so Mexico is noted for its wonderful churches; and I am old-fashioned enough to think that in the loving care with which these churches were built and in the skill which was lavished on the carvings in wood and stone with which they are adorned, there is more of true civilisation than there is in the Woolworth Building or the Grand Central Terminal of New York City.

Some of the Mexican churches can boast of an antiquity which is not generally associated with the New World: I saw one which dates from the year 1598, and is still in a good state of preservation.

In the course of three hundred years no less than nine thousand churches were built in Mexico, a creditable record, I think, though Mexican Government officials sometimes scoff at it. Among the scoffers is one Dr. Moisés Sáenz, a Methodist min-ister of Jewish descent who is at present Sub-Secretary of Edu-cation in the Calles Government, despite the law which prohib-its clergymen of any denomination from holding office under Government. As the Calles Government has done less in the matter of education than even the Government of Porfirio Díaz, Dr. Moisés Sáenz has abundant leisure to carry on propaganda work in America and at one meeting which he addressed in an American University, he sneered at the craze for church build-ing from which the Spanish conquerors of Mexico had suffered. Presumably he would have preferred "sky-scrapers" to churches, but I don't think that he will find many Europeans to agree with him.

Besides the churches, there are numerous chapels, wayside shrines, and domestic images. In the *patio* of the large building where the British Consulate General in Mexico City is situated, there is a large statue of the Blessed Virgin with fresh flowers before it all the year round. I do not mean that the Consul-General puts the flowers there, but, if he did, the fact would be less significant than the truth, which is that they are put there by some humble Mexican porter or caretaker, for in the first case it would be the whim of an individual foreigner, whereas in the second place it is an indication of the faith held by a whole people.

This superabundance of religious memorials makes all the more remarkable the entire absence at the present moment of priests, monks, and nuns, not only from the streets but from churches, convents, and other ecclesiastical buildings. Throughout all Mexico's many degrees of latitude and longitude, one never sees the clerical dress or the religious habit of nun, monk or friar. Even an Anglican Bishop, who once landed at Vera Cruz in the dress of his order, was instantly arrested and dragged before a magistrate who lectured him severely on his impertinence in thus violating the law which prohibits the wearing of religious dress.

Mexico is under an Interdict such as that pronounced against England in the time of King John. Baptisms do not take place in public. The marriage ceremony is performed by laymen; but it is validly carried out if the married pair intend to have the ecclesiastical ceremony performed as soon afterwards as possible. Holy Communion is given by laymen. There is never any priest to bless a coffin as it descends into the grave. Priests are not allowed to assist at religious processions, even at those held inside churches. The dark soutane of the priest and the red robe of the acolyte are never seen.

Most of the churches are open, but they are like those deserted "mystery ships" which are sometimes encountered at sea, ships with no officer on the bridge, no steersman at the wheel, no sailor in the fo'castle, not a living soul aboard though the table has been set for dinner and the bread cut.

The sanctuary lamp is extinct, in some instances perhaps for the first time in three hundred years. No candles burn before the images of the Saints. All the doors are wide open. The first deserted church I entered was in Guaymas, Sonora, the birthplace of President Calles, who is responsible for this throttling of Mexico's religious life. It is dedicated to St. Francis and is built in the well-known Spanish colonial style, a long rectangle with two towers at one end and a high, narrow, egg-like dome at the other. Of course, towers and dome are alike surmounted by crosses. It is the old Spanish mission type of church which is so common in California. As usual, it is built on the principal plaza, and is by far the best building in town, which is as it should be, for originally it was the *raison d'être* of the town and of the plaza. It was built by some Franciscan missionary, and houses grew up around it. I was never able to see the local priest, though I was told that he was still hiding somewhere in the town. In January, 1927, he was arrested, and detained for some time in prison; and presumably he is again "wanted" by the police, for all priests who refuse to register are supposed to be sent to Mexico City.

It was on a Sunday morning that I arrived in Guaymas, and, when I entered this church, I found there two or three women and one man, but the altars looked cold and deserted; there was no light and no service. On my way back to my hotel, I was astonished to hear the ringing of a bell, apparently a church bell. I returned rapidly to the church, but it was as deserted as before; and I soon found that the bell belonged to an engine on the Southern Pacific Railway which was manoeuvring on the line, and at the same time ringing a bell, as the custom is in Mexico and the United States. In Mexico bells are rung by engine drivers, hotel keepers and town criers; and I have also seen church bells on the top of the look-outs from which sentries gaze in Sonora, towards the devastated lands of the Yaqui Indians, but on church towers and altar steps the bells are dumb.

While waiting in the church on this occasion, I noticed on one of the altars a statue unusual in the Catholic churches of Great Britain, Ireland, and the United States, a statue of the Risen Christ, triumphant, glorified, the banner of the Resurrection in his hand. *Sit omen.*

CHAPTER II

EL PASEO DE LA REFORMA

EL Paseo de la Reforma, one of the principal streets in Mexico City, has been converted by successive anti-clerical Governments, into a sort of Siegers Allee lined on both sides by extremely inartistic statues of those Mexicans whom Mexican anti-clericalism thought worthy of such honour. I use the word "anti-clericalism" to describe the party which has ruled in Mexico for the last seventy years, save during the thirty years that the Díaz regime lasted and during other brief intervals, as it would be incorrect and misleading to apply to that party the name "Liberal" and "Constitutionalist" which it applies to itself.

Who are the Mexicans thus honoured by statues? Not poets, explorers, or missionaries, not great Archbishops who built churches, schools and hospitals in distant parts of Nueva España, not great Viceroys who ruled wisely; not great Catholic Presidents who raised the prestige of Mexico higher than that of any other Republic in Latin-America. No, mostly Mexican soldiers who were indistinguishable from bandits, and who killed other Mexican soldiers, equally indistinguishable; Mexican politicians who assassinated other Mexican politicians; Mexican statesmen who stole millions of *pesos*, and thousands of ecclesiastical buildings, and gave great chunks of the national territory to the United States, in exchange for large sums of money.

These are, of course, the sort of gentry we would naturally expect to see commemorated in a Republic which has, throughout its whole history, been torn by civil war and dominated by one military clique after another; which has had seventy-two Presidents in seventy years, if we deduct the period of thirty years during which it was ruled by Porfirio Díaz. Germany points to the Thirty Years' War as an exceptional period in her history; Mexico points to the thirty years' peace as an equally exceptional period in hers. France had her Hundred Years' War; Mexico has had her Hundred Years' Revolution.

The heroes commemorated in the Mexican Siegers Allee are nearly all in uniform but, as a rule, they are bandits rather than soldiers, or, at best, they are corrupt and ignorant politicians who would never be regarded as soldiers either in the United States or in Europe. The uniform does not make the soldier any more than the cowl makes the monk; and if one sees a great deal of the uniform in Mexico, that is due to the longing of Mexican politicians to acquire the title of General and to wear the corresponding dress. Some of the heroes commemorated in el Paseo de la Reforma make the same impression on Mexicans as would be made on Londoners by a statue of Mr. Saklatvala replacing that of Nelson on top of the pillar in Trafalgar Square.

One bronze gentleman on this Paseo is wearing a hussar's jacket—or so, at least, it looked to me—and a sailor's wide trousers. With his arms he is making gestures expressive of exasperation; and an unfriendly critic might say that he felt his position acutely, as prisoners are sometimes supposed to do in the dock, and wanted to be removed from that pedestal.

Another gentleman has his hands tied behind his back, but there is no indication of what his crime was. Some of the figures represent prancing warlords or orators in full blast. Several of the orators are indulging in impressive gestures or exhibiting parchments meant, I suppose, to represent treaties they made with Washington although these treaties always involved the sale of national territory to the United States.

Martial figures lean in picturesque poses on their swords. One hero, with an antique revolver in his hand, looks very angry about something. Another, in a sudden access of fury, is drawing a knife. It is a characteristic gesture among representatives of "advanced" thought in Mexico, but personally I would prefer to see statues of nuns teaching little girls to pray and friars teaching peons to plough.

The greatest monument of all is devoted to President Benito Juárez in the Avenida Juárez, a beautiful little park between the Paseo de la Reforma and the Avenida F. I. Madero, which we owe not to Juárez but to the unfortunate Empress Charlotte. This monument takes the shape of a colossal statue which must have cost as much as the Albert Memorial in Hyde Park, though the principal achievement of Juárez consisted in beginning that religious discord which has kept the country in hot water ever since (excluding always the Díaz period), and which may only end with a regrettable event to which it will have powerfully contributed, the disappearance of Mexico from the list of independent nations. Juárez triumphed, it is true, but only because the United States had provided him with arms and ammunition.

The next greatest statue is that of Cuauhtemotzín, the cannibal Emperor of the Aztecs, the last champion against Cortés of the most awful system of human sacrifices that ever existed on the face of the earth, a system in comparison with which the religious systems of Greece and Rome were mild and harmless. But the best statue and the third most artistic of its kind in the world is Tolsa's equestrian statue of Carlos IV in the Plaza de la Reforma; but this was, of course, put up by the Spaniards.

The really great men of Mexico are conspicuous by their absence from the Paseo de la Reforma. The names that Macaulay's schoolboy knew so well must not be whispered to the Mexican schoolboy, for a process of Indianization and de-Christianization is afoot, and the names of the Conquistadores are taboo.

Hernán Cortés is not to be seen (thank God!) in this Rogues' Gallery on the Paseo de la Reforma; but he does not need a monument; Mexico City, the great plateau, the ring of mountains, the volcanic peak of Popocatepetl and the snowy summit of Iztaccihuatl; these are the best monuments the great Marquis of the Valley could possibly have.

The anti-Spanish and anti-clerical gang might, however, have left his bones to rest in peace; but that gang was so determined to desecrate those bones that they had to be removed secretly and by night from the tomb where they had reposed during four hundred years. The place where they are hidden is known only to a few persons.

As for the great Conservative Dictator, Porfirio Díaz, he has no statue of course anywhere in Mexico.

On the Paseo de la Reforma there are a few statues to ecclesiastics, for, from very shame, some of them could not well be excluded, and if perchance one of them came to life and descended from his pedestal, he would promptly be arrested for violating the law which forbids the wearing of clerical dress. But we do not see any statue of Fray Junípero Serra who walked barefoot to the California hills, or of the Franciscan who first discovered that great marvel of nature, the Grand Cañon of the Colorado River. Prancing Generals are commemorated but we do not find anywhere statues to the friars who first penetrated into what is now Texas, New Mexico and Arizona, though they added to New Spain immense territories which those prancing Generals afterwards lost. This is not rhetorical exaggeration; it is sober, historical fact. By their journeys, their explorations and their discoveries, those humble friars doubled the size of Nueva España, while, on the other hand, the proud politicians, the raucous orators, the astute diplomatists, the powerful statesmen, and the belted Generals lost, literally, more than half of that Mexico which freed itself from Spain about a hundred and seven years ago. But the Friars have no statues, while the politicians and the Generals have. Worse than that, those Friars who opened schools all over the colony, reduced the native languages to writing, and accomplished the formidable task of civilising the aborigine, are branded to-day as the representatives of an antiquated and unsuccessful system while disastrous personalities like Benito Juárez and Plutarco Elías Calles are hailed even in England and North America as constructive statesmen, reformers, builders of Empire, bearers of the light.

The Friars tracked the great rivers to their sources. One of these reached the place where the Californian city of San Francisco now stands. All of them built churches and schools, around which towns afterwards grew up. All of them preached the Gospel to savage tribes. Many of them died the death of martyrs. They are not commemorated, but the men who did their best to de-Christianize and re-barbarize the natives *are* commemorated.

There are no memorials to the great Archbishops who built universities two hundred years before Harvard was even heard of, and who founded schools, orphanages and hospitals, but there are plenty of memorials to the anti-clerical demagogues who appropriated for their private profit the endowments on which these institutions subsisted.

The only two priests who are plentifully commemorated throughout Mexico and who even have towns called after them, are the two leaders of the independence movement, *el cura* Hidalgo who failed to prevent the massacre of unarmed Spaniards by his Indian followers, and his disciple José María Morelos, defeated through his own imprudence.

This erroneous impression that anti-clericalism in a Catholic country means progress, education, democracy and "big business" is responsible to a large extent for the consistent support the United States has given to the anti-clerical forces in Mexico during the last seventy years, and, consequently, for the almost hopeless plight in which Mexico finds herself to-day; but most of the Statesmen at Washington now see that Mexican anti-clericalism is really a huge parasite, incapable of constructive work, and only able to subsist by preying on the values created in the past by the Spaniards, the Church and the Catholic Presidents. To this point I shall devote my next chapter.

CHAPTER III

THE PARASITE

WHAT is called Liberalism in Mexico is a parasitical growth which, having preyed for some seventy years on the civilization built up by the Church and the old Spaniards and the Catholic Presidents, is now fastening on to the economic structure erected by American enterprise in Tampico, in Durango, in Chihuahua, on the Mexican West Coast, and on the banks of the Rio Grande. But, whereas Uncle Sam regarded this parasite without alarm and even with complacency so long as it confined itself to devouring the wealth of the Church, and firmly believed it when it described itself as a great creative force, the very antithesis of the lazy monks on whom it preyed, he regards it with horror and aversion now that it is devouring the wealth of American capitalists in Mexico. To change the metaphor, Uncle Sam saw nothing wrong with Mexican Liberalism when its hands dripped with the fat of sacrilege, but at the end of 1926 when its hands dripped with the oil of John D. Rockefeller, he was so scandalized by the sight that a landing of United States marines was expected every moment at Tampico.

This Oil question is now settled, it is said, but the Agrarian question has not been settled yet. From 1915 up to the present, the Mexican Government has seized nearly half-a-million acres of land belonging to American farmers in order to give it to the peons, but, so far, it has paid no compensation to the owners, while, on the other hand, the peons have made little or no use of the confiscated land, and are getting out of Calles' Socialistic Paradise into the United States with an alacrity which reminds one of people escaping from a house on fire.

This parasitical growth is incapable of creating or of building up or even of repairing: it can only destroy.

One curious result of its destructive activities is that a Mexican Minister of Finance is to be envied by all other Finance Ministers and Chancellors of the Exchequer in the world, inasmuch as when he has to think of the imposition of new taxes, he need never worry about protests from his fellow-citizens because few of them produce taxable values. He has only to select as his victims foreign industrialists or capitalists who are occupied in exploiting the mineral or agricultural wealth of the country; and the louder the foreigner squeals, the greater the Finance Minister's satisfaction, as this gives him an opportunity of striking a patriotic attitude, and declaring that he will stand no nonsense from foreigners who seek to plunder and enslave the free people of Mexico.

The whole activity of the Mexican Government is directed to getting a share in the profits made by foreign capitalists, foreign merchants, and foreign landowners, without paying anything themselves or doing any work. Mexico is full of minerals and of latent wealth, but the officials of the Mexican Government never, never help in its exploitation. On the contrary, they go around scowling darkly at the *Gringo* while he plans and works and risks his life and his money. If he succeeds, they yell for a division of the profits, and if they do not get all the profits, they go away muttering ominously that they will not allow their beloved country to be plundered any longer by foreign bloodsuckers and adventurers.

Parasites the Mexican "*Constitutionalistas*" undoubtedly are, and they are in a luckier position than their Comrades of Muscovy, for whereas the Red Muscovite has to stew in his own juice, the Red Mexican, not having any juice of his own to stew in, squeezes all the juice he wants out of the foreign capitalist, the Spaniard, and the Church. Both the Russian and the Mexican Reds are lucky in having as the scene of their operations and the subject of their experiments, a self-supporting country filled with mineral wealth, for, if they carried out their interesting experiments in a country like England, those experiments would quickly end in the starvation of the experimenters and of their victims.

What have the Revolutionaries done for Mexico? I defy the reader to indicate any substantial benefit which they have conferred on that country. There is an impression abroad that they have helped education, but as a matter of fact they have sucked for seventy years at the life-blood of education in Mexico. In Sonora which is now (March, 1928) being swept by fire and sword as it was swept in March 1927, there are many old ruined schools, established by the Franciscans 250 years ago; and I find that in 1785 a Bishop of Sonora built "seven primary schools, two grammar schools, and one college" for the Yaqui Indians, yet despite the eloquence of these two facts, placed side by side, one finds American Radical periodicals complacently stating that, thank God, Calles is at all events "keen" on education and "uplift," so far, at least, as the Indian is concerned. "Ultimately," says the *New Republic*, "what the Calles Government demands is an opportunity to educate the Mexican Indian."

The various Radical Governments of Mexico have, as a matter of fact, confiscated all the schools which the Church had established for the education of the Indian. It would not be so bad if the confiscated schools were used for public purposes, but very often they are sold and the proceeds appropriated by "patriots"; and, during the last seventy years, there has been continuous confiscation of the houses on whose rents educational establishments depended for their endowments.

All the good architectural work in Mexico is the work of the Spaniards, the Church, Maximilian, or Porfirio Díaz, in other words of the Catholics, for though, while he was President, Díaz was not a practising Catholic, he did not enforce the anti-religious laws, with the result that Catholic life flourished under his administration.

All the good industrial works—railways, bridges, machines, harbour-works, oil works, pipe-lines, factories, etc.—are due to foreign capitalists, mostly American and British. All that the "*Liberales*" and the "*Constitutionalistas*" do is to shoot one another, to murder innocent people, to plunder the national exchequer, to extort money from the industrious Catholics and the still more industrious foreigners, and, having done so, to take off their *sombreros*, wave them aloft, and yell "*Viva Méjico!*"

In almost every Mexican town and city the best buildings were built by the old Spaniards, the Bishops, the Abbots, or the Catholic Presidents; but nearly all of them are now occupied by "patriots" or (what comes to the same thing) by Red Municipalities or other public bodies. Despite careful search I failed to discover a single building that the "*Liberales*" have built. The great public library in Mexico City was once the Church of St. Augustín. The municipal Museum of which Guadalajara is so proud was a seminary built, centuries ago, by pious Spaniards for the education of priests, and it is still full to-day of religious books, paintings and statues for, in the matter of art and literature, "*Liberalismo*" is as sterile as it is in the matter of education, industry, agriculture, and political economy. Among the historical records which this Museum contains is an edict signed by Benito Juárez, the first anti-clerical President, graciously donating this Seminary with all its endowments to the Municipality of Guadalajara.

It is a beautiful old Spanish building with several restful *patios* full of verdure and of brightly-coloured flowers. On the ground floor there are cloisters with groined ceilings; and cool stone steps lead to other cloisters on the upper storey. But though the Municipality got this building for nothing, it is unable to keep it in repair, and half of it is in a ruinous condition, being probably inhabited by underpaid municipal employees if one can judge by the rubbish, the pots and pans, the rags hung out to dry, and the other evidences of human occupation.

Having been deprived of this Seminary, the Catholics then built another, but Carranza confiscated it in 1914 when he entered Guadalajara, and converted it into a barrack. In the middle of 1927 it was the H.Q. of General Jesús M. Ferreira, Chief of the Military Operations in the State of Jalisco.

Opposite the Cathedral in Guadalajara is the Archbishop's house, a fine stone building simple in style and provided with very thick walls as a protection against the earthquakes. Needless to say, the Archbishop is not living in it. It was appropriated long ago by the Government and is now the Municipal Building. The present Archbishop rented another house some distance away, but though it is a very humble and ordinary-looking dwelling and was rented, not bought, it also will be confiscated, for it is empty at present and its doors are sealed with an official seal, and bear, besides, a formidable official document. While in Guadalajara I heard that Government officials had entered it and were busy carrying off the furniture and the library to their own houses. If they did so, then they ran true to form, as "patriots" who afterwards occupied high positions in the Carranza Government plundered shamelessly the library of the Bishop of Monterey in 1914.

As for the Archbishop of Guadalajara, he is living in disguise on the mountains, and putting up with every kind of discomfort for the sake of his flock.

One public building, indeed, the "*Constitutionalistas*" of Guadalajara have attempted to erect, the House of Congress intended for the State Legislature, but it is in the same condition as the Parliament Building in Mexico City, in other words it is uncompleted and uncompletable, for though great sums of money are voted annually, the building operations make no progress for the simple reason that most of this money is stolen.

All over Mexico we find the same lamentable story of pillage and ruin. There is, in Querétaro, a Franciscan friary built in 1693, and interesting to Americans as having been the mother house which sent out some of the Californian Missions. It was confiscated and sold by Juárez; then repurchased by the Catholics and re-opened in 1885 as the College of Pio Mariano. But in 1914 it was again confiscated, this time by Carranza; and on this occasion a number of valuable pictures were stolen from it while it was garrisoned by Carranza's Yaqui Indians. It is now a barracks. There are many such instances of the Catholics buying back their own buildings at enormous prices—only to see them confiscated again, a few years later.

Bishop Creighton, the head of the American Episcopal Church in Mexico City, told me in June, 1927, that Calles had offered him four Catholic Churches but that he had manfully refused to take them. "Anyone can get a Catholic Church now," he said; and then he went on to tell me how Bishop Reilly, the first Episcopalian Prelate in Mexico had got the beautiful old church of San Francisco in the *Avenida* which was formerly known as the *Avenida de San Francisco* but which as I have already pointed out, is now called after another (and very different) Francisco. This Church was given to Bishop Reilly by Benito Juárez, always generous where other people's property was concerned. Bishop Reilly then wandered off to Egypt and became so interested in mummies that he forgot all about his flock in Mexico City, not, however, a very numerous flock, for it only consisted of a few hundred Yankees and Englishmen—none of them much addicted to religion. The result was that the Catholics bought back their church again at a stiff price.

There was a touch of dignified regret in Bishop Creighton's voice as he told me this sad tale of a lost opportunity but I wonder what the Episcopalians would say if Tammany Hall were to give the Cathedral of St. John the Divine to Cardinal Hayes as a Christmas Box and the Cardinal were afterwards to sell it back to Bishop Manning at a pretty high figure. Yet the two cases are in some respects identical; and if they are not regarded in the same light by Anglo-Saxons, that is because the Anglo-Saxon would use two sets of scales, one for weighing attacks on Catholics and Latins, the other for weighing attacks on Protestants and "Nordics." A good instance of this occurred when, in April

1928, the *Daily Express* of London was induced by a letter from the Hon. Mr. Evan Morgan to investigate the treatment of the Catholic Church in Mexico. It sent its New York correspondent to Mexico City, where he asked Calles personally how many Catholic priests had been shot. Calles agreed that possibly fifty had been shot. Now, if President Cosgrave had put fifty Protestant clergymen to death in one year, there would have been no need for the son of a Peer to direct the attention of the *Daily Express* to these unusual occurrences.

The College of San Augustín in Querétaro was built in 1731, but is now the Post Office and Federal Building, the Government being apparently unable to build a Post Office and Federal Building for itself. One wonders sometimes what those great creative geniuses the "*Liberales*" would have done if the Church and the Spaniards had not preceded them in Mexico, for in that case, President Calles would probably be living to-day in a tent or an adobe hut or an Aztec ruin. Of the two houses in which he does live, Chapultepec Palace was built by the Emperor Maximilian, and the Government building which is his town residence was constructed by the Spaniards whom Calles regards with such supreme contempt.

To return to Querétaro, the old ecclesiastical seminary is a fine example of early Spanish Colonial architecture. I need hardly add that it has been stolen and is now used for Government offices. The men who stole it were apparently unable to build, but they have certainly the gift of language for they have bestowed on it a euphonious title—*el Palacio de los Poderes del Estado* (the Palace of the Powers of the State). In Guadalajara I saw a Jesuit College which was stolen by Juárez, and I could hardly believe my eyes when I saw above the main door, in huge letters, the following inscription, which is a quotation from Juárez himself: "He who steals the goods of others, the same offendeth against charity." It was not ironical, however: Juárez was not advanced enough for irony: like Calles and Obregón, he was simply an ignorant bandit.

To continue my tale of confiscation, the episcopal palaces at Zacatecas and at Puebla have both been made into barracks. Where they did not confiscate, the "Patriots" hacked and mutilated, for in many of the nationalized churches and monasteries, gold work and precious mosaics have been scraped off and sold. This work of destruction has been going on at such a rate since the beginning of the present persecution that the Minister of Education, a cultured unbeliever of the Lunacharsky type, has appealed to the people to safeguard for artistic reasons the treasures in their churches. He does not realise, apparently, that the harm is all done by the soldiers and workmen whom he and his friends have de-Christianized and re-barbarized.

This work of destruction has been going on since the time of Juárez, and it was Juárez who began it by seizing many of the jewels, pictures, and other artistic treasures in the great Cathedral of Mexico City.

The Cathedral of Morelia was once celebrated for its massive silver communion railing and other ornaments of the same precious metal. All these, to the value of $400,000 were removed, by order of the Federal Government, on the 23rd of September 1858 because the church had refused to pay a war contribution of $100,000.

"Disappeared during the Revolution of 1860." These are the words used in a guide-book about the rich silver ornaments "worth many thousands of *pesos*" which once decorated the High Altar of the Cathedral in Guadalajara; and, unfortunately, the same phrase can be used of many artistic treasures which have vanished from other Mexican Churches. One trembles to think of how often we shall see, in future guide-books, the corresponding phrase "Disappeared during the religious persecution of 1926."

It is the same story in every part of Mexico; and it is such a long story that a large book could be devoted to it alone, but I have only space here to give a few cases taken at random.

The Church of Santa Rosa in Querétaro dates from the year 1699 and was long famous for the gold leaf on its altars. It no longer enjoys this fame, for those altars have now been destroyed for the sake of that gold leaf. When the religious persecutions began under Calles in 1926, so many valuable objects were stolen from the Cathedral in Mexico City that it was closed. But Calles has the key, and I would be very much surprised if, when this venerable church is opened again, its few remaining treasures are found to be intact.

Another phrase which one often finds in Mexican guidebooks is this: "After the promulgation of the Reform Laws, this church passed to private ownership," the private owner being always a "patriot" whose bank account benefited by the transaction. Some of those churches became Masonic lodges. There is one in Tacuba Street, Mexico City, which is now a "Library of the Social Sciences," in other words a Marxist library. In 1925 I happened to be in Mexico City soon after a Catholic Church was seized by a group which was acting for Calles, and I studied the *modus operandi* on the spot and with great care. The Church was called *La Soledad* and apparently it was seized by two schismatic priests, Pérez and Monje. In reality these men had no followers at all and were assisted by policemen disguised in civil dress. But despite this assistance, they would have been expelled had it not been for the fact that the uniformed police drove out the Catholics, and that, when the latter renewed the attack, the City fire brigade came to the help of the besieged schismatics and turned a stream of water on the Catholics who were thus prevented from occupying their own Church.

Calles was really behind the whole plot, for he meant to inaugurate his attack on Catholicism by the establishment of a Schismatic Church, but, in view of the excitement aroused among the regular congregation of *La Soledad*, it was impossible even for Calles to maintain in that church two profligate priests who had no lay followers at all. What, then, did the President do? Did he return the Church to the Catholics? No, he closed it; and *La Soledad* is to be made into a Museum. Pérez has now got another church, one which had previously been used by the Government as an agricultural Museum. Thus, the churches built by Catholics may be given to schismatics, not directly but after having been used for some time as Government buildings. In this way are churches confiscated by a sleight of hand worthy of a conjuror at a village fair.

Not only are churches seized but schools, orphanages and hospitals are also seized, not for the benefit of the public but for that of corrupt politicians. The list of such cases, even in the City of Mexico alone, would be too long for this book, so that I can only mention one.

Exactly four hundred years ago, a Franciscan lay-brother called Pedro de Gante founded in the City of Mexico a famous High School for Girls, the *Colegio de Niñas*. This magnificent educational institution was closed and confiscated in 1861 by the so-called "Liberals," and was afterwards sold to a German Association which converted it into the Deutsches Haus, a German Club. In a word, all the schools and colleges run by religious men and women, in the whole of Mexico, together with episcopal palaces, almshouses, hospitals, and orphanages were nationalized and converted into barracks, prisons, and public buildings of other kinds.

I have before me a list of twenty-seven *Colegios* or High Schools founded in Mexico City by the Secular or Regular Clergy of Colonial times. They have all disappeared or been converted into barracks or prisons owing to the confiscation of the houses whose rents furnished their endowments; and those houses were invariably seized by "patriots" for their personal gain. The father of M. Limantour, the Finance Minister of Porfirio Díaz, got no less than forty such houses, with the result that his descendants are wealthy. But it ill becomes Mexican "Liberals" who enjoy such wealth to reproach the Mexican Church for inactivity in the matter of education.

In the time of Porfirio Díaz, when the religious laws were in abeyance, the Catholics re-purchased in many cases their own schools and colleges from the people who had seized them or from others who had bought them from the original confiscators. They generally took care, however, to re-purchase them, not in the name of any religious community or of any ecclesiastic but of some Catholic laymen. To prevent this, the Constitution of 1917 specifically states that confiscated property must always remain public property; and that if it passes into the hands of private individuals, these individuals must be supporters of the administration. This law has led, by the way, to much unpleasantness for English and American Protestants who had purchased in good faith the confiscated property of religious institutions. Going on a general rule that the sales of religious property are only make-believe sales unless the purchaser is a follower of Calles, the Mexican Government has seized many of the properties purchased by English and American Protestants who have of course appealed to their respective representatives. Those representatives have made the usual remonstrances, which have elicited the usual evasions from the Mexican Foreign Office. It is hard to save anything round which the tentacles of the great Parasite have closed.

Even at the moment of writing, April 1928, there are wholesale confiscations and expropriations going on in Mexico. I have before me a copy of the *Excelsior* of March 1st in which there is mention of 130 cases of nationalization of private property belonging to the clergy. The *Excelsior* of March 14th relates how on the previous day the Government authorities in Tampico took steps to nationalize "the edifice which is to-day occupied by the Chief of the Military Operations but which was previously the Catholic College," the reason being that the College had belonged to the late Mgr. Montes de Oca, Bishop of San Luis Potosí whose heirs are declared to be rebels. Here we have the case of a saintly Bishop establishing a College at his own expense. This College is seized by a lawless General, whereupon the Government hastens to confiscate it, and in the end it will probably become this General's private property. Yet the *New Republic* assures us that "ultimately what the Calles Government demands is an opportunity to educate the Mexican Indian!"

An even more scandalous case was the seizure by the authorities of the Josefino College, a Catholic school for girls, and of the Great Seminary in Mexico City on the grounds that their inmates were circulating subversive propaganda, although this "propaganda" consisted, as a matter of fact, in the official photographs of the murder of Father Pro which I describe in the third part of this book. These confiscations have produced a poisonous swarm of new functionaries, the parasites of parasites, members *de los Servicios Confidenciales de la Secretaría de Gobernación* (of the Confidential Services of the Secretariat of the Home Office), spies to watch spies, spies to watch gendarmes, and a dozen other new species of Government employee which could not be matched elsewhere in the world, save perhaps in Bolshevist Russia. These worthies are not only a source of expense to the State (now on the eve of bankruptcy), but they are a scandal by reason of their drunken orgies, and, moreover, they plunder and steal the "nationalized" property which they are supposed to guard. Sometimes they quarrel over the spoil, and begin to shoot one another and for an instance of this, the reader might consult the *Excelsior* of 31 March 1928, always remembering that this paper as well as all the other Mexican newspapers have to be exceedingly careful owing to the censorship and to the summary expulsions of independent journalists which took place during the last three months of 1927.

In the issue referred to we get a long and edifying story of how on March 30th a Captain Novaro Hernández shot dead a Colonel Porfirio Rodriguez owing to a dispute arising out of the stealing by these "agents of the Confidential Services of the Home Office" of property belonging to the nuns who were driven out of the Josefino College. The tragedy took place in the Home Office itself, and it is not the first tragedy of the kind which that institution has witnessed, for some years ago Jesús Z. Moreno, a member of Parliament was shot dead in the same building by Tejeda Llorca, a Senator.

I am not going to give an account of this murder, for such murders are commonplace occurrences in Mexico. The first day

I arrived in Mexico City in 1925, two great brave Generals suddenly opened fire on each other near the War Office with the result that one was killed, the other committed suicide, and six bystanders were wounded by stray bullets. My only reason for referring to the murder of 30 March 1928 is because it led to a disclosure in the Press of the thefts which are committed by high officials in these "Nationalized" Colleges.

"Ultimately what the Calles Government demands is an opportunity to educate the Mexican Indian!"

I cannot easily forget this soothing phrase of the *New Republic*.

In view of the foregoing, it seems almost incredible that an intelligent people like the Americans should fail to see that the only constructive force in Mexico is the Conservative force, and that the so-called "*Liberales*" and "*Constitutionalistas*" are shams, but history shows us that for a long time the Government at Washington acted as if it believed the "Liberals" and anti-clericals to be the one progressive force in the country. It may be of course that Washington feared the Conservative, Catholic force would make Mexico too strong and too prosperous and that it consequently encouraged a party which could be relied upon to keep Mexico weak and divided; but at all events the fact remains that America's consistent support of anti-clericalism in Mexico is accountable for the parlous position of that country to-day and for the fact that it is ruled by the ludicrous and sanguinary crew which now occupies Chapultepec Palace.

This question of America's support of anti-clericalism in Mexico is so important in itself and in its relation to the present chaos in Mexico that I shall deal with it in the next two chapters.

CHAPTER IV

AMERICA'S SUPPORT OF ANTI-CLERICALISM IN MEXICO

As I have already pointed out in my preface, it may be set down as a general rule that, for the last seventy years, America has backed up every anti-clerical movement in Mexico and has, on the other hand, thrown every obstacle in the way of Catholic *émigrés* who sought to overthrow the anti-Catholic Governments which, with the help of the United States, had established themselves in Mexico City.

I hasten to explain that by America, I do not mean the majority of the American people or the America of to-day. I mean that unofficial body of great bankers, manufacturers, capitalists, politicians and publicists who have, up to the present, directed from behind the scenes the foreign and domestic policy of the United States. As I shall show later, this body is undergoing a change which will, within the next twenty years, make it unrecognisable; and, indeed, all America is changing far more rapidly than any other country in the world and far more thoroughly than Great Britain has changed since 1830. But very often the Mexican policy of America was simply the personal policy of the President, and the general public of the United States took no more interest in it than they took in the Tsar's policy towards Afghanistan. Even then there was continuity in that policy owing to the fact that all the Presidents have been

Protestants and Anglo-Saxons, save Roosevelt who was a Protestant of Dutch descent.

The traditional policy of America was, I repeat, to back up anti-clericals and revolutionaries in the Catholic countries of the New World just as Gladstone backed up Garibaldi and Mazzini in the old. There was one exceptional period, namely the period of thirty-odd years during which Porfirio Díaz ruled; but it must be remembered that, though Díaz did not persecute the Catholics, he did not, on the other hand, remove the anti-clerical laws of Juárez from the statute-book and did not allow the Catholics to form a political party. Despite this, he was a constant target for those restless Americans who can never refrain for a moment from meddling in the affairs of a Conservative Government in some foreign country but who make no protest when a Socialist and anti-clerical Government is guilty of the same acts of repression as the Conservative Government committed. For example, these cranks conducted a violent propaganda against Díaz some twenty years ago because he expatriated the Yaqui Indians of Sonora to Yucatán, and one of them wrote on this subject a heartbreaking but inaccurate book, somewhat after the style of *Uncle Tom's Cabin*, but none of them made any protest whatever when, in the spring of 1927, Calles and Obregón devastated Sonora with fire and sword, slaughtered great numbers of the same Yaqui Indians, and expatriated most of the remainder to an unknown destination. Whenever the *Ruráles* or rural police of Díaz treated poor, dear Communists or Revolutionaries roughly, these Yankee cranks made the whole United States ring with their protests; but when Calles put to death in two years more than a thousand men, most of them youths with very high and noble ideals, the cranks not only maintained silence themselves but succeeded in imposing silence on the American Press as well. I should add that most of these political cranks are also religious cranks; they were shocked at the connivance shown by Díaz to Catholic monks and nuns who established themselves in Mexico despite the prohibition of the law; and

though they are illogical, they are extremely numerous, powerful, wealthy and well-organized, whereas the Catholics, though
numerous, "swing no political weight" as Catholics, being
divided among the two great political parties. Even the Knights
of Columbus are in both camps, and are consequently negligible
from the political point of view.

Comparatively poor, the Catholics are unorganized, and
consist largely of unabsorbed foreign communities—Italian,
Polish, Mexican, French, Canadian, Hungarian, Lithuanian,
etc. The members of these foreign communities use their native
language to an extent that is not always realised by Europeans,
but which is a matter of importance in the present instance since
it involves their reading small "foreign language" newspapers
printed in America. The great newspapers can consequently
afford to treat with indifference their protests on the Mexican
question since they are neither subscribers nor advertisers, while
the Protestants are both.

Although it is over one hundred and twenty years since
America cut the political painter which connected her with England, she has not cut the intellectual painter yet, and the anti-
Spanish and anti-Catholic propaganda manufactured for political purposes at the time of the Reformation and the Armada is
even stronger to-day among the Ku Klux Klan and the Baptists
of the South than it is in England herself. This is in accordance
with the law whereby the English traits left in the American
character are exaggerated, temperance becoming, for example,
prohibition, and popular Protestantism becoming, in the words
of Dean Inge, "barbarism and belated obscurantism." There
will probably be a change in twenty years' time when the English tradition has died out or lost its force and when the children
of the shy and tongue-tied foreigners to whom I have just
referred become active monolingual Americans; but it is impossible of course to prophesy what form this change may take.
Certain it is, however, that up to the present the Baptists and
Methodists have dominated the United States. They "put over"
Prohibition; they have given a puritanical tinge to all American

legislation; and they have admitted to the White House only Protestants of Anglo-Saxon descent for even Roosevelt was partly of British origin. Had Al Smith been born in a parsonage like Taft and Wilson, the Democrats would never have had the slightest hesitation in nominating him.

To return, however, to the assertion with which I began this chapter, America has undoubtedly backed up every anti-clerical movement which has taken place in Mexico during the last seventy years, has backed them up when they were anti-Government movements, supported by a small minority of the Mexican people, and continued to back them up after they had become Governments, still supported by a small minority of the Mexican people.

This being the case, one would expect that the Mexican Bishops would be anti-American, but they are not. Bishop Banegas of Querétaro declared himself satisfied that, even when they interfered in Mexico, the American people and government were always actuated by good intentions and by a sincere desire to help the Mexicans. He ascribed their mistakes to the efforts of the Mexican "Liberals," who supplied them with much information which, though wrong, happened to agree with the inherited prejudices of the *Americanos*; and as the Mexican Conservatives held proudly aloof, the Americans got only one side of the question.

Had he known the United States better, the Bishop might have added that behind much of the American interference was a real love of freedom and a genuine desire to help what seemed to be an oppressed minority. America used to be always on the side of minorities, but it must have occurred to her more than once during the last decade that there is something wrong in that theory for, if minorities are right especially when suffering persecution, they may be wrong when inflicting persecution as in Russia, and if it is proper to send a Commission to far-off Rumania in order to investigate the grievances of the religious minorities there, it is still more proper to send a Commission to

Mexico next-door in order to investigate the grievances of a religious majority.

It must be admitted that in the case of Mexico there were special reasons why America should take the side of the people who called themselves "Liberals" and oppose those who called themselves Conservatives and Catholics. As Bishop Banegas has just pointed out, those so-called "Liberals" supplied the Americans with most of their information about Mexico; that alone would be a sufficient reason for the *Gringo* to look upon the affable "*Liberale*" as a friend and the haughty *Conservativo* as a foe; but there were other reasons. Among them was a fear that the Catholics were incurable Monarchists who would infallibly establish an absolute monarchy, form a great army, conceive great schemes of conquest, and become a menace to the simple, God-fearing farmers of the United States. In the time of Napoleon III the Americans were particularly afraid that the Mexicans would form European alliances, give concessions to bellicose Frenchmen and Austrians, and thus introduce to the New World, complications of a most undesirable kind.

To this a Mexican might reply that the United States has been a far more dangerous neighbour to Mexico than Mexico has ever been to the United States, for America has already annexed half of Mexico, and may yet annex the other half. A Mexican might also fail to see what right the United States has to dictate to Mexico with regard to her form of government, and he might maintain that, of all forms of Government, the Monarchical suits his country best. In support of that statement he could mention the fact that Mexico enjoyed its greatest prosperity under its two Emperors and its one Conservative Dictator Díaz, who was practically an Emperor.

Mexico's first Emperor was Iturbide, and Mr. D. J. R. Poinsett, the American Minister at his Court, was certainly no friend of his: indeed it is pretty certain that he had been sent by President Monroe to do Iturbide all the harm he possibly could. He organized a number of York Rite Masonic lodges with the idea, according to some Mexican historians, of creating dissension;

and it must be admitted that Masonry has been a source of dissension in Mexico ever since: Calles is a mason.

Poinsett visited Lorenzo Zavala and other "Liberals" who were in prison. Zavala was a violent anti-clerical, and that he was also a friend of Poinsett is evidenced by his "*Manifesto de los Principios Politicos del Excelentísimo Señor D. J. R. Poinsett, por su amigo el C. Lorenzo de Zavala*" (Mexico, 1828).

In November 1927 an appeal was made by a number of distinguished Mexicans to Mr. Dwight W. Morrow, the American Ambassador in Mexico City, on behalf of Father Pro and his three companions who were awaiting their death sentence for a crime which they had never committed. Mr. Morrow took no notice of the communication, and started off on a joy-ride in Calles' million-dollar Presidential train, a few days after these four prisoners had been butchered without trial.

But, to return to Poinsett, he is charged by Bustamante ("*Campañas de Calleja*") with all the disorders that followed Mexican independence.

Later on, the Southern States looked with covetous eyes on Mexico, which they regarded as good, potential slave territory that would enable the South to hold its own against the North, by returning to Washington more senators and representatives pledged to support slavery. It was with this object in view that they acquired Texas, but it must also be admitted that in this case the activities of British agents in Mexico precipitated annexation. The North, on the other hand, always opposed the annexation of Mexican territory as such annexation would make the Southerners too strong, and, though the Slavery issue has disappeared, the North still retains its hatred for annexation while the South has lost all desire for it. Protestant missionaries in Mexico have always favoured intervention when there was a chance of destroying the Catholic Church, and opposed it when there was a chance of it strengthening the Catholic Church. They favoured intervention in 1914 when the Catholic President, Victoriano Huerta, was in power and many of them accepted commissions in Carranza's rebel bands; but in 1927 when there was a possibility of President Coolidge intervening for the sake of the Oil and Land interests, all the Protestant organizations of the United States successfully opposed such interference, because it would incidentally benefit the Catholic Church.

The Zapotec Indian Juárez who was the first "Liberal" leader to carry out a wholesale pillage of the Church, had the fullest sympathy of President Buchanan; and Mr. Lewis Cass, the American Secretary of State wrote, 27 December, 1858, to a special agent whom he despatched to Mexico; "The Liberal party in Mexico has our hearty sympathy."

At this time Juárez was established in Vera Cruz, always a hot-bed of radicals and anti-clericals. Buchanan gave him valuable assistance in return for which he agreed to the McLane-Ocampo treaty which, had it been accepted by the U.S. Senate, would have placed Mexico practically under the control of the United States.

Miramón, the Conservative General who had established himself in the Federal Capital, felt it necessary to dislodge Juárez from Vera Cruz since at that time that gate-way to Mexico City was an even more vitally important point than it is now. Its import duties furnished much, if not all, of the revenue, and through it came all supplies of arms and ammunition. Miramón might control all the rest of the country, but without Vera Cruz, he must eventually succumb. To dislodge Juárez it was necessary, however, to attack by sea as well as by land, not only because of the necessity of cutting Juárez off from all his sources of supply, but also because of the necessity of hastening the operations, as a long campaign conducted by troops from the highlands would surely result in those troops being decimated by yellow fever. An agent of Miramón secured therefore some vessels in Cuba, had them armed, loaded with supplies, and sent to Vera Cruz in order to co-operate in the land attack on that port. But when they arrived off the Mexican coast they were seized by the ships of the American Navy and taken to New Orleans whence they were sent later as a present to Juárez. As a result of this, Miramón was compelled to abandon the siege of Vera Cruz; and his position soon became utterly hopeless as the United States prevented any supplies being sent to him while Juárez was permitted to receive all he desired. This action of Buchanan was a deciding factor in the duel between Miramón and Juárez, for had the American President not intervened, Juárez would have been driven from Vera Cruz and his cause ruined, perhaps for all time, while Miramón would have been able to establish a Conservative Republic or a Porfirian dictatorship which might have made Mexico as prosperous to-day as Argentina.

As I shall point out later, President Wilson acted in 1914 in very much the same way as Buchanan acted. In 1914 the Conservative General in Mexico City was President Victoriano Huerta, and his "Liberal" and anti-clerical rival was Venustiano Carranza who was at the head of a rebel band, not in Vera Cruz, but in Sonora. President Wilson allowed Carranza to import from America all the arms he wanted, but prevented Huerta from importing any arms even from Europe, for when a German ship laden with rifles for Huerta arrived at Vera Cruz, the United States navy prevented it from landing its cargo, and even seized Vera Cruz itself, thus forcing Huerta to resign. In neither case, it must be admitted, did the people of the United States take any interest in the proceedings of their President. In his annual message of 1859, Buchanan recommended intervention but his recommendations were wholly disregarded by Congress, which did not even notice them in any of its proceedings.

Exactly as the triumph of Carranza brought with it a reign of pillage and terror, so did the triumph of Juárez bring with it a similar reign of pillage and terror which so disgusted the decent people of Mexico, that they approved of the negotiations carried on by Estrada for the selection of Maximilian as Emperor. Thus the opposition of Buchanan to the moderate Conservative Miramón led to the appearance of an Emperor.

At this time the United States was rent asunder by the Civil War and could therefore do nothing in Mexico, but it never ceased to recognize Juárez as the official President of Mexico, though he could only assert his authority in a remote spot on the banks of the Rio Grande where he and a few of his Mexican supporters were protected by a handful of American desperadoes, who were always ready to convoy Juárez across the river in case the imperial troops appeared.

When the Civil War ended, Napoleon ceased supporting Maximilian but America did not cease supporting Juárez, and preventing the luckless Emperor from getting any supplies. The United States did not actually intervene, but its frequent military demonstrations on the frontier did Maximilian almost as much harm as intervention. General Sheridan tells us in his *Memoirs*, that he used two army corps to "impress the Imperialists as much as possible with the idea that we intended hostilities," and that he demanded from them war material given them by the Confederates. He also tells us that "as the summer wore away, Maximilian gained in strength until all the accessible portions of Mexico were in his possession, and the Republic under President Juárez almost succumbed." Then General Sheridan made another demonstration as though preparing to cross the frontier, interviewed Juárez in an ostentatious manner, and let it be known that he waited only the arrival of troops "to cross the Rio Grande on behalf of the Liberal cause." These stratagems were successful: the Imperialists withdrew in a panic from northern Mexico, and the "Liberals" were able to organize an army. Then General Sheridan goes on to say that "Thus countenanced and stimulated, and largely supplied with arms and ammunition which we left at convenient places on our side of the river to fall into their hands, the Liberals under General Escobedo, a man of much force of character, were enabled in northern Mexico to place the affairs of the Republic on a substantial basis. . . . During the winter and spring of 1866 we continued covertly supplying arms and ammunition to the Liberals—sending as many as 30,000 muskets from Baton Rouge Arsenal alone—and by midsummer Juárez, having organized a pretty good sized army, was in possession of the whole line of the Rio Grande."

From what Sheridan tells us, it is not difficult to see that, without American aid, the "Liberals" would have been permanently eliminated from the problem, yet the Mexican "Liberals" of to-day maintain that Juárez won without assistance from anybody outside Mexico.

Juárez had cried "No Re-election!" like the others, and, like the others, he had himself re-elected, just as Obregón, who also poses as a strong opponent of Presidential re-election, is having himself "re-elected" to the Presidency in July, 1928; but as a matter of fact there is neither election nor re-election, it is simply a case of mounting the Dictatorial "throne."

Juárez left a country completely ruined and at the mercy of innumerable armed bands supporting a precarious existence by pillage, and of several contending leaders who sought to seize his mantle. From among these leaders Porfirio Díaz emerged triumphant, and ruled the country more or less wisely for some thirty years. During that time the relations between the Dictator and America were good, perhaps because Díaz posed as an anticlerical and a Radical and was certainly not a practising Catholic, though he connived at the re-establishment of the religious orders in the country, and allowed the anti-religious laws to fall into desuetude. Finally, as I have already pointed out at the beginning of this chapter, an outcry was raised against him in the United States by those "unco guid" people who now maintain absolute silence about the misgovernment of Calles, but I must admit that many American newspapers kept silent then as they are keeping silent now, thus showing that they had not been caught in the toils of any propagandist, and that the only charges against them were an obstinate unwillingness to reckon with realities and an utter failure to realize their responsibilities. Nevertheless the attack of the "unco guid" on Díaz was a far more serious matter than is the present attack of the Catholic Press on Calles, and that for the simple reason that America is a Protestant country. Díaz was accused of supporting a system of peonage or slavery inside the country; and though the accusations made against him on this head were greatly exaggerated, there is no doubt that he failed to give proper attention to the peon.

It is somewhat amusing now to read the criticisms that used to be passed at that time on President Taft for shielding that Man of Sin, Porfirio Díaz, and preventing godly revolutionaries of the Calles type from using Texas as a jumping-off ground for an attack on him, as the organizations which indulged in these criticisms are largely responsible for paralyzing all action against poor, dear Calles by President Coolidge, and the sealing of the frontier against Catholic gun-runners. But, as I have already remarked, the enemies of Díaz were far stronger at the White House then than the enemies of Calles are to-day. Finally President Taft winked at the preparations which were openly made by Francisco I. Madero on American territory for the overthrow of the aged Dictator; and so powerful is the United States that the wink of an American President is enough to unseat a Mexican Dictator.

A short time before his fall, Díaz celebrated with great pomp the centenary of Mexican Independence, and a ceremonial meeting between himself and President Taft was part of the pro-gramme. The two Presidents met on the bridge of El Paso, but no report of what they said to one another has ever been pub-lished. They may have confined themselves to vague and polite generalities, or Taft may have complained of the Mexican pro-ject to let a Japanese Colony establish itself on Magdalena Bay in Lower California and of the anti-American policy of M. Limantour, the Mexican Finance Minister, who was obsessed by a determination to replace all American interests in Mexico by French interests. A short time before his death, Díaz was visited, in Europe, by a Mexican Bishop, (who does not wish his name to be mentioned,) and the ex-Dictator informed this Bishop that he had left Mexico because he had been threat-ened with American intervention if he did not do so.

CHAPTER V

PRESIDENT WILSON AND MEXICO

FRANCISCO I. Madero proved to be not only a dreamy incompetent but actually of weak intellect, and he was soon overthrown by General Victoriano Huerta, a strong Catholic and Conservative who afterwards, it is said, disposed of Madero in the manner customary in the country when the retiring executive fails to reach the coast in time to escape his pursuers. President Wilson took a strong personal dislike to Huerta, determined to get rid of him, and did get rid of him by intervention of the most flagrant kind while all the time declaring that he would not intervene. This sentence gives the key-note to the whole story; and in all the annals of diplomacy, or even in the wildest works of that fiction which deals with international diplomacy, there is no more ludicrous and incredible story than that of Huerta's expulsion from Mexico by the Professor of the Fourteen Points who later on won the Great War after having been re-elected on the slogan of "He kept us out of the War." That story is not told by enemies of President Wilson or of America: it is told in the impartial pages of the *Fall Committee Report* published by the Government Printing Office at Washington in 1919. I shall devote the present chapter to this expulsion of Huerta because President Wilson placed in power the Socialist and anti-clerical gang which has not only persecuted the Church ever since, but has also murdered American citizens at the average rate of five per week, confiscated their property, torn up their contracts, trampled on their rights, worked against American interests all over Central America but especially in Nicaragua; been pro-German during the Great War (Obregón was on the "Black List" of both England and America); and has filled up its spare time in the composition of insolent notes to Washington.

The State Department has the following table of crimes committed against Americans alone, from 1914 until a few years ago:

- 546 murders,
- 855 robberies,
- 668 assaults,
- 106 kidnappings,
- 847 property seizures,
- 508 "agrarian expropriations,"
- 550 trespasses,
- 109 deportations,
- 55 expulsions,
- 6,487 arrests.

This table is incomplete for, instead of keeping a strict account against the day of reckoning, the Mexican Section of the State Department has sometimes to ask the Mexican Government for figures as to the amount of American land stolen during such and such a month, and on such occasions the Mexican Government is always anxious to oblige, though the figures it supplies are not to be relied upon. It is enough, however, to show that Uncle Sam made a bad bargain when he "swopped" Díaz and Huerta for Carranza, Obregón and Calles.

President Wilson based his objection to Huerta on the grounds that Huerta had committed one murder, but he embraced the notorious bandit Francisco Villa, who had openly committed hundreds of murders and gloried in having done so. We find him ignoring his own able diplomats in Mexico and sending thither, as his manner was, a series of unofficial observers, all of them ignorant of every language save English, innocent of diplomatic usages, and complete strangers to the country. One was the late Mr. William Bayard Hale, an unfrocked Episcopalian clergyman who turned out to have been a German spy, but who was unfrocked not for espionage but for immorality. Another envoy was Mr. John Lind, who in addition to being as ignorant of Spanish and of Mexico as his predecessors, harboured an intense antipathy to Mexico and to the Catholic Church. This gentleman's mission was, if you please, to request President Huerta to resign!

The rest of President Wilson's information about Mexico came from John Reid, the Bolshevik journalist, whose gravestone occupies a prominent place near Lenin's mausoleum in the Red Square at Moscow. When Mr. Reid returned from a journalistic raid into Mexico, he was sent for by President Wilson, who seemed to be more impressed by his gorgeous word-pictures than by all the solid information that he got from Mr. Henry Lane Wilson, the United States Ambassador in Mexico.

The British Minister, Sir Lionel Carden, took the side of Huerta and prophesied with extraordinary accuracy the mess into which Wilson's policy would land Mexico. Great Britain consequently recognised Huerta and her example was followed by Spain, Germany, France and Japan; but Wilson, who had by this time developed a temper worthy of Kaiser Wilhelm II, continued his attempts to make Huerta resign and even induced the British Government to recall Sir Lionel Carden. Why, exactly, the British Government gave way is not quite clear, for it was in the right and Wilson was in the wrong. Perhaps it foresaw the approach of the Great War, then very near, and feared to antagonize President Wilson, but American writers like Mr. J. Fred Rippy, author of *The United States and Mexico*, take a view less flattering to British complacency; they assert or hint that the English Government yielded in return for Wilson's action in killing the bill for exempting from the Panama Canal tolls all American ships, a bill which would have unfairly handicapped British shipping.

In any case, Great Britain yielded, and all the other European nations followed her lead and ceased to support Huerta, whose position was consequently hopeless.

I have already pointed out how President Wilson permitted Carranza to import all the arms he wanted while preventing Huerta from doing so; but as this was not enough to overthrow the latter, Wilson sent the American Fleet to bombard and occupy the vitally important port of Vera Cruz, his pretext being the refusal of Huerta to salute the American flag in satisfaction for some unintentional discourtesy to American marines at Vera Cruz. Although in this matter the Mexicans were not in the wrong, they were willing to apologize, but President Wilson eagerly seized on the opportunity to capture Vera Cruz despite the fact that such drastic action was against all the pacifist principles which he so eloquently expounded in his speeches. In one of those speeches he dwelt feelingly on "the futility of force," and in another speech, delivered afterwards, he declared that he would never countenance armed intervention in the affairs of another State.

We find him letting loose chaos in Mexico before first getting out the American civilians, who had to be rescued by British ships. We find his Secretary of State, the "silver-tongued" Fundamentalist, William Jennings Bryan, asking President Huerta for favours by cable after having begun to make war on him.

All these charges will be found in the American Government publication to which I have just referred. It is not I who make them. They are made by eminent Americans, and have been published at the order and at the expense of the United States Government. Europe has commented little on this extraordinary page of history, probably because of the fact that when President Wilson was making such a sorry exhibition of himself, Europe was watching the approach of the tempest which was to devastate her from 1914 till 1918, and foresaw that she would be obliged to borrow money from Uncle Sam.

What the Fall report says of President Wilson's responsibility for the overthrow of Victoriano Huerta and the elevation of

Carranza to the Presidency is confirmed by Mr. Henry Lane Wilson, the American Ambassador in Mexico in 1914-1915. In a book on Mexico which was published in 1927, Ambassador Wilson says of Victoriano Huerta:

"He was a devout Roman Catholic, a believer in the Díaz regime and policies, and with all his faults, I am convinced that he was a sincere patriot, and, in happier times, might have had a career honourable to himself and useful to his country. He fell from power, a victim of narrow-visioned American diplomacy, and died a sacrifice to the same overweening jealousy and egoism which, with the power of a great people behind it, had brought about his downfall. . . . Perhaps no other Mexican Cabinet has contained men of such exceptional ability and high character as did the Cabinet of General Huerta."

Ex-President Theodore Roosevelt was, as we should expect, even more outspoken. He wrote as follows to the *New York Times* of December 6, 1914:

"The act of permitting the passage of arms across the frontier, on the part of Wilson, meant that he not only actively helped the insurrection, but without any doubt provided the means of achieving success, in so far as he actively prevented Huerta from organising an effective resistance. The defenders of Wilson allege that he could not have prevented the passage of arms across the frontier. Our reply to that is: Wilson did, at times, prevent such gun-running. He thus proved that he was actively interested in arming the revolutionaries, and when he so desired he gave permission, when he wished otherwise, he refused it; he was therefore absolutely responsible for this.

"The United States would not have had the least responsibility for what has been done to the Church, if the faction which committed these outrages had not been enabled to triumph by the United States. But since the United States took part in a civil war in Mexico, in the manner in which Wilson and Bryan obliged our government to take part, this country, through this act alone, is responsible for the horrible injustices, the terrible outrages, committed by the victorious revolutionaries against hundreds of believers of both sexes.

"Not long ago, President Wilson, in a speech delivered at Swathmore, Penn., declared that 'in no part of this continent can any government survive that is stained with blood,' and in Mobile he said: 'We shall never forgive iniquity solely because it may be more convenient for us to do so.'

"At the very moment he was pronouncing these high-sounding phrases, the leaders of the faction which he actively aided, were shooting down hundreds in cold blood; they were torturing men supposed to be wealthy; they were casting forth from their homes hundreds of peaceful families: they were sacking the churches and maltreating priests and religious in the most infamous manner, from assassination to mutilation and outrage.

"In other words, at the very time the President assured us 'that in no part of this hemisphere can any government endure if it be stained with blood' he was helping to put in power a government that was not only stained with blood but was stained with stains worse than those of blood. At the very time he announced that 'he would not continue relations with iniquity even if it were more convenient to do so,' he not only consorted with iniquity but openly supported it and put in power men whose actions were those of ferocious barbarians."

Ex-President Roosevelt's last message to the American people contains the following paragraph:

"Mexico is our Balkan Peninsula, and during the last five years, thanks largely to Mr. Wilson's able assistance, it has been reduced to a condition as hideous as that of the Balkan Peninsula under Turkish rule. We are in honour bound to remedy this wrong."

Mr. Charles Evans Hughes, formerly Secretary of State, spoke to the same effect on the 31st of August 1920. He said that:

"The conduct of the administration of Mr. Wilson in Mexico constitutes an intricate chapter of errors. The administration did not limit itself to refusing to recognize Huerta who had been recognized by Great Britain, Germany, France, Spain and Japan. The administration set out to destroy Huerta. ... By destroying the Government of Huerta, we left Mexico a prey to the horrors of revolution. We were then told (by Wilson) that Mexico had the right to spill all the blood that seemed to her necessary for the attainment of her ends. In October 1915, Wilson placed an embargo on all arms except those destined for the partisans of Carranza. ... This can only be called an absolute lack of political rectitude."

In the course of the same speech, Mr. Hughes said:

"In the spring of 1913 Mr. John Lind was sent to the City of Mexico with the object of asking Huerta to resign. It was an unjustifiable mission. The administration used all its endeavours to overthrow the Government which then existed in Mexico. In the spring of 1914 Vera Cruz was captured. ... We were told at that time that our object in going to Vera Cruz was to make Huerta salute our flag. We were told that we had gone there to show the Mexicans that we were in earnest in asking Huerta to resign. In other words, we took possession of Vera Cruz in order to depose Huerta; the flag incident was only a pretext. All we gained was the ridicule and the contempt of the Mexicans. In this manner we roused the indignation of the Mexicans and could not rescue our own people in Tampico without running the risk of losing more lives than we saved. We seized Vera Cruz in order to drag Huerta from his post, and we left other nations to save our own citizens. What a masquerade of international politics!"

The above quotations prove pretty conclusively, I should think, that the anti-clerical gang which at present rules Mexico was placed in power by President Wilson. Carranza then came into power to an accompaniment of outrages on monks and nuns such as no civilized country had witnessed for the previous two hundred years. Even Bolshevist Russia never attained the high level reached by Venustiano Carranza. Although not anti-clerical himself, Carranza became a helpless tool in the hands of the anti-clericals who nationalized churches, monasteries, and ecclesiastical buildings of every kind and indulged at the same time in a perfect orgy of looting. By this time, however, the Great War had broken out, and Europe had other matters to think of.

In 1917 Carranza assembled at Querétaro an assembly which drew up a new Constitution, known as the Querétaro Constitution or the Constitution of 1917; and it is on the anti-religious articles in this Constitution that Calles bases his own Bolshevist and anti-clerical laws.

The Querétaro assembly was incompetent, however, to draw up a constitution, as it was not a Constituent Assembly and did not comply with any of the conditions laid down in the Constitution of 1857. It was not a Constituent Assembly because it formally excluded all the other political groups which existed in the country, consequently the "reform" did not ema-nate from the national will: it was merely the work of a small group of armed men. The only persons allowed to vote in the so-called Constituent Assembly were men who could prove that they had added materially to the triumph of the revolution. Finally, the new Constitution was never submitted for ratifica-tion to the people or to the State Legislatures, as the law required; it was imposed by force.

The Querétaro Constitution was not only anti-Catholic, it was also Bolshevist; it aimed not only at the destruction of the clergy but also at the destruction of the capitalists. The Carran-zists wished to force all labour into the Red Labour Unions, and were therefore inimical to free labour. They also advocated a division of the land without payment of compensation to the plundered landowners; and this part of their programme has been carried out with such tactlessness, violence and injustice by President Calles that the lot of the peon and the workman has been made worse instead of better. All this makes more incomprehensible than ever the action of the American Government in supporting such a gang while steadily refusing to recognize the Soviet Government of Russia; the most probable explanation is that President Wilson did not foresee in 1914 the Red feature of the Carranza movement, and that President Coolidge does not like to encourage a counter-revolution in Mexico lest it makes things worse instead of better.

Not only did President Wilson fail to foresee the religious persecution which would inevitably follow Carranza's triumph, even the American Catholics failed to foresee that persecution; I remember that, as late as 1924, I had a long argument in New England with an American Jesuit, a Democrat in politics, who stoutly defended Wilson's support of Carranza! Sooth to say, neither the President of America nor the average American knows much about Mexico; and as the American public is sick of Mexico and never reads Mexican news, the newspapers no longer give any Mexican news, and no longer send to Mexico their best correspondents, or even their tenth best. In the same way, the Mexican section of the State Department in Washington was, until recently, composed of gentlemen who did not speak Spanish and were totally unfamiliar with Mexican conditions. Only one of them had ever been in Mexico City, and this one had only been there for three days!

I acquit President Wilson, therefore, of any charge of religious intolerance. He acted in utter ignorance, and imitated, sub-consciously, the policy of his predecessors, while, without realizing it, he was also influenced perhaps by the traditions of his Orange ancestors in Ulster, and by the wonderful Propaganda with which England bombarded Spain and the Vatican throughout all the seventeenth century. In fairness to the American Protestants, it must be conceded that this English propaganda and the later propaganda based on it were amazingly good, even better, indeed, than the English Propaganda against Germany during the Great War. Was not the Ulster Protestant more industrious than the Kerry Catholic, the Scotch Calvinist than the Sicilian, the stern New England Puritan than the easy-going Neapolitan? If England went ahead at a great rate after the suppression of the English monasteries, why should not Mexico go ahead in the same way after the suppression of the Mexican monasteries?

In America these arguments have greater force than in Europe, owing to the almost supernatural power attributed to the dollar. Some clergymen there appear to imagine that wealth is one of the marks of the true Church, and I actually heard one clergyman reel off for my edification the names of the multi-millionaires belonging to his Communion, as a Franciscan might reel off the names of Saints belonging to his Order. Moreover, a comparison between Mexico and the United States is not fair, since about fourteen million out of the fifteen million people in Mexico are natives or *mestizos*, and not therefore so easy to educate or civilize as the Whites.

In any case, this question of the comparative merits of Catholic and Protestant civilizations is too complex to be solved by quotations from *Westward Ho*. Moreover it soon became clear to all Americans that, even after the suppression of her monasteries, Mexico did not go ahead, and that Mexican anti-clericalism was impotent for constructive purposes and potent only for evil and for destruction.

"We are in honour bound to remedy this wrong," said Mr. Roosevelt, but President Coolidge has adopted a policy of "watchful waiting" and there is great reluctance to criticize him or to hurry him, not only for the reasons I have already given, but also because of a deep respect for the Presidential office that has now grown up in America, and which may be observed even in the articles of such journalistic filibusters as the *New York Journal*. The President occupies in America a position like that which King George would occupy in England, if he were also

Prime Minister; and in some respects it is an unfortunate arrangement as it leaves no place for a big political leader at the head of a Ministry and liable at any moment to get a good, healthy heckling on the subject of his home or foreign policy. Mr. Baldwin and M. Poincaré have to submit to this process, which has generally a beneficial, tonic effect on them as well as on their critics.

I have now shown how President Wilson, the Professor of the Fourteen Points who won the Great War and afterwards re-divided Europe, drove out of Mexico a Conservative Catholic President who was personally distasteful to him but under whom, in the opinion of the American Ambassador, Mexico would have enjoyed another spell of prosperity such as it enjoyed under Porfirio Díaz. In my next chapters I shall give the characters of the gentlemen whom President Wilson placed in power.

After several years of office, Carranza began to see that the anti-religious articles in the Querétaro Constitution were a mistake, and to harbour an idea of amending them; but Calles and Obregón objected to this, and in the end drove the President from the Federal Capital. He perished miserably in a wretched hut at Tlaxcalantongo where he was shot by several murderers despatched for that purpose by Obregón. Such at least is the report current in Mexico City and it is certainly in accord with Mexican Presidential practice; but, though I have met several people who assured me that full proofs of Obregón's guilt exist, I have never seen those proofs myself.

Obregón succeeded Carranza, and continued the anti-clerical tradition. In 1924 Calles succeeded Obregón; and in July 1928, Obregón will succeed Calles. Obregón and Calles constitute, therefore, a Duumvirate Dictatorship of a peculiar kind; and these two will succeed each other until one or the other dies. Democratic Government does not of course exist; votes cast at Presidential elections are not counted.

PART II

THE PERSECUTORS

Chapter I

SONORA

To understand Calles, one must first understand Sonora, the home of the wild Yaqui Indians and of the wilder men who now rule *la República Mejicana*. As a glance at the map will show the State of Sonora is situated in the northwest corner of Mexico, washed by the Gulf of California, and bounded on the north by Arizona.

Of the Yaquis I shall say little, as they are outside the limits I have assigned to myself in this book, and consist in all of only fifteen hundred fighting men; nevertheless, they deserve a few paragraphs to themselves, being one hundred per cent American and the old proprietors of Sonora. Small attention was being paid, however, to their ancient rights when I first entered Sonora, in April 1927, for Mexican troops, to the number of 17,000, were then engaged in hunting down the Yaquis as if they were wild beasts. Some of them had been killed. Others had been shipped to an unknown destination from the ports of Guaymas and Mazatlán. A few had taken refuge in the United States. But many were resisting, though broken up into small bands of horsemen widely scattered throughout a difficult mountain country, and their resistance was not altogether passive judging by the appearance of the country when I entered it. Forty-five railway bridges had been destroyed; and in the train by which I travelled there were two armoured cars, one in front and one in rear, each containing a score of soldiers whose Mausers projected through the loopholes and whose intent faces showed that they were not enjoying the ride. As a matter of fact, railway travelling in Mexico was anything but enjoyable in the spring of 1927 and it is worse now, in the spring of 1928, for owing to the destruction of several large bridges in Jalisco, it is impossible to reach the Federal capital by the West Coast railway, and, even along the route which is still open, the traveller is never quite sure whether the train will be (1) blown up or (2) merely derailed. There is also the possibility of his being hit by a stray bullet, for as in England bad boys sometimes throw stones at trains, so in Mexico bad men occasionally send a bullet through them. Some months after I passed this way, an American schoolmistress on a holiday trip was killed on this line by a rifle bullet which came through the carriage window at which she was seated; and some months before I passed, a train had been derailed, attacked by rebels, and set on fire, with the result that all the passengers as well as the military guard had been shot or burned to death. The soldiers were responsible, however, for the death of the passengers as, instead of fighting in their armoured cars, they had taken shelter behind the women passengers in the train, and at the same time continued firing, with the result that the rebels were compelled, in self-defence, to kill everybody.

The country through which we travelled had apparently been starved by nature as well as desolated by war; but nature's parsimony in the matter of rain could easily have been made good by irrigation such as that which has converted the Imperial Valley of California into one of the richest agricultural districts of the United States. But the Mexicans have no time for irrigation themselves, and they are now killing all the American attempts at irrigation by means of a law, the *Ley de Extranjería*, which forbids any foreigner to hold land within fifty kilometres of the sea-coast or one hundred of the frontier. Any foreign farmer who already holds land within this forbidden zone cannot bequeath it to his children or sell it to another foreigner; and, as no Mexican can buy, the land will simply revert to the Great Sonoran Desert, and all the magnificent work done on the Mexican West Coast by small American farmers will have been done in vain.

The district through which we passed seemed to feel that it was already doomed, for it consisted entirely of a great ashen-coloured plain upon which a hot sun beat down relentlessly. There was no vegetation save *cacti* and thin, dusty bushes. On both sides of the railway was desolation, on one side the desolate Gulf of California, on the other side the desolate Sierra Madre Occidental. And the railway itself was a desolation, for nearly all the stations along the line had been burned by the Yaquis.

We stopped every ten minutes at a military post which was always a combination of field-work, fortress, and encampment, but which sometimes looked like a squalid Indian village composed of thatched huts not as high as one's head. Sometimes there was a kernel of blackened masonry that had once been a railway station. Sometimes this kernel was a stately old Spanish Presidio in which the Mexican soldiers crouched, as Bedouins might crouch in the ruins of a Greek temple. But though these forts thus differed in some respects from each other, they all possessed certain military features in common. They were all surrounded by trenches and barbed-wire entanglements; and in the centre of each was a look-out post, sometimes on the roof of a house, sometimes on the top of a tower, sometimes on the top of some scaffolding, and in it there was always a sentry, rifle in hand, shaded from the sun by a strip of matting, and with his eyes fixed intently on the foothills of the Sierra Madre. Alongside him was suspended a bell, obviously of ecclesiastical origin. The Church bells in Mexico no longer call the people to prayer; to ring them for religious purposes is, in fact, a criminal offence. But they are rung for other purposes; they are the tocsins of war.

Another trait these posts have in common. In all cases the *cacti* and other vegetation have been cleared away for a distance of five or six hundred yards all around—a field of fire.

At some of these forts I saw the word "Battalion" displayed, but "Battalion H.Q." must have been meant as there was never more than one company of soldiers in any of these places. The bivouacs were of the most primitive description—boughs of trees sometimes, with ancient coats and blankets spread over them to exclude the burning rays of the sun. In every encampment there was a swarm of women and children, for when the Mexican warrior takes the field, he always takes his family with him. His wife looks after the Commissariat, and acts as tailor, cook, washerwoman, and (when necessary) Red Cross nurse.

The soldiers were all pure-blooded Indians, not of the Yaqui tribe, for even the *Yaquis Mansos*, or tame Yaquis, had been placed under arrest or supervision all over Sonora for fear that they might assist their wild brethren of the hills; and none of the officers whom I saw could be described as white. The men wore all sorts of uniform. Some were in khaki drill of military cut. Some were dressed exactly as workmen, in white calico or in blue overalls, with nothing to indicate their military character save the prodigious supply of ammunition which they carried in belts around their waists. These were probably the *Agraristas*, rural communists whom Calles is seeking to rally to his side by giving them huge chunks of other people's land, exactly as Lenin won the support of the Muzhiks in 1918 by encouraging them to divide the estates of the landlords.

Some of the soldiers wore broad-brimmed *sombreros* of straw; others *sombreros* of felt; others, again, military caps. On the march, with their domestic animals, their women, and their children, these troops gave the impression of a savage tribe migrating. The improvement that has taken place in the appearance of the soldiers in the Federal District does not extend to Sonora.

What caused this little war, which afterwards broke out again, in the spring of 1928? The answers I got to this question were various, but always uncomplimentary to the Mexican Government (of which I regard Obregón as being practically a

member). Some people said the Mexicans had deliberately broken faith with the Yaquis. Others said that a war was forced on
the Yaquis by Obregón who, in view of the coming elections to
the Presidency, wanted an excuse to get an army sent into
Sonora, so that he could get control of it, for in Mexican elections rifles count, not votes.

It surprised me, however, to find that the United States took
so little interest in this Yaqui war. Only a few hours to the north,
American schoolboys were intent on *The Last of the Mohicans*,
and apparently unaware that the real thing was going on so
close to them. Only forty-eight hours to the north, the film
actors of Hollywood were staging sham dramas of Indian war,
and paying not the least attention to this real drama; in fact, they
were absolutely ignorant of it. The explanation is, I suppose,
that men, as well as boys and women, tend to cultivate the arti-
ficial instead of the real, that minor poets find it easier to copy
major poets than to study nature and life.

But even politicians who pride themselves on their cosmic
breadth of view are sometimes as narrow as minor poets. When
I was in Los Angeles, Mr. Upton Sinclair and a number of other
Radicals were orating on the subject of two men, Sacco and
Vanzetti, who had been condemned to death in Massachusetts,
and they always denounced as a reptile and an enemy of the
Cause anyone who interrupted to ask about the Yaquis and the
Christians who were being slaughtered at that moment in
Mexico.

On the other hand, the woes of the Yaquis are sometimes,
as I have already pointed out, the burden of Communist, Pacifist, Methodist and Humanitarian oratory—but only when their
oppressor happens to be a Catholic Conservative. Some twenty
years ago the Humanitarian, religious, and Socialistic Associations of the United States rent their garments, poured ashes on
their heads, tore their hair, wept tears of blood, and went
through all the other motions symbolical of immeasurable woe,
because Porfirio Díaz was making a mild attempt to transplant
those Yaqui Indians to Yucatán where they could get plenty of

work in the *henequén* fields. Now that Calles is slaughtering those same Indians like wild beasts, we do not hear a word of protest from these sensitive associations.

What is the explanation? Can it be because Porfirio Díaz tolerated the Church while Calles persecutes it? Or is it because the members of these wealthy and sensitive associations are, after all, very simple souls who take people at their own valuations, that they are like the book-reviewers who only read the preface and base their review on that? A Tsar comes before them for judgment. They consult their little note-books and say "Hem! Declares he is an Autocrat. Must be a bad man, tyrannical, bloodthirsty, etc. We will denounce him whatever he does."

Or a Lenin. Again the note-book. "Says he is a plain, simple man, opposed to bloodshed in any shape or form, and filled with affection for the common people. Obviously we must praise him; he's all right."

Bluff, honest old Porfirio, the Mexican Mussolini, never talked of liberty or the Proletariat, hence he was naturally denounced as a superstitious tyrant and a cruel slave-driver when he attempted to transplant the leisurely Yaquis in the direction of work. Calles, on the contrary, has proclaimed, *urbi et orbi*, that he is a Proletarian and a Friend of the Poor. He admits that he is the best friend the Indians ever had; and when flatterers assure him that he is of pure Aztec descent, he does not correct them. In public orations he sometimes turns a moist eye towards the vanished glories of Montezuma, and never, never, has he a good word to say of Cortés or the Spaniards, or the religion introduced by the Spaniards. "Hence," say the seventy-one humanitarian Associations of the United States, "this man is a sincere lover of the poor, dear Indian, and those irresponsible newspaper men who accuse him of murdering the Yaquis are base calumniators."

If they went more deeply into the subject, they might change their opinion; but, in the mad whirl of modern life, Americans have no time to go deeply into any subject save that of money-making. I cannot say that I have got very deeply into the subject of the Yaquis myself, but I saw in Sonora a number of things which made me doubtful of Calles being the best friend of the Indian. One sometimes sees in Sonora, the ruins of the old churches and schools built by the Franciscans for the Yaqui Indians in the sixteenth century; and it is quite certain that the Yaquis have now been thrown back again into a barbarism worse in some respects than that from which the Franciscans rescued them, that they have lost almost all the religion they ever had, and are acquiring again that taste for blood which made them the most sanguinary savages of the New World. I cannot therefore agree with those American Humanitarians and other cranks who regard as benefactors of the Indians the men who have destroyed their churches and schools and who consider the Franciscans as a retrograde and noxious influence.

Sonora is at once the most advanced and the most backward of the Mexican States. It contains the most savage Indian tribe in the whole Republic, and at the same time it is more affected than any other part by the feverish activity of the Colossus on its northern frontier. Mr. John Lind, the unofficial envoy of President Wilson, the Colonel House of Mexico, had a delightfully simple theory to the effect that always and at all times the people living in the north of a country are superior to the people in the south. This may or may not be true in Norway, from which Mr. Lind's ancestors hailed, but it is certainly not true in Mexico where the best men have come from the south and the worst from the north. Velásquez and Porfirio Díaz, both came from Oaxaca: Carranza, Calles, Obregón, and Serrano came from the North. Oaxaca is a centre of consolidation, Sonora a centre of disintegration—possibly because of the vicinity of the United States.

What is good for one country is not necessarily good for another; what cures the smith, kills the tailor; and American influence has, generally speaking, been bad for Mexico. It led the first Mexican republicans to draw up a constitution which did not suit them; and it has been responsible for much of the trouble in Mexico since. This has been well pointed out by a

Mexican lawyer, Mr. T. Esquivel Obregón, in his *Constitución de Nueva España* a paper read before the third national juridical congress.

Carranza's Constitution of 1917, about which I have already spoken, is also spoilt by American influence, in this case the influence of American Prophets who are certainly without honour in their own country, which would probably have clapped them into jail or exported them to Russia, their spiritual home, if they had not crossed the Rio Grande in the nick of time. Some of these philosophers were what is known in America as draft-dodgers—in other words, they escaped military service in the United States when that country entered the World War, by the simple process of bolting across the frontier. Others of them were simply thugs. All of them professed, however, to be austere Marxists; and all of them had a good deal to do, indirectly, with the drawing up of the Querétaro Constitution which is the cause of the present difficulties not only between Chapultepec and Washington but also between Chapultepec and Rome.

Calles, though he does not speak English, was born near the southern border of Arizona, and has been all his life associated with Americans of an undesirable type. When he was a boy in Sonora, that State had been demoralised by Sonorans who had come back from California, and was being invaded by very tough Americans from California, Arizona, and New Mexico, as mines were being opened up by American capitalists; and, for some reason or other, a western mining camp attracts every sort of international criminal, male and female, as surely as a dead horse attracts vultures. This influence from north of the border made Sonora the hotbed of revolution which it has been for the last thirteen years, and made Calles and his Sonorans what they are. The industrial civilisation of the Anglo-Saxon is sometimes as fatal to solitary tribal settlements of Indo-Iberian stock as the rich assortment of drinks and diseases which Anglo-Saxon pioneers bring with them. Before the Americans came to open mines and to build the Southern Pacific of Mexico, Sonora was peopled by isolated, patriarchal communities which were peculiarly unfitted to stand the rude impact of the north. Owing to the difficulties of communication with the Federal Capital, they had become weakened, physically and mentally, by constant inbreeding. The Americans woke them up, it is true, but they also unsettled their faith without giving them a new faith, and imparted to them a restlessness which does not seem to have done much good to them or to Mexico. From that restlessness were born Calles and Obregón, Gómez and Serrano.

But even now, the average Sonoran town would be regarded by a New Yorker and, indeed, by an Old Yorker, as a sleepy, one horse, dead-and-alive place. From an architectural point of view, the old church, built of adobe, is still the one redeeming feature. The barracks, and the Government offices, and the official residences can also boast of graceful lines which recall the old Californian missions, the explanation being that the Government has, in the name of the Sovereign People, bagged the Bishop's Palace, the Franciscan monastery, and one or two old convents.

Most of the houses are of adobe, and not one of them has a bath or a latrine. Only about a dozen have glass in the windows, the police commissioner's, the padre's, and the houses of nine or ten shop-keepers. The population is ninety per cent Indian or *mestizo*, and nine per cent Chinese. In summer-time the younger children are almost completely naked, and there is much ophthalmia, dirt, and skin disease. The roads are extremely bad, very dusty in the hot season and very muddy when it rains. There are few old towns, however, where one does not find an ancient Spanish house, its shady *patio* filled with flowers and trees; but a new house built by a *revolucionario*, one never sees, for, as I have already pointed out, the Mexican *revolucionario* is a parasite, intellectually impotent, utterly unable to create, to build, to plant, to sow, to organize or to do anything whatever save rob people and cut their throats.

On the other hand there is the American element, mostly from California and Arizona. Even at the present moment,

Arizona is none too tame, but when Calles was head of the police in the frontier village of Agua Prieta, that wretched little place was overrun not only by Mexican bandits but also by American desperadoes, for most of whom the principal attraction of Agua Prieta consisted in the fact that, if they killed their man on one side of the international street, they could escape the consequences by crossing to the other side. Agua Prieta was, in fact, a den of drunkards, smugglers, card-sharpers, horse-thieves, filibusters, murderers, criminals, and bad men generally. It is necessary to bear this fact in mind if we wish to understand the mentality of President Calles.

That remarkable but obnoxious man was born and had all his early training in the only part of the North American West which is still entitled to use as a prefix the adjective "wild." As police inspector, first of Agua Prieta and afterwards for all Sonora, he was brought into daily contact with the most desperate characters; and, even if he himself were not a super-tough to start with, he would have had to become one in order to survive. He owed his success, however, to Oriental craft rather than to Occidental courage. It is also very necessary to remember that the Americans he knew at this period, including the American officials on the frontier, were mostly "grafters," and cut-throats of the worst type, for it was from them that he got his idea of America, a very erroneous idea and one which may ultimately be the cause of his ruin. In the same way he may have also met at this period, on that wild frontier, bad priests who gave him a very erroneous idea of the Catholic Church.

In the cinema the Wild West is always picturesque and often chivalrous, but the specimens which the Mexican Wild West have sent to Chapultepec are simply ignorant and savage. Imagine what the United States would be if it were ruled by Chicago gunmen of the worst type and of foreign origin, and you will have a good idea of the present state of things in Mexico, for Mexico is ruled by its gunmen.

This may seem to be an exaggeration, but it is literally true, as may be seen by the most cursory examination of the records of Mexico's present rulers.

I shall begin that examination by an investigation of Calles's own record, for Calles is not only the Dictator of Mexico, but is likely to continue dominating the country even after he resigns the Presidency in favour of Obregón, a much weaker man. Calles is also the driving force of all the present religious persecution and the author of the Agrarian and Petroleum legislation which has caused such difficulties with the United States. It is only right, therefore, that I should investigate Calles's career first.

CHAPTER II

THE MURDER GANG

IT might be supposed by quiet people leading sheltered lives in Sussex, Massachusetts, and such-like civilised places, that the members of the murder gang alluded to in the title of this chapter were in jail or on the hills, with the police after them, but, unfortunately, this is not the case, the gang in question being the government of the country, and the most prominent members of the law-abiding, conservative community being in prison, in exile, or "on the run."

As I have already pointed out, all the members of this murder gang came from Sonora. All three Presidential candidates in 1927 were from Sonora, and all of the three candidates who ran in 1923 were also from the north-west. In one respect Sonora resembles the small State of Georgia in the Caucasus, for as Georgia sent forth Stalin and the clique which now dominates the Empire of the Tsars, so Sonora sent forth Calles and the gang which now dominates the Empire of the Aztecs. Moreover, as Stalin has wisely placed Georgians at the head of all the more important Government offices in Moscow—and especially at the head of the vitally important OGPU—so Calles and Obregón have, with touching nepotism, placed Sonora men in charge of the more important Government offices in Mexico City, especially the War Office and the Prefecture of Police.

I would not push the parallel too close, however, for whereas Stalin, Bukharin, Chicherin and half-a-dozen other Bolshevik leaders are educated men who have read Karl Marx in the original, and who are (some of them at least) genuine enthusiasts, Calles, Obregón, Morones and all the other Mexican Marxists, are dishonest, insincere, financially corrupt, less than half educated, and more than half savage. It is true that Calles pays marked attention to the Bolshevik Legation, but this is only to strengthen his influence with the CROM and the *Agraristas*, and it failed to impose on Madame Kollontai, the Bolshevik Representative, who has now left Mexico. In an interview she gave to a German paper on her way back to Russia, she briefly described Calles and Co. as "a gang of brigands."

This is a correct description. To show how correct it is, I need only mention the fact that Calles, who entered politics without a *centavo* and whose official salary was never large, is now a very wealthy man and owns the large hacienda of *Soledad de la Mota* in the State of Nuevo León; while Obregón who began life with a small farm of a dozen acres, is at present one of the largest landowners in Mexico. Chicherin, to do him justice, showed that he was a sincere Communist by giving all his land to the peasants; but though Calles insists on cutting big chunks for the peons out of other people's estates, he has not allowed an inch to be deducted from his own estate or from the estate of Obregón.

In this section of my book I shall deal, at considerable length, with the early life of Calles and with the Sonora gang and with Sonora itself, for a study of all these is necessary to render credible many incidents that would be otherwise quite incredible, among them the appalling cruelty of the Dictator, his barbarity, his ignorance, and his utter failure to understand even the ABC of Constitutional Government. Unless one knows the conditions under which the present rulers of Mexico were brought up, one would find it difficult to believe some of the brutal acts perpetrated by the Sonorans; one would find it difficult, for example, to believe that the head of the Police, a General, would strike in the face with his whip and without provocation, a lady who called at his office to request that he would order the reopening of a church which the police had closed. Yet this, General Roberto Cruz did, and it is one of the least of Roberto's crimes. His greatest crime was probably the murder of Father Pro Juárez and his three companions on the 23rd of November, 1927, and this crime, which I shall describe in detail, was marked by features which would horrify even Felix Dzerzhinsky. As will be seen, the four prisoners were given no trial, and, though they strongly protested their innocence, Cruz informed the newspaper reporters that they had confessed themselves guilty. He was present at their execution, uniformed, powdered, perfumed, gloating; and, after the execution, he actually had himself and his fellow-executioners photographed on the blood-stained ground, he with a cigarette between his thick, sensual lips. Such things would be impossible of belief unless the reader were first given a careful account of the circumstances and the society which have produced such monsters.

The savagery which distinguishes the Sonorans is so great that we cannot judge the present Mexican Government by ordinary standards, not even by Balkan standards; and consequently, it would be one of the most absurd things in the world to hazard any prophecy about Mexico. To show how unsafe prophecy is, even the prophecy that Calles and Obregón will keep together, I need only point to the history of Mexico during the last fourteen years, the period during which the present murder gang from the North has been in power. It is so dreadful a history that even the Balkans of fifty years ago might legitimately object to any comparison, and it would, indeed, be more correct to compare the Mexico of the Sonoran period to those bloodthirsty but decadent Khanates, some of them situated in Northern Africa and some in Central Asia, which were conquered by France and Russia in the course of the last century.

In Mexico we find the same sudden permutations and combinations as we find in those doomed Principalities, the same swift uprisings and savage repressions, the same instantaneous conversion of friend into foe, the same appalling cruelty and bloodshed. But of course there are also differences. In the mongrel rulers of Mexico, we find a strange smattering of agnosticism, Marxism and Constitutionalism and a great deal of lip-service to progress, science and democracy. To make the mixture more horrible still, we find these medieval brigands sending each other expensive American motor-cars before sending each other assassins; we find them vowing eternal friendship, in exclusive interviews granted to the special correspondents of New York papers, just before they start murdering one another; we find the Sultan getting his official photographer to "snap" the contorted features of a disobedient Grand Vizier as that gentleman stands at dawn in front of a firing squad and with his back to a wall. One has an uneasy feeling, while witnessing such things, that the marvels of modern science can be utilized just as well by a modern Nero or Caligula or Caesar Borgia as by a tame, respectable modern who pays income tax, lives in the suburbs, and goes every morning to the City.

In the year 1915 we find Carranza, Obregón and Calles fighting shoulder to shoulder, like brothers, under one banner. A few years later we find Carranza lying dead in a wretched hut at Tlaxcalantongo, where he was murdered by paid assassins of the faithful Obregón. A little later Sultan Alvaro Obregón ascended the vacant throne with Calles on his right hand and Adolfo de la Huerta on his left, these being the trustiest of all his Janissaries. But in less than a year, Adolfo declared war on Alvaro who was only saved by the intervention of President Coolidge, who supplied him with arms, ammunition, and aeroplanes. In January 1927 Calles was supported by his two Generals, Francisco Serrano and Arnulfo Gómez (both Sonorans) and he must have trusted these Generals implicitly for he had given to Serrano command of all the troops in the Valley of Mexico, and to Gómez the command of Vera Cruz, the gateway to the capital. Yet, before the end of the year, Calles had Serrano assassinated at Cuernavaca, and Gómez was hunted down like a wild beast in the mountains and finally trapped and shot, the click of the official photographer's camera being drowned by the reports of the five rifles which sent five bullets through his breast.

CHAPTER III

CALLES

I AM not prejudiced against President Calles; in some respects
I even admire him ever since I had an opportunity, in the year
1927, of investigating his early life and adventures, and of conducting those investigations in the sleepy little one-horse town
of Guaymas, Sonora, where, in the year 1870, he first saw the
light. A full and accurate account of this illustrious man's career
would be every whit as interesting as the imaginary adventures
of Gil Blas or Hadji Baba of Ispahan; but, unfortunately, Mexican adventurers who attain high position seem to become
ashamed of their humble origin and their early struggles, for the
autobiographies which they give out for publication are as col-
ourless as the autobiographies in *Who's Who*. Of course there is
this to be said for that system that at all events it keeps them out
of jail, for if they gave as frank an account of their career as, say,
Benvenuto Cellini gives of his, they could hardly escape imprisonment or assassination, unless, indeed, they took the precaution before publication to change their names and go to the
Galapagos Islands or some equally remote place.

Plutarco Elías Calles, the head of the Sonoran clique and the
Stalin of Mexico, is half Syrian and half Yaqui, and is illegiti-
mate. His father belonged to that strange race which calls itself
Syrian, and which has added an important, but poisonous, ele-
ment to the ethnological hotch-potch that makes up Latin
America. America does not allow any more Syrians to enter the

territory of the United States; and she acts very wisely in keeping them out, for, though I have come across them all over Mexico, Central America, and South America, I never once heard them spoken well of anywhere.

They are charged with dishonesty in business; but an even greater offence in the eyes of the easy-going Latins, is their low standard of life and their habit of combining in family groups which undersell all rivals, kill all competition, and get control of almost any branch of trade. Their exact ethnological composition is, by the way, somewhat of a mystery, for though in Syria there are Arabs, Jews, Turks, Armenians, Greeks and other races, there is not, so far as I was able to discover, any race which calls itself Syrian. In Brazil, Turks and other Mohammedans from Asia Minor call themselves *Sirios* in order to disarm the hostility of an ultra-Catholic people and to give the impression that they belong to a Christian race which groaned for centuries under the domination of Stamboul; and Calles, who is known in his native town as "*El Turco*" (The Turk) may really be of Turkish descent. If so, that helps to explain the intense hatred for Christianity which is one of his most prominent characteristics.

Most authorities agree, however, that he is the son of an Armenian pedlar, and if this is so, one can understand the mysterious disappearance of every record relating to his birth, for according to the Mexican Constitution, the son of an alien is ineligible for the Presidency. Writing in the February (1928) *Reflex*, a Jewish monthly published in the United States, a Mr. Adolphe de Castro, himself a Jew and formerly American consul in Madrid, claims Calles and Aarón Sáenz as Hebrews, and declares that the existing persecution is "an act of retributive justice rare in the annals of history." However that may be, there is no doubt that Calles hates Christianity.

A more amiable feature in his character is that strong family affection which, as I have already indicated, binds together all Syrian immigrants in Mexico, making them a State within a State. His half-brother, Arturo Malvido Calles, is Mexican

Financial Agent in New York City, where he has to deal with extremely delicate financial matters, and has the rank of Consul General. From the Mexican point of view, New York is the most important foreign city in the world; that is why Plutarco Elías entrusted it to his half-brother. Thus we have Plutarco holding the highest post a Mexican can hold in Mexico, and Arturo holding the highest post a Mexican can hold abroad; while a relative, Pancho Elías, has been twice Governor of Sonora, and other relatives of the President are comfortably provided for. It must be a great consolation to the Mexican people to know that, much as they themselves suffer from poverty, they are nevertheless maintaining in luxury all the members, legitimate and illegitimate, of this interesting family from far-off Syria; and that even if Brother Plutarco is ever ejected from Mexico—which Heaven forfend!—their judicious investments in the United States will enable them to pass the rest of their lives in opulent tranquillity.

The reader may wonder, by the way, why, save the great man himself and his children, no member of the Presidential family bears the Spanish name of Calles. Possibly the President's mother was a Calles, for all the Indians have Spanish names; but in any case the Castilian name Calles is much more suitable to the ruler of a Spanish-speaking people than the Syrian name Elías, just as the good old Russian name of Trotzky is much more suitable to a Muscovite *magnifico* than the Jewish name of Bronstein.

After a slight smattering of education at a school in Hermosillo, Plutarco began life as a Primary School teacher in his native town of Guaymas; but his convivial habits and the disappearance of certain funds that had been entrusted to him, as treasurer, by the Guaymas Teachers' Association, soon led to his being ignominiously "fired." Through the influence of a kind uncle, he afterwards obtained the position of municipal treasurer in Guaymas; but in a short time he was "fired" from this post also, owing to the discovery of an inexplicable shortage in his accounts; and he would even have been prosecuted, had not the same kind uncle generously come forward with a promise to make good the deficiency.

He did not keep his promise; but long afterwards, when Calles stood as a candidate for the Governorship of Sonora, the Municipality, dazzled by his oratory and by the success which had accompanied him so far (and rather scared by the number of murders he had committed) wiped out this indebtedness and this blot on the Callista escutcheon.

For the moment, however, the prospects of our hero were bleak, and he experienced for a time that annoying difficulty in finding another billet which similarly forgetful financiers experience even in this country. Finally he was forced to descend somewhat in the social scale and to accept a job as bartender in the "Hotel Mexico," a new, but already disreputable, establishment which his brother Arturo had just opened on the Plaza of Guaymas, opposite the venerable church of San Francisco.

Here, perhaps, and not in the hereditary hate of the Moslem for the Giaour, nor in the obscure labyrinths of theological, historical, or sociological controversy, will the future historian seek for the origin of our hero's anti-clericalism. The good Padre of San Francisco may have objected to the unholy uproar in Calles' "pub" of a Saturday night which had insensibly merged into a Sunday morning; and it must be borne in mind that since all this happened in the days of Porfirio Díaz, the Padre was a man of some local consequence. If this theory is correct, Calles has had his revenge, however, for when I recently visited the church of San Francisco it was deserted, and when I inquired discreetly about the Padre, I was told that he was in hiding and had been for some time in jail. On the other hand, Arturo Malvido Elías, as we have just seen, is now the Mexican Financial Agent in New York. Thus are the benefactors of struggling genius rewarded and its enemies crushed!

In a short time Plutarco Elías became owner or part-owner of the "Hotel Mexico" and as he added a gambling table to its other attractions, he had to keep his wits about him, for a low-class drinking-den which is at the same time a gambling-hell does not, as a rule, attract a very select clientele, at all events in the Wild West of Mexico.

But, perhaps, after all, this severe training was the best that this remarkable man could possibly have had for his subsequent political career. In the first place historians will probably date from this period our hero's ardent teetotalism; and doubtless they will attribute it to the fact that nightly observation of the pernicious effect of bad liquor on the human system cannot have been lost on that acute and powerful intellect. As frequently happens in such cases, self-denial has been rewarded even in this world, for the warm friendship of the American Prohibitionists has been of inestimable political service to our hero, whose strict teetotalism gave him a great advantage, besides, in his contest with the alcoholic Serrano towards the end of 1927.

Valuable, too, in their influence on his future Presidential labours, were the nightly struggles with inebriated guests (each with his hip-pocket revolver). These strenuous exercises must have kept Plutarco in excellent physical condition, must have accustomed him to think and act quickly, and to shoot at sight, may even have imparted to his sombre visage and menacing gait that truculent air of the "chucker-out," which is still discernible by the initiated even at the most august diplomatic functions, and which has not, so far, been neutralized by the Presidential sash nor by all the glories of Chapultepec.

Very different, of course, is the training of a United States President nowadays; but then, "North is North and South is South," as Governor John Lind would probably have sung if he were a poet.

One of the least pleasant characteristics of the Oriental race to which our hero belongs is an inveterate habit of having an accidental fire in their houses after having first taken the precaution to insure them heavily, and this characteristic President Calles does not lack, for, after having insured his saloon with two American Companies, he "had a fire," as the phrase goes, a very thorough one too, for the house was so completely gutted that not even a stone was left for the veneration of posterity; and when the other day I myself, accompanied by a few members of the local CROM, made a pious pilgrimage to this hallowed spot, I found it was occupied by another building.

Calles maintained of course that the fire was accidental, but the Insurance Companies refused to pay up, and even indulged in nasty insinuations. Finally, after the dispute had gone on for some time, a composition was effected and the future Dictator received something, but not so much, alas! as he was entitled to.

We next find our hero in charge of the ranch of Santa Rosa, which belonged to his uncle. (Notice how, with characteristic family affection, the relatives of Calles helped him as he afterwards helped them; this helpfulness is very characteristic of the *Sirios*.) Under his expert management, the ranch soon went bankrupt, and was finally mortgaged to another relative, Pancho Elías, who afterwards became Governor of Sonora. Then he was for a time in charge of a flour mill at Fronteras, but that also failed. This would probably have been the end of him, for family affection has its limits even among the *Sirios*, had it not been for the fact that, ever since he was a teacher, he had dabbled in politics; and that his tall stature, his impressive appearance, his grim face, his powerful voice, and his rough eloquence caused him to be much in demand at political meetings.

Just after the flour mill followed the ranch into the bankruptcy court, the revolution of 1910 took place, and furnished Calles with many opportunities for demonstrating from the top of a soap-box how the country could be run on sound business lines. Naturally, he was in the ranks of the "advanced" thinkers, and his doctrine, like that of the dreamy Madero, was strongly impregnated with Socialism.

When Madero came into power, he offered Calles the arduous post of police inspector at Agua Prieta on the Arizona frontier. Calles accepted the post, but, as the salary was exiguous, he also opened a store, a public-house, and a gambling saloon, and went halves with one Tomás Rosas, a local butcher, who specialized in the slaughter of cattle stolen from the American side of the border. This little arrangement with the butcher, though it must have been profitable to Calles in his private capacity, was naturally intolerable to him as a Police official; but he finally quieted his conscience by reporting Rosas to the American authorities, after which he drove him out of the town, and calmly annexed his business.

As a soldier, Calles was not a success. His first defeat took place at the village of Cutchverachi in the year 1912, when he was already a Colonel. He had marched at the head of forty Federalists against a rebel leader called Francisco Escandón, who had appeared on the frontier; but, though Escandón commanded an army of only twenty men, he not only routed Calles but also captured him. Calles is said to have pleaded piteously for his life, and to have even gone down on his knees to do so, but Escandón was pitiless until a Spaniard called Huerta, who was acting as a medical officer in the rebel force, begged that Calles should be allowed to go free. The result was that Calles became the bitter enemy of Huerta, and that he even went to the trouble and expense of having him kidnapped from Douglas, Arizona, and hanged in the Plaza of Agua Prieta on December 15, 1918. A Sonoran who knows him well, tells me that on that occasion he rose at five o'clock in the morning to gloat in solitude for hours over the limp body swinging from a gibbet in front of his police station. I am averse to putting in these ghastly touches, but to omit them would be to leave my reader under a false impression regarding Calles' character. It is history, not I, that deals harshly with this Mexican Dictator. Indeed, I omit quite a number of murders with which he is credited, because I wish to give him the benefit of the doubt.

And now for a word about this kidnapping of Mexicans by the Mexican authorities from the territory of the United States. As I have already pointed out, it is quite a common practice, partly because there is a large Mexican population north of the border, and partly (I regret to say) because the officials on the north side of the frontier are often as corrupt as those on the south side. Even in the month of October, 1927, a Mexican

General who escaped into America from Calles was kidnapped, conveyed back to Mexico, and assassinated; while, about the same time there was a regular panic among the Mexican refugees in San Antonio, Texas, owing to the activity there of the Mexican Secret Police.

Calles' dealings with corrupt and bribable Americans on the frontier must have given him an erroneous impression of the United States generally, and this may be his ruin, so that his peculiar training in Sonora has its bad points as well as its good. That erroneous impression must have been heightened when, in Mexico City he afterwards came in contact with low-class American journalists impatient at the small remuneration offered by the Press and anxious to become advisers, publicity men, or propagandists for the Mexican Government. Some of the American Oil agents are equally contemptible: I do not of course refer to the official agents; I refer to the numerous, unofficial agents which Oil considers it necessary to maintain in the Mexican Capital.

The Teapot Dome scandal throws a strong light on the corruption which prevails among American Oil magnates in America: what, then, must the state of things be in Mexico, where every kind of swindling can be covered up on the plea of secrecy? The American novelist, Joseph Hergesheimer, gives in his novel *Tampico* a good idea of this corruption, which involves forgery, the theft of confidential documents, and even murder. At the present moment there are scores of secret agents employed by the Oil men. Some of them are hunting after compromising letters which are floating around. Some of them are forging State papers. Americans are working against Americans as well as against Mexicans; and nearly all of them are swindling their employers.

Calles knows a great deal about these people, for some of them have offered to serve him. He found Mr. Sheffield as upright as the highest type of English public servant; but he cannot have been favourably impressed by some of the other Americans who came to see him. American Chambers of Commerce frequently organize joy-rides to Mexico City, are dined and wined and made drunk by the Mexican authorities, and are then addressed by Calles, who finds it difficult as a rule to conceal his contempt for them. Even the American Federation of Labour sent an important delegation to attend Calles' inauguration as President, and allowed themselves to be filled up with alcohol and official propaganda. The intellectual Radicals of the United States are more dignified; and several articles by a prominent Radical writer, Mr. Carleton Beals, which have appeared in the *New Republic* (New York, July 6, 1927 and August 17, 1927) contain denunciations of the Calles regime which are as strong as anything I have written in this book.

Calles and most Mexicans have a sincere contempt for the United States; and it would be interesting to speculate on what the result of this feeling will be when America gets control of Mexico; for that she will eventually be forced to establish a protectorate over the country is pretty certain. In that case she will not (according to English critics) have the advantage of that prestige which the British rulers of India enjoyed among the natives, that reputation for truthfulness, strict impartiality, incorruptibility and justice. Moreover, the better class Mexicans will consider that their civilization is better than that which flourishes north of the Rio Grande; that they are more courteous in their manners; and that their appreciation of literature, art, and music is higher than that of the *Gringo*. In Mexico, the United States has certainly a problem which will leave her little leisure to put things right in other parts of the world.

Calles' next defeat was inflicted on him by a General Ojeda, another revolutionary who had entrenched himself in Naco, Sonora, and whose programme apparently consisted of the three words "Agin the Government." Calles attacked him at the head of a much superior force, but was routed and forced to cross the frontier and take refuge in Douglas, Arizona. The State Department at Washington has still, by the way, in its Mexican archives, a request from Ojeda for the extradition of one Calles, a horse thief, on the charge of having fled to Douglas astride of a stolen mule.

But before the request could be answered, Ojeda was "on the run" himself, and Calles was back in Mexico arranging with Obregón that treaty of friendship and alliance which has proved so profitable to both these distinguished politicians.

CHAPTER IV

MORE CALLES

FROM Agua Prieta, Calles was promoted, with the rank of Colonel, to Hermosillo, the State capital, whence he ruled all the police of Sonora, as choice a band of cut-throats as one could find anywhere in the world.

Under him, at Nogales on the Arizona frontier, was Captain Arnulfo Gómez who had, as a boy, been a pedlar, but who was afterwards to rise high, and finally to die at the hands of a firing squad on a charge of rebellion. When he was a Police officer in Nogales, he was a faithful follower of Calles as the following incidents show. I give them to illustrate the character of both Calles and Gómez, as well as to indicate the amenities of life on the Mexican-American frontier at that particular period.

One half of Nogales is Mexican and the other American; and, in the American half, there lived at this time an expelled Mexican journalist called Sanchez, better known by his nick-name of *"El Chorizo,"* who published lurid weekly attacks on Calles in a little Spanish paper called *The New Era*, printed of course on the north side of the frontier but circulating surreptitiously throughout Sonora. Calles, who is morbidly sensitive to newspaper criticism, and who may even object to the present book, seems to have instructed Gómez to "get" Sanchez by hook or by crook, with the result that Gómez did "get" Sanchez, not by hook, indeed, nor yet by crook, but by lasso!

Sanchez had a habit of walking at a certain time every day along the American side of the international street to which I have already alluded; and, on learning of this, Gómez had a heart-to-heart talk with sundry American authorities; and here I might pause to remark that in this part of the States some of the American officials are accused by the Mexicans of being very corrupt. Possibly they have been demoralised by contact with smugglers, bootleggers and Mexicans; and they themselves are very often more Mexican than American. I have been told of many instances in which they allowed Mexican detectives to arrest political prisoners on American soil and to carry them across the border; and some of these incidents are of quite recent occurrence.

Gómez also had a talk with a certain Mexican soldier who was very expert with the lasso; and, one day when the unsuspecting Sanchez went for his usual *paseo* after having dined particularly well at his usual tavern, *Las Emociones*, he was suddenly lassoed, dragged to the Mexican side of the street through the wire fence which separates the two Republics, and at once murdered in the presence of many American spectators. A copy of the latest issue of *The New Era* containing the usual virulent attack on Calles, was then nailed to his forehead, and the body was left lying there all day.

It is the custom of the Sonora gang to leave the dead bodies of their victims lying thus in public places: in this respect that gang is no better than the Chinese Communists on the Yangtze. In October, 1927, the dead body of a General Huerta was left lying for a whole day propped against a tree in the market-place of Nogales, and photographs taken of it as it lay there, surrounded by children, and bearing insulting inscriptions written on slips of paper, appeared in many of the New York papers about a week later. Even now (April 1928) dead bodies of Catholic guerillas are exposed in the same way all over Jalisco and other States.

I have described above the sad fate of "*El Chorizo.*" That neat piece of work seems to have encouraged Colonel Calles to send

Captain Gómez another obnoxious journalist for treatment. The second victim was one Manuel M. Huguez, managing editor of *The Voice of Sonora*, a little newspaper published in Hermosillo, the capital of Sonora, and somewhat critical at times of Calles, then chief of police there and the superior of Gómez.

Acting with his usual resolute illegality, Calles had this pestiferous scribe placed on board a northward bound train; and, when he reached Nogales, Captain Gómez and the American Immigration authorities took very good care that he did not get any further. Gómez had received instructions to "eliminate him at the first opportunity," and this opportunity soon came in the tavern of one Pedro I. Torres, who has been described to me as "a spy of Calles."

"This tavern," continued my informant, "was patronised by Huguez, who was a notorious drunkard; and on one occasion when the unfortunate man was under the influence of drink, it occurred to him to give a cheer for General Maytorena."

It was a fatal brain wave, for Calles was a deadly enemy of Maytorena, consequently the scandalized Torres immediately arrested Huguez and dragged him before Captain Gómez, whose sentence was as short and as much to the point as that passed on himself the other day in the mountains of Vera Cruz. "Take the newspaper gent to the cemetery," he said significantly: and three soldiers at once did so.

Now, the only kind of business that has flourished in Mexico for the last sixteen years is the undertaker business and those "businesses" which are dependent on it, that is, coffin-making, grave-digging, etc., and, for the last sixteen years, the only "live" place in a Mexican city has been the cemetery. Nogales was no exception to this rule. In anticipation of "rush" orders, a number of graves had already been dug in the crowded cemetery of Nogales, and at the foot of one of those graves, Huguez was permitted to drink a bottle of whisky which the soldiers had considerately purchased for him *en route*, with the money they had found in his pocket. When he had finished the bottle, he was shot.

Meanwhile, Calles was dreaming of something better than the control of the Sonora Police; he was aspiring to the Governorship of the State; and, finally, he proposed himself as Governor without, however, resigning his official post. This was, of course, a flagrant breach of the Constitution; but, then, the whole career of Calles is paved with breaches of the Constitution, even as a certain place is said to be paved with good intentions. Having counted the votes himself, he announced himself well and truly elected, and nobody ventured to disagree with him since he was the Chief of Police, with a long list of murders to his credit. It was about this time, too, that the Guaymas municipality hastily decided to erase from their records all reference to the shortage in Plutarco's accounts and to declare that he left their service without a stain on his character.

From the Governor's palace in Hermosillo to the Chapultepec Palace in Mexico City is only a step, especially now when Sonora dominates Mexico; and, as Calles had by this time made an advantageous pact with Obregón, we soon find him President of Mexico.

But though the news of his "election" to the Presidency was received with great delight by the American Federation of Labour, which hailed him as "the Labour President," he is not a person in whom American or European democrats can take much pride.

Plutarco Elías Calles personifies, in fact, one of the strongest objections that are urged by absolutists against the elective system of Government, the charge that, under this system, a man is sometimes raised to high office not because he is fitter than anybody else to discharge the duties appertaining to that office but simply because he can talk. Here we have a man who, having failed disastrously in everything to which he put his hand, succeeds in taking charge of everything.

Even as a parent he cannot be regarded as a success, for on May 18, 1927, when I entered the Mexican town of Nogales, one of his sons reeled out of a night-club at three o'clock in the morning, and had to be kept in order by the repeated discharge of a policeman's revolver close to his ear. Yet Plutarco Elías now poses as the father of his people.

As treasurer of the Guaymas Municipality he appropriated the funds entrusted to him, with the result that, instead of being in jail, he is now in charge of the national treasury from which he has paid out millions of *pesos* to finance revolution in Nicaragua and communistic propaganda in Mexico and Central America.

His failure as a teacher has encouraged him to "reform" the whole educational system of Mexico, which is now much worse than it was in the days of Porfirio Díaz when, Heaven knows, it was bad enough.

Moisés Sáenz, Sub-Secretary of the Department of Education in Mexico, puts the total number of schools in Mexico in 1926 at 12,257, but many of these exist only on paper. Emilio Rabasa gives the number of schools at the conclusion of the Díaz regime as 12,518 (*La Evolución Histórica de México*); but there were probably more, for religious schools were very numerous at that time, though, being illegal, they were not included in the official reports. In a message to Congress in September, 1926, Calles boasted of having closed more than 120 colleges; but did not speak of having opened any. It is true that he opened a number of agricultural colleges, but these turn out politicians, not agriculturists.

The failure of Calles as a farmer has led him to put into execution a mad-cap agrarian scheme which is ruining agriculture in Mexico.

His failure as an industrialist has led him to issue edicts which are destroying all the Mexican industries.

He never went to any Christian church and is apparently not a Christian at all, but that has not prevented him from founding a Christian Church of his own, *la Iglesia Católica Apostólica Ortodoxa Mejicana* (the Catholic Apostolic Orthodox Mexican Church) as he calls it, one of the most misshapen ecclesiastical abortions that ever came into this world. Yet this monstrosity is regarded with reverence and hope by many Protestant theologians north of the Rio Grande, and one American Episcopalian clergyman has joined it and been made a Bishop.

He never studied economics, but that has not prevented him from embarking on an economic revolution which is inflicting untold hardships on the Mexican people. He poses as a friend of the Indian, yet in 1912 and again in May, 1927, he made a fierce and inexcusable attack on the Yaquis.

He poses as a friend of Labour, and has been saluted by the A.F. of L. as a "Labour President," "a lover of Liberty and Humanity," a "Man of Destiny," yet he is only using Labour for his own ends, as Lenin did. On July 2, 1914, he broke, by means of rifle bullets, a strike of workmen which took place in the mining works of a personal friend of his at Cananea, Sonora. He made the troops fire on the strikers, with the result that several were killed; he then forced the men to return to work at three *pesos* a day; and when their women-folk invaded the workshops in order to make them come out again, he had forty of these women arrested and lodged in jail. At present he has deprived Mexican workmen of nearly every kind of freedom, freedom of speech, of the Press, of religion, and of education for their children—unless, of course, they speak in favour of him, attend the Mexican Church which he has founded, and send their children to his anti-Christian schools.

Let us pause here for a moment to examine the system of education which this unsuccessful teacher has forced on Mexico. It is, in one word, a thoroughly Bolshevik system. In January, 1927 there was issued a decree of the Ministry of Education relative to the books to be used in Mexico's grammar schools; and one of the books is *Lecturas Populares*, a series of selections edited by Esperanza Velásquez Bringas, a prominent official in the Ministry. The first part of this volume includes shorter compositions by such writers as Anatole France, Tolstoy, Andreyev and Romain Rolland. The second part is entitled "The Revolutionary Ideology," and contains an address by President Calles, a few remarks by Eugene V. Debs, an exposition of socialism by

Mr. Wells, a pronouncement by Henri Barbusse, and a prose poem by Jean-Jacques Rousseau. Ultimately the child is introduced to Felipe Carrillo Puerto (a fanatical Bolshevik leader of Yucatán), Karl Marx, Lenin, Kropotkin, Louise Michel and Rosa Luxemburg.

Even more striking is the *Catecismo de las Doctrinas Socialistas* issued by the Government printing office of Saltillo, Coahuila in 1926. This document, the title-page assures us, is "arranged in conformity with the catechism of Christian doctrine, as per the Jesuitical ritual of the Roman Catholic Church, which is a necessary arrangement on account of the fanaticism of the present generation."

This means that the book is a parody of the Christian Catechism. The Ave Maria is parodied as follows:

> Hail Socialism! Thou art full of love, fraternity is with thee, and thou art powerful among all the oppressed, and great therefore shall be the fruit of thy doctrinal womb.
>
> Holy Liberating Cause, Mother of Humanity, do not abandon us now nor at the hour of our social emancipation.

To a Roman Catholic, and therefore to ninety per cent of the Mexican people, this is blasphemous; and the parodies which I have seen of the Lord's Prayer would be regarded as blasphemous by any Christian body.

Calles poses as the friend of the Downtrodden and the Oppressed, and insists on bestowing large chunks of other people's land on peons who do not want them, yet, as I have already pointed out, he himself owns the vast hacienda of *Soledad de la Mota* in the State of Nuevo León. In addition to this, he has still the extensive business interest he acquired in Agua Prieta, when he was Police Inspector there. One of these interests is a tannery which has, so far, netted him over half a million dollars. He had himself appointed a director of the Banking and Loan Association of Sonora. He has several fine farms in the Agua Prieta district. He owns vast mining interests in Pilares de Nacozari, and he holds a majority of the shares in the mine *El Tramador*. He calmly took possession of certain public lands in Vera Cruz as soon as he had learned that they contained rich oil deposits. Early in 1923 he formed an oil company in partnership with Obregón and a number of other friends. One of those friends was the unfortunate General Francisco Serrano whose shares in this company were, presumably, confiscated by Calles as his vast estates were certainly confiscated, and I should not be surprised to find that all this loot now belongs to Calles personally or to some of his friends, for, as we shall see later, Calles gave the blood-stained but expensive motor-car of Serrano to one of Serrano's murderers, though, from a legal point of view, he had absolutely no right to dispose in this way of Serrano's property.

The Oil Company to which I have just referred is known as "the National Oil Company of Tabasco and Chiapas," and it is not the only Oil Company in which Calles is interested.

It would be idle to deny, of course, that Calles is in some respect a remarkable character. He reminds me indeed of Oliver Cromwell, if I eliminate Cromwell's military genius, his personal bravery, and his religious fanaticism, for Calles is a bad General and a worse soldier, and his fanaticism is all anti-religious. He possesses, however, in a high degree three characteristics of the Lord Protector—craft, cruelty, and an intense hatred of the Catholic Church. With his craft there goes a capacity for judging character which has enabled him to collect around him men almost as bad as himself, but nevertheless devoted to him. Of these men—Obregón, Amaro, Roberto Cruz, and others—I shall speak later.

Calles is very far from being as educated or as intellectual as Cromwell. He is to the last degree obstinate, and he is by disposition an extremist like López of Paraguay, or Rosas of the River Plate, or the men who "put over" Prohibition in the United States; (the New World seems, by the way, to have a curious tendency towards Extremism.)

His detestation of intoxicating liquor led him, when he became Governor of Sonora, to issue his famous "decree number one," which imposed the penalty of death on anyone caught selling intoxicating liquor. People laughed at first, for Mexico is in some respects an easy-going Latin land: everyone drinks pulque, mescal, tequila and aguardiente, and even Obregón is fond of the flowing bowl. But the laughter ceased when the Callisto police began putting tavern-keepers up against a wall and shooting them. Of one such case, at all events, there is no doubt, that of "*El Corcholito*," a *mestizo* who brewed as well as sold a concoction of unusual potency in Hermosillo. When he fell dead, his infant son was clinging to his legs, and covered with his father's blood, but the gendarmes were not affected by the sight. The indignation caused by this execution would have overwhelmed a weaker man, but Calles did not even stoop to explain, though he might have pointed out that such severity was justified by the harm that aguardiente was causing among the Indians, then on the war path. Like Lenin and other great Leaders of the "Proletariat," Calles has all the temper of an autocrat.

Curiously enough, this Draconian severity has only made Calles popular with the Puritan extremists who really govern the United States, I mean the Methodist-Baptist organisations which are responsible for Prohibition, and which have permanently barred out Al Smith from the White House. A love of extreme measures is a craze with these organisations, and indeed, with Americans generally: see their craze for Prohibition, cleanliness, disinfection, speed, work, sport, "records" of all kinds, and the sterilization of criminals. The American Prohibitionists have even proposed to add a deadly poison to alcohol so that it cannot be drunk in any form; and the number of lives which have been lost so far in the hopeless attempt to make the United States "bone dry," surpasses the number of casualties in some of Europe's "little wars."

When Calles was governor of Sonora, he expelled every priest from that State, so that the present persecution throughout all Mexico might easily have been prophesied; but Americans take no interest in Mexican State Governors, even when they are potential candidates to the throne of Montezuma: they are infinitely more interested in sport, aviation, the scandals of Hollywood, and the doings of Big Bill Thompson of Chicago.

Calles is one of those unwise extremists who never know when to stop, who push onward and onward so long as their victims give way, even though this retreat leads into a quicksand where both pursuers and pursued will likewise perish. If the victim is weak and friendless, Calles blusters amazingly; but if the victim is supported by formidable exterior forces, armed with military and financial power, Calles invariably gives way. He belongs, therefore to a class of bully more common among degenerate Asiatic races than among Americans and Europeans. Now, it is fatal, of course, to yield to a bully: compliance only inflames him more and more; but several of his victims did yield to Calles. One was the English manager of the Light and Power Company of Mexico City, a very large concern registered in Canada, which runs the whole tramway system of the Capital. In 1924, this Company was confronted by a formidable strike which had behind it the whole power of the Government, for Calles finds the support of Mexican strikers an easy means of winning popularity since the capitalists in Mexico are invariably foreigners. Instead of allowing the strike to be fought out in the usual way, the Dictator sent for the manager, received him in his most truculent manner, and said to him: "I will give you three days to agree to the demands of the strikers; and if, at the end of that time, you have not done so, I will take over your whole business and expel you from the country. Good day."

The manager gave way there and then; and this triumph led Calles to interfere with the foreign banks. He violently claimed for the banks' Mexican employees, an amount of control which no bank could possibly give to its clerks. Every foreign bank would have to employ a very high percentage of Mexicans; and its books would have to be open to investigation by its Mexican clerks who would also be entitled to an impossibly large percentage of the profits. Again, Calles reckoned on winning popularity among Mexican labour without antagonizing Mexican employers; and he also knew that while, owing to the Monroe doctrine and to the debilitation and impoverishment caused by the Great War, Europe could not intervene, President Coolidge would also refrain from intervention. But international Finance can do a great deal of harm, especially to a country like Mexico, by simply sitting still with folded arms; and, inside of twenty-four hours, the banks had brought the tempestuous Dictator to his senses by putting up their shutters, closing their doors, and preparing to withdraw from the country altogether. With ludicrous panic and alacrity, Calles gave way; whereupon the banks reopened again.

But he immediately afterwards tried to save his face by attacking an enemy which he regarded as weak and friendless, the Church; he made demands to which the Church could not possibly yield, without stultifying itself, proving false to its Divine mission, and surrendering to Caesar the things that were God's, but the Bishops were unsupported by bayonets, and got no encouragement from the American Press, and no sympathy from any European Government, even from the Government of Spain. The Church closed its doors, like the banks, by proclaiming an Interdict, but this only made Calles laugh, for he had never been to Church in his life, and had never, probably, received any Sacrament of the Church, not even Baptism. Moreover, he has been encouraged in his war on the Church by the expressions of admiration he has had from many religious organisations in the United States and of many Communist and Masonic organisations in Europe, and by the almost complete silence of the great secular newspapers everywhere. Small secular newspapers in Ireland and Belgium and, of course, Catholic religious newspapers all over the world have attacked Calles, but the combined circulation of them all would hardly equal that of one of the big dailies in New York, London and Paris which have apparently closed their columns entirely to all news of the religious persecution in Mexico. Instead of bringing trouble on Calles, the persecution of the Church has even helped him in his confiscatory and retrospective legislation on the subject of the oil lands, ranches, and haciendas held by Americans, for any attempt of President Coolidge to intervene vigorously with regard to these matters would be regarded by powerful Protestant organisations in America as an inspiration from Rome; so that President Coolidge, being a canny New Englander, does next to nothing for any American interests in Mexico.

Coolidge and Calles seemed, indeed, to swap roles in the most curious manner, for at the end of 1926 it was Coolidge, the man of few words, who blustered and collapsed, and Calles the "dago" of many words who kept silent and won. With regard to the effect of the confiscatory laws on American interests in Mexico, Mr. Kellog had used such strong language in December, 1926, that a landing of United States marines was expected every moment at Tampico; but this menacing gesture was followed immediately by a pitiable collapse from which Uncle Sam has not yet recovered. As a matter of fact, the old gentleman was suddenly hit on the head from behind by the combination of Protestant, Pacifist, Prohibitionist, Humanitarian and Bolshevist associations to which I have already alluded; but as to what subsequently happened, the reader will have to see chapter I, part IV of this book wherein I deal with American-Mexican relations, for that subject is too large to be dealt with at the tail-end of a chapter on Calles.

The result was that during the year 1927, Calles swelled, metaphorically speaking, to twice his natural size, interfered in Nicaragua; aspired to the leadership of a Central American confederation against the *Gringo*; paid marked attention to Madame Kollontai, not because he admired her or the Soviet Government which she represented, but because he knew her to be *persona non grata* in Washington; and gathered around him at Chapultepec as choice a collection of Yankee Communists, thugs and army deserters as had ever met before on the soil of Mexico.

At the same time he exhibited the prudence of the bully, afraid that his victims might hit back, by refraining from the enforcement against the American Oil Barons of the confiscatory legislation which he had made.

With the Church, of course, it was a different matter. The more clearly he perceived the weakness of the Church in material things, and the reluctance of any temporal Power to support her, the more outrageous became his assaults on her, until by the spring of 1928 the persecution had reached a point never attained, in some respects, by the persecution of Nero or Diocletian.

For some reason or other, Calles has an intense hatred of the Catholic Church, a hatred quite as great as that of Cromwell. An American journalist in Mexico City once had an opportunity of discussing the whole religious question with President Calles, or rather of listening to Calles on that subject for an hour and a half. This correspondent was a Protestant and he was not particularly interested in religious matters, but he came away from that interview in a cold sweat, and confessed to me (when he had recovered his speech) that he had been appalled by the abyss of hate which lay behind the Dictator's words. "I saw behind his words," he said, "not only a life-time of hate, but many generations of hate. Moreover, in his whole mentality he is strikingly un-Mexican."

Another friend of mine, a foreign diplomatist who had to see Calles frequently, confirmed this statement and added that, every time the Catholic Church was mentioned, the President grew black in the face and pounded the table with his fist. "Of all the members of the Government," added my diplomatic friend, "Calles is the only one who takes the matter to heart in this way. The others are mostly actuated by greed."

I should put it somewhat differently however. I should say that while the others are actuated only by greed, Calles is actuated by both greed and fanaticism.

CHAPTER V

OBREGÓN

CALLES and Obregón together form a rotativist Dictatorship of a kind very unusual in history, and unique in the world at present. It is said that in a secret compact which was made, over ten years ago, between these two men, it was laid down that they should succeed one another alternatively, and in 1924 Calles did succeed peacefully to the chair vacated by Obregón, after a farcical election at which a Conservative, one General Ángel Flores, had the temerity to offer himself as a candidate. Soon after the election, Flores was assassinated. In 1927 Obregón offered himself as candidate for re-election, and was strongly supported by Calles, despite the fact that the re-election of a President is forbidden by the Constitution, and is detested so much by the people that the words "*sufragio efectivo—no reelección*" (an honest suffrage—no re-election) is printed to this day on all Government notepaper, on passports, and on official proclamations, like the words "Liberty, Equality, Fraternity" in France, and the words "Workmen of the World Unite," in Soviet Russia.

True, a servile Parliament had agreed in November, 1926, that the words meant only "no immediate re-election," and that an ex-President was eligible if he presented himself after an interval; but it was the business of a Constituent Assembly to clear up this point, not that of a Parliament. In any case Calles violated the Constitution by the support he gave to Obregón. He gave Obregón unlimited credit at the Bank of Mexico, made the Treasury defray the expenses of the Obregónist Conventions throughout the country, and allowed those Conventions to be presided over in twelve States by the State Governors and to be packed with Government officials. At that time I myself saw Obregón's election literature posted on the armoured cars that accompany all railway trains and on the old Church of San Francisco in Mexico City, a church which is now Government property quite as much as the armoured cars. All this was, of course, flagrantly illegal; but Calles revels in flagrant illegality.

Gómez and Serrano, the "anti-re-electionist candidates," as they called themselves, protested against these illegalities, and Gómez even went so far as to publish his protest, in the *Excelsior* of 28 June, 1927; but the answer of Calles took an unexpected form; he accused both Generals of rebellion. Serrano was shot at once, and Gómez shared the same fate after having been hunted down in the mountains where he had taken refuge.

I shall give a detailed account of these happenings later on: here I only mention them to show that, in all probability, there is a pact between Calles and Obregón; and that it is unhealthy for any politician to get in the way of that pact by standing for the Presidency. Three men have already lost their lives by doing so; and the absence of any opposition candidate at the present moment, though the Presidential elections take place in July, is an eloquent proof of what I say. A soldier of the Great War would say that the approach to the Presidency is like an exposed point commanded by an enemy sniper: it is ominously deserted save for three dead bodies lying on the ground.

The Calles-Obregón dictatorship has every chance of lasting as long as the Díaz dictatorship, though its effect on Mexico will probably be as harmful as the effect of the Porfirian regime was beneficial. Calles and Obregón have complete confidence in each other; and they supplement each other in a remarkable way. If one of them lack any wickedness, the other is sure to have it. Calles gambles but does not drink: Obregón drinks but does not often gamble. Calles is a bad soldier but a crafty politician, while Obregón is a good soldier but a poor politician.

As a politician, Obregón has some curiously soft streaks in his character, especially when it is a question of enforcing drastic laws calculated to offend affable foreign diplomatists, pious Mexican ladies of good family, and wealthy corporations, whereas Calles on the contrary, seems to take a positive pleasure in being bluff, brutal and offensive. He is like the dourer kind of Scot while Obregón, who is said to be descended from an Irish exile named O'Brien, has something of the physical pugnacity and the moral weakness that often distinguishes an attractive kind of Southern Irishman. A foreign diplomatist once put the same idea in fewer words when he said that Calles has moral but not physical courage, whereas Obregón has physical but not moral courage; but I do not like to use the word "moral" in connection with either of these gentlemen.

Like the devil-may-care character that he is, Obregón does not worry much about the religious question; and, once he got safely into Chapultepec Palace, he would probably come to terms with the Church were it not for the fact that Calles will certainly remain at his side in order to keep him up to the mark, and that he, Obregón, has now committed himself far too deeply to the Church's enemies. Most of the *corps diplomatique* and some of the Mexican hierarchy think differently and point to Obregón's laxity on the Oil question, the Land question, and the Church question during his last period in office, but in Obregón's election address of June 1927 there was an unaccustomed hardness. The voice was that of *el modesto agricultor de Cajeme*, but the words were those of *el Turco de Guaymas*. In other words, that election address was as anti-clerical as Calles himself could have desired. It was filled with a panic fear of what he called "Reaction," and panic fear is at the root of all persecution: the persecutors are more subject to it than the persecuted. And Obregón has not only the Catholics to fear; he has also to fear his own partner, who would strike him down without a scruple if he stopped the persecution. Here also there is a dead body in the trench, the dead body of Venustiano Carranza; and it will be safe to assume that, for the next six years, Obregón will simply be a figure-head, and Calles will be the master. Twice Obregón got into touch with the exiled Bishops, once in the autumn of 1927 and once in the spring of 1928; but as the Bishops said that the anti-religious laws would have to be rescinded, the negotiations went no further.

The career of Alvaro Obregón has been quite as shady as that of Plutarco Elías Calles, but Alvaro has always had a better Press, thanks to his genial and liberal way with newspaper men, though, as a matter of fact, he is *un faux bonhomme*, and not of Irish descent; these big and boisterous men are often the falsest and most cunning of all.

He has been particularly well advertised in the United States and in Europe, not only in newspaper articles but even in books; and I regret to say that in connection with this advertising campaign there are many stories of financial corruption. One English journalist is said to have received 50,000 *pesos*, and a large number of American newspaper men were at one time on Obregón's pay-roll. A high American official in Mexico City once confessed to me that this was the case. "How often," he said, "have I seen newspaper men come here with high professional ideas, to which they do not live up for long! In the beginning, several trenchant paragraphs appear in their newspapers; then there is a long silence; and, after that, alas! the usual praise of Obregón."

Obregón has many American friends who are even more powerful than newspaper men. One of them is Mr. Shoup, President of the Southern Pacific Railway, another is Mr. John Hays Hammond, and a third is Mr. Henry Payne Whitney. Mr. John Hays Hammond, who was associated with Cecil Rhodes in South Africa and who was imprisoned by President Kruger after the Jameson Raid, is a very large land-owner in Mexico. He and Mr. Henry Payne Whitney hold the Richardson Ranch in Sonora, which comprises some six million acres; both are in partnership with Obregón, and both are doing their best to make that corrupt politician President of Mexico, because they know that, if he does get elected, he will repay them a hundredfold. With them is Mr. Shoup of the Southern Pacific Railway, which recently spent $10,000,000 connecting Tepec with Guadalajara. Mr. Shoup and a group of very wealthy friends of his in California hope to make millions if Obregón lets them exploit the properties adjoining the railway system. I need hardly add that the estates of these gentlemen are untouched by the Agrarian Law which has ruined so many small American ranches on the West Coast; and of course the estates of the President, of the Calles family, and of Obregón are also untouched.

Mr. John Barton Payne and Mr. Beecher Warren are likewise on Obregón's side; as also are many small American capitalists and officials in Arizona and California. I was told in Mexico City that Obregón's personal friends among Americans on the Arizona frontier and in California helped very much to stop the gun-running carried on by the friends of the Catholics and the Yaquis in the spring of 1927, gun-runners being frequently caught, and dumps of arms being often discovered.

Nevertheless, Alvaro Obregón is quite as disreputable a character as his colleague, Plutarco Elías Calles—which is saying a good deal.

We first hear of him as the owner of a farm of about 50 acres, the *Quinta Chilla* near the obscure village of Huatabampo in Sonora. Then he became the municipal President of Huatabampo; and might have remained in that position till this day were it not for the rebellion of Madero. Previous revolts against the authority of Porfirio Díaz had left him cold—because they were fore-doomed to failure: on one occasion, indeed, he promised to join an insurgent leader, but failed to do so, and even took the opposite side, with the result that the *insurrecto* was defeated and killed. The Madero revolution was quite a different matter, however, being backed up by powerful interests in the United States and well supplied with arms and ammunition which were allowed to cross the frontier without let or hindrance on the part of the American authorities.

Having appropriated the sum of 3,000 *pesos* which he found in the municipal treasury (he did not take more because that was all there was), he spent it on the arming and equipping of a gang of Weary Willies at the head of whom he presented himself, sword in hand, to the Governor of Sonora who saluted him as Lieutenant-Colonel; gave him back his 3,000 *pesos* (under the impression that they were his private property); and named his followers "the Fourth Battalion of Sonora."

Thus began Obregón's Napoleonic career. He was successful as a soldier; and he had the discernment to strike a bargain with Calles, whom he created General and placed at the head of all the Police in Sonora, when he himself marched south against Carranza.

As a result of that campaign, he was President for one term, and it was during his Presidency that the disgraceful murder of Mrs. Rosalie Evans took place and the breaking off by Mr. Ramsay MacDonald of diplomatic relations between Great Britain and Mexico. *The Rosalie Evans Letters* place Obregón in a bad light; they show us that Obregón was reluctant to protect Mrs. Evans against the Bolshevik villagers who had illegally seized part of her estate; that he took no steps to punish her murderers; and that he resented the plain speaking of the British *Chargé d'Affaires* on this subject.

Obregón induced the United States to renew diplomatic relations by saying that the article in the Constitution which referred to Petroleum lands was not retroactive, but when Calles came into power he explained that the article and the law based on it were retroactive.

In these circumstances, it is difficult to understand the optimism with which some American newspapers and some foreign diplomatists look forward to Obregón's accession to power in July 1928, though of course it is easy enough to understand the joy of Obregón's rich Yankee friends.

During the war, Obregón was a bitter enemy of America, and therefore a friend of Germany, to which he sent so much goods that he was listed in the Black Book both of the United

States and of England. On account of his being thus officially listed, he was once refused bags which he wanted to buy for his agricultural produce by two large British firms which are established in Mexico, and which employ, between them, some seven thousand men. Obregón has never forgiven these firms, and has not only boycotted them ever since, but has even succeeded in having the duty on imported bags lowered, in order that they may be ruined. In other words he is bitter, small-minded, and ready to injure even his own country if he can at the same time injure a personal enemy.

His return to civil life, on leaving office, was hailed by many newspapers in the United States as an astounding and auspicious event; and it is not often indeed that a Mexican President does leave office without a row; as a rule he leaves Chapultepec for the cemetery. He returned, like Cincinnatus, to the plough, in other words to his great estate of 12,000 acres at Cajeme. Enthusiastic journalists followed him thither, and described afterwards how he employed over one thousand men and how favourably Cajeme, with its cultivated fields, its flour-mills, and its bustle contrasted with the arid deserts of Sonora. But *el modesto agricultor de Cajeme*, as Obregón is called by ironical Mexican journalists, is a humbug who owes most of his popularity abroad to skilful propaganda. His delight in country life is a pose for the edification of the United States, which seems to have a traditional sympathy with republican Presidents who were born in a log cabin and passed their boyhood splitting rails. Instead of rejoicing in country life, Obregón disliked it and manifested extreme anxiety to return to Chapultepec where he could squeeze more money out of the Mexican people.

While waiting to get back, he borrowed large sums of money from the Government bank (for agricultural purposes of course); and induced the Department of Agriculture to spend over half-a-million *pesos* on the port of Yavarros, simply because that port is convenient to his estate. As there are only fourteen feet of water on the bar, which is continually shifting, this money might as well have been thrown into the sea, though it might be better to spend it on Guaymas, Mazatlán, Manzanillo or some of the other Pacific ports, which badly need improvement.

CHAPTER VI

THE MEN AROUND CALLES

THE men around Calles are worthy of him, though some of them are still worthier of comic opera.

Luis León, who was for some time Minister of Agriculture, has no acquaintance with the science of agriculture, or with any animal used in agriculture save the ordinary domestic bull, for until he entered politics, he was a professional bull-fighter.

Another Minister, who posed as being peculiarly the friend of the Poor, kept up four separate and expensive establishments in the Federal Capital, with a mistress and a Rolls Royce in each; and though he murdered one of those mistresses some time ago in a fit of jealousy, the matter was easily hushed up.

As General Francisco Serrano and General Arnulfo Gómez were both Sonora men, and as they were, until the middle of 1927, faithful henchmen of the President, I shall glance at their careers also.

Serrano, as a boy, had been a fiddler in a disorderly house, but he afterwards joined a circus, and, by sheer force of character, raised himself to the position of chief clown. From the position of chief clown in a circus to that of General in the Mexican Army is an easy transition, for, in order to become a General, one has only got to equip a few scallywags and lead them to the assistance of some politician who happens to be in difficulties. Now, Serrano joined Obregón when Obregón was in very great difficulties, and it was he and not Obregón who deserves the credit for the latter's famous march of 8,000 kilometres from Sonora to Mexico City. He was rewarded with the portfolio of War Minister in Obregón's Government, and he retained that position for some years despite the fact that his private life was not quite what Americans or Englishmen would call respectable. In fact, his addiction to drink, gambling and debauchery was so notorious that even the Mexicans noticed it, and when the election campaign began in June 1927, his two rivals, Obregón and Gómez, made pointed reference to these little weaknesses. The first posters of Gómez bore a portrait of himself with the words "*El hombre sin vicios*" (the man without vices) underneath, the allusion being to the rival who had all the vices; and the original draft of Obregón's election address contained such a violent attack on the private life of his former Minister for War that, in order to prevent the immediate outbreak of hostilities, the more crafty Calles persuaded his hot-headed colleague to omit most of this onslaught.

Even while occupying the position of Minister of War, Serrano could not observe the usual conventions of polite society. Once on a night of revelry, he threw a nude woman out of a window, and though she was seriously injured by the fall, Serrano continued to hold his post. Whenever he contracted debts in a tavern, a brothel, or a gambling-hell, he had an easy way of signing a cheque on the War Office for the amount telling the debtor to collect it there next morning; but after that impecunious and long-suffering institution had paid out over two million *pesos* in this way, even Obregón became scandalized, with the result that Serrano was sent to Europe for a year and a half on an ideal sort of official mission with no duties attached to it but with full pay and all travelling expenses.

This singular forbearance on the part of President Obregón was probably due to his feeling of gratitude towards this drunken soldier for his past services, but it may also have been due to the fact that he himself had mixed occasionally in Serrano's revels. At one time, indeed, Obregón, Calles, Serrano and a few other choice spirits were in the habit of gambling heavily together; and in one night Serrano lost 75,000 *pesos* to the famous Mexican bullfighter Gaone, who won 100,000 *pesos* in all on that occasion from these three gay and disreputable adventurers.

As will be seen later, Serrano's decision to stand for the Presidency brought on him the wrath of the Duumvirs; had it not been for that unfortunate decision, he might still be holding a high position and at the same time getting as much amusement out of life as ever.

Although, as we have just seen, Gómez presented himself, somewhat pharisaically, to the electorate as "the man without vices" (*el hombre sin vicios*), and though I am told that the Catholics finally decided to support him, *faute de mieux*, he also was a typical Sonoran politician and had long been a tool of Calles. The Catholics say that during the Jalisco insurrection he made friends with the Catholic *insurrectos*, and afterwards betrayed them to the Government. In his boyhood he had been a pedlar; and he really seems to have had fewer vices than Serrano, though of course that does not mean that he was a saint.

The two men who have done more than any others to maintain Calles in power are General Joaquín Amaro and General Roberto Cruz. Amaro is the Minister of War, or Secretary for War, to use the Mexican title, a man of about thirty-five years of age, and a pure-blooded Indian. He acts not only as Minister of War but also, on occasion, as Commander-in-Chief, and throughout the year 1927 he was in charge of the operations against the Catholics in Jalisco, Zacatecas, Colima, Michoacán, and several other States, and is still in charge of these operations. In this work he has not been conspicuously successful, partly no doubt on account of his eagerness to make money by sparing land-owners able to pay heavy bribes. At first he decided to form concentration camps, and to waste all the country outside them, his object being to leave the guerillas nothing to subsist upon; but finally he spared the crops and herds and haciendas of such *hacendados* as paid him enough to equip a certain number of soldiers; and I heard that much of this money went to himself.

The Catholic insurrection I shall deal with later; here I shall confine myself to saying that it was badly organized and badly conducted, and that Amaro showed no military talent by the way he handled it. This insurrection is much worse now, that is, in the spring of 1928, than it was in the spring of 1927; but, though Amaro does not shine as a fighter, he has succeeded at all events in keeping the army solid behind Calles, for the last two years. Some battalions broke away, it is true, at the time of Serrano's murder, but they soon returned to their allegiance; and at the time of writing (April 1928) the army is all on the side of the Dictator. This is a very exceptional circumstance in recent Mexican history, and speaks well for Amaro, who probably pays the soldiers and does not steal their boots as Mexican Generalissimos generally do.

When one speaks of the Mexican "army," one should use inverted commas, as when one speaks of the "Liberals," "Constitutionalists," "Patriots" or "Congress" of Mexico; for everything save the Church is opera bouffe. The "soldiers" are generally men of the worst antecedents, many of them being actual criminals wanted by the police, for, in organising his revolutionary forces, Carranza recruited all the bandits in the country, took all the able-bodied criminals he found in the jails, and attracted to his service as officers such evil-doers as had had the wit to keep out of jail.

An entertaining book could be filled with the humorous stories which are told of the Mexican army. One story told to me by an American settler on the West Coast was about a Mexican General at Chihuahua who was amazed, one day, to receive five hundred thousand *pesos* to pay his troops who had not been paid for years; and who had been "living on the country" since the days of Díaz. Evidently there was a revolution brewing, and the President of the moment was anxious to make sure of the troops near the American frontier.

When he had recovered from his astonishment, the General immediately brought the money across the frontier to El Paso, where he deposited it under his own name in an American bank. In Juárez, on the way back, he seized a goods train and had it brought to Chihuahua, where he discovered to his disgust that it was laden with soap—a luxury which this hardy warrior never used. But, as there was no help for it, the General called together his soldiers, showed them the train, and said "*Hijos mios!* I know that your salaries are in arrears, and that most of you are bare-footed; and I deeply regret that I am unable to pay you. But here is soap! It is yours. Sell it and make all you can out of it, or, alternatively, boil your blasted heads in it for all I care."

For the next ten days Chihuahua and its environs were full of soldiers selling soap at prices which can only be described, in the language of the trade, as "an alarming sacrifice." But they never thought of using it on themselves.

As might be surmised, the officers are generally of the same type as the men, being without military training. Some are bandits, like Pancho Villa, who won his spurs in the revolution by conspicuous ferocity and cruelty.

Less than three years ago, Amaro was himself a professional bandit in the State of Michoacán, and his speciality lay in wrecking trains and robbing ranches. It would hardly be correct to say that he was "on the run"; on the contrary it was the wealthier inhabitants of that State who were "on the run" with Amaro after them. At that time he wore in the lobe of his right ear an ear-ring, the symbol in Mexico of a professional bandit; and though he wears it no longer, he is still a bandit and the lobe of his ear is still pierced. I may add that he learned to read and write only after he became a Cabinet Minister; but probably his illiteracy was a recommendation in the eyes of his astute Syrian employer, for a more educated General might have been ambitious, like Gómez and Serrano.

English manufacturers will be pleased to learn that he is an enthusiastic admirer of their cloth, their leather, their cutlery, and their polo sticks—for he is passionately fond of polo. His wife is, by the way, a white woman, and a good Catholic, like the wife of Roberto Cruz and like the wives of nearly all the other Sonoran chiefs. When she accepted him, it was only on condition that they would be married in Church; but here a difficulty arose owing to the old Indian padre who had been asked to perform the ceremony refusing to do so on the ground that Amaro had been living with an Indian woman. Amaro overcame the old man's scruples, however, by sending six armed soldiers with orders either to fetch him or to shoot him in case he refused to come. From this it may be seen, first that the Indian padre is sometimes weak, and, secondly, that Amaro is somewhat of a Sheik. Young, handsome, and resolute, he gives some astute American diplomatists the impression that he will one day have a shot at the Presidency, but though, after Obregón and Calles, it might well seem impossible that intellectual or educational deficiencies should bar anybody from Chapultepec, Amaro's intellectual and educational cargo is rather too light, just as Pancho Villa's was.

Next to Amaro, the subordinate whom Calles has found most useful to him is General Roberto Cruz, the chief of Police. As I shall have something to say of Roberto when I come to describe the religious persecution, he shall not detain us long in this chapter. Naturally brutal and cruel, he was at first a terror to the criminals who swarmed in the Mexican capital some years ago; and gruesome tales were then told of how on their way to the Penal Colony in the Islas Marías, boatloads of them disappeared mysteriously. Calles encouraged this taste for illegality in his subordinate, and has now involved him in so many frightful murders, that there can be no forgiveness for him in case of a Catholic triumph. "They never pardon who have done the wrong," and consequently Cruz will never pardon the Catholics whom he has oppressed. Even if tried to-morrow by Mexican law and under an impartial administration, his life would infallibly pay the forfeit of the murders he has committed, despite the fact that Calles made him commit them.

He is not anti-clerical, but has become so through panic fear of a Catholic revolution. In short, he is tied, hand and foot, to Calles, so much so that, in September 1927, he betrayed to Calles his best friend, General Serrano, owing to his dread that Serrano's triumph would mean the establishment of a just administration.

Hence it is that he guards the villainous dictator as he would guard a jewel of great price, that he unearths all the plots against him, and seizes all the secret printing presses of Calles's enemies, even the presses which only turn out religious propaganda. In his panic terror, he tortures prisoners, strikes ladies, shoots and stabs like a maniac. Decidedly he is a useful tool; and the dictator showed perspicacity when he selected him.

CHAPTER VII

HOW CALLES DEALS WITH RIVALS

CALLES and Obregón are the Duumvirs who rule Mexico, though of course they do not call themselves Duumvirs: on the contrary they attribute their rotatory "election" to the votes of the people, votes which are not counted at all. But woe betide anybody who puts up as opposition candidate. General Francisco Serrano and General Arnulfo Gómez did so in June 1927 and were both killed before the end of the year. For a few months they were allowed to hold election meetings and all went well, save that, as I have already pointed out, Gómez complained publicly of the support which Calles was openly but illegally giving Obregón. This action did not increase the popularity of Gómez with the Duumvirs, already incensed against him owing to the fact that he was gaining over to his side many military men (civilians do not count in a Mexican election), by his slogan of "No re-election."

The Duumvirs determined therefore to eliminate both the Opposition candidates, and, to do them justice, they struck with a rapidity and a skill which Lenin himself could not have bettered. Their *coup* was, in fact, a model of its kind. In preparation, in timeliness, in execution, in swiftness, and, above all, in the indispensable propaganda which followed close on the assassinations, it was a veritable masterpiece. Instead of having the two candidates arrested and tried, they sent soldiers to shoot them without trial. The remarkable event which occurred in Mexico during the early part of October 1927 was not an unsuccessful insurrection on the part of Serrano and Gómez, it was a successful *coup d'État* on the part of Calles and Obregón.

Serrano, who had a weakness for alcohol, gambling, and gaiety, had gone to his country house at Cuernavaca for a merry week-end, and had brought with him thirteen civilian friends. On the other hand, Calles, Obregón, General Amaro, and General Alvares, had got together, like conspirators, in Chapultepec Palace. An absolutely reliable force of troops under General Claudio Fox and General Juan Dominguez was sent to arrest and murder Serrano and all his guests; and they not only carried out their mission but robbed and tortured their victims as well. One of those victims was a youth from Torreón who was acting as one of the election campaign managers for Serrano. He seems to have joined Serrano by chance on the eve of the Cuernavaca picnic and to have been invited to take part in it, and to have had no idea that his employer intended to carry out a revolution next August. The wrists and ankles of this youth were so tightly bound with wire that, when the corpse was delivered to his family, his father fainted while making an unsuccessful attempt to undo the wires.

Serrano had received a blow from a musket on the head, before being riddled with bullets; and, though he had 17,000 *pesos* in his pockets when he left the Federal Capital, the pockets were empty and turned inside out when the body was handed over to the relatives. This mark of a pocket turned inside out should, by the way, be assumed as a crest or heraldic device by the Duumvirs, for it will be remembered that when they had the unfortunate Don Venustiano Carranza murdered in a wretched hut at Tlaxcalantongo, it was placed on record afterwards that "the trousers pockets were turned inside out." Yet for the unworkable Constitution which this verbose and misguided old gentleman drew up in 1917 in flowery language but with no authority from the people, Calles and Obregón profess a reverence like that professed by pious Moslems for the Koran!

A pocket turned inside out would certainly be the most suitable sign under which Calles and Co. could do business; and I am afraid that Mexico will look like a pocket turned inside out before these two gentlemen have done with her.

Enrique Monteverde, Serrano's private secretary, was murdered with his master, and, like him, robbed of all his money. He had 5,000 *pesos* in his pockets when he left Mexico City; but when his body was brought to the military hospital, his pockets also were empty and turned inside out.

The pickpocket in both cases seems to have been General Fox, for next day he was buying jewellery—for lady friends, it is to be presumed, as Mexican Generals generally spend their blood-money in this way. His fellow-assassin, General Juan Dominguez, was not left out in the cold, however, for Calles sent him a special order authorizing him to take possession of Serrano's expensive motor-car.

Of course Calles had no right to confiscate private property in this way; and his assassination of the thirteen civilian guests of Serrano was a clear breach of the Constitution, which insists emphatically that under no circumstances shall civilians be tried by a military court. But, during the month of October, thousands of civilians were executed throughout Mexico after trial by court martial or, more frequently, without any trial at all. In Mexico City, three Congressmen, Barros, Valle, and Mangel were arrested and executed despite their constitutional immunity as deputies; but, in order to cover up this flagrant violation of the Constitution, Calles ordered Congress next day to expel these dead men and predate their expulsion. Congress meekly obeyed, owing to the fact that in obedience to a previous order of the Dictator, it had purged itself of all deputies who were not tools of the Duumvirate. The army, the civil service, and the Press had been similarly purged; so that there now exists in Mexico a Dictatorship like that which rules Russia.

And many of the methods of that Dictatorship are absolutely Russian especially the practice of assassination by civilian Communists, in other words by members of the CROM, which is under the direct control of Luis N. Morones, ex-Minister of Commerce, Industry and Labour, and which corresponds somewhat to the Communist party in Russia. Members of this organisation put Rosalie Evans to death, and have committed a long series of murders in Mexico, more especially in the State of Pueblo; but not one of them has ever been put to death for these murders or even arrested.

One of their victims in October 1927 was Charles Robinson, who was both a Congressman and a Colonel in the army, but who obtained leave of absence from the army when he entered Congress, and therefore enjoyed personal immunity against arrest. Because he was opposed to the re-election of Obregón, he was killed like a dog in the street by a member of the CROM.

It is true that Gómez and Serrano intended to revolt, but they had decided to wait till July 1928, when the Presidential elections would be held, so that all the world might see from the unfair way in which the elections had been conducted that revolution was the only means by which they could prevent a pair of scoundrels from ruling Mexico alternatively for many years to come.

Here we have, by the way, an explanation of the political instability which prevails in Latin America where the crux is not the revolutions but the unfair elections by means of which corrupt and mendacious Governments can remain in power indefinitely if they are not turned out by revolution.

It must be admitted, I repeat, that Calles acted on this occasion with great resolution, rapidity, and unscrupulousness. A mutiny took place in Mexico City after the news of Serrano's execution had been received, but it was partial, unorganized, and therefore unsuccessful. It would have been very different if led by Francisco Serrano, who had, only four months earlier, been the G.O.C. of all the troops in the Valley of Mexico, and who had endeared himself to the soldiers by his military talent as well as by that reckless generosity which is so often found in association with alcoholic excess. Calles, as I have already pointed out, is neither a soldier nor a drinker, but he had taken care to summon to his side Obregón, who is both; and these two, with Amaro and several other Generals in whom absolute confidence could be placed, formed a fairly efficient G.H.Q. in Chapultepec Palace until all danger had passed.

The outer world knew nothing of what was happening, for Calles had isolated Mexico by stopping all unofficial telegrams as well as all letters and all railway trains. Then he told his story to the American public, and in American journalism it is of vital importance for a man in Calles' position to tell his story first, as an American editor generally sticks to the first interpretation which he publishes, being unwilling to confess that he has been duped. Now, Calles presented his case to the American public with such skill and moderation that it is impossible to give all the credit of this presentation to himself: he must have been "coached" by the renegade Americans whom he has about him, and who know perfectly how to manage the Press of the United States. He deplored the attempt that had been made by a couple of disloyal Generals to prevent the people from peacefully electing a new President. He declared that he had frequently been warned of their treasonable preparations, but had withheld his hand in the hope that they would reform and be good. He made a pathetic reference to his own unwearied and unselfish efforts to secure the purity of the election and the integrity of the ballot-box.

This was exactly the right note to strike in the United States, for it prevented the Pacifists from inquiring too closely into the methods which the President had employed in squelching the "revolt," while at the same time those methods recommended themselves to that worship of autocracy, efficiency, ruthlessness, and success, which is becoming more and more a Yankee characteristic. For some weeks after the crushing of the revolt, the Press of the United States was full of admiration for "Mexico's Man of Iron." In an article under that heading which appeared soon afterwards in the leading newspaper of New York, the phrase was repeated, in various forms, about twenty times; and the writer waxed enthusiastic even over Calles' defiance of the United States. "The iron in Calles' unyielding nature," he says, in an English that is not quite perfect, "has also been bared in the relations of the Mexican Government with the American State Department over the enforcement of land and oil laws. . . . But Calles never budged."

As for the handful of terrorized American correspondents who were left in Mexico City, they were down on all fours in front of this Iron god. To find a parallel for the panegyrics they cabled, one would have to go back to the files of the *Moniteur* in the days of the first Napoleon; and it must be remembered that England is dependent on these enthusiasts for all her Mexican information. Even in private letters home, the members of the English colony in Mexico refrain from criticism for they know the excellence of the censorship that has been established in Mexico City, but in private conversation with trustworthy countrymen they maintain that Calles has played ducks and drakes with the constitution which he professes to worship.

If Calles were to read these strictures of mine, he would, I think, laugh good-humouredly, for he has won the hand. He took advantage of the Gómez-Serrano disturbance to purge the Army and the Congress and all the Public Offices of his opponents. He ordered the Legislature to prolong the Presidential term to six years—and it did so. He has thoroughly mastered the native press and the foreign journalists. Up to October the first, 1927, he was seriously annoyed by adverse criticism, very ably written, which appeared occasionally in the two greatest newspapers of Mexico City, the *Excelsior* and the *Universal*. He tried at first to bring pressure to bear on these papers through the Labour organization CROM, which, acting through Communist compositors, threatens editors with a strike if they persist in criticising the Calles Dictatorship; and a strike, I might remark parenthetically, is no joke in Mexico, for if the printers walk out of a printing-office, the red flag of the CROM is hoisted over the door, and a gendarme takes his stand beneath it till the strikers win; in other words the Government takes the side of the strikers. But the compositors of the *Excelsior* and the *Universal* could not be seduced from their allegiance to papers that treated them well, and nothing could be done. The October *coup* gave Calles a chance to get rid of all his journalistic critics, and he made good use of that opportunity. In fact he has expelled every one of them—Felix Palavicini of the *Universal*, (founder and occasional contributor but not actually connected with it,) Edward Pallares also of the *Universal*, Luis Elguero of the *Excelsior*, José Salada Álvarez who was Secretary of Foreign Affairs in the time of Porfirio Díaz, and all the rest. Their expulsion marks the extinction of the last spark of independence in Mexican journalism; for, despite the fact that they had to exercise great caution, their articles on Mexican affairs were extraordinarily valuable and illuminating. I shall give here an extract from one, which appeared in the *Universal*.

"What we lack are moderate laws, firm guarantees for work, security for investments and a social equilibrium. What we have in excess are radical laws, fantastic doctrines, social demoralization provoked by political deception, uncertainty regarding property, wages, conditions of life and education, and, above all, great lies advanced as gospel, and great errors disguised as principles of redemption.

"To the naked, incontestable facts of depopulation, misery in the fields, diminishing production, forced importation of food, clothing and medicines there comes the persistent, increasing power of radical laws and means of restriction and regulation."

This is the truth about Mexico, and Mexico is not lost so long as she produces men who can write like this at a time when it is very dangerous to do so, men who are not only an honour to journalism but who would also make good Cabinet ministers and upright judges. North Americans are too often inclined to assume that Mexico contains no men fit to rule, but this is a great mistake for I have myself seen in Mexico many conservative lawyers, authors, journalists, and publicists, who in mental calibre, in educational training, in executive ability, and in the finished courtesy of their manners, are at least the equal of any statesmen I ever met with in Washington. One of these men is Señor Elguero, who enjoys a high reputation in Mexico, Central America and Spain on account of his editorials, his dramatic works, and his high character as an individual.

But such men are out of power; and cannot get in, so long as the Calles-Obregón pact remains in force.

CHAPTER VIII

THE CAUSE OF THE PERSECUTION

SUCH is Calles. How could a Christian Church place its organization under the control of such a man? Yet the Catholic Church of Mexico would do so if it obeyed the anti-religious laws which Calles has drawn up and promulgated.

The men around Calles are equally unfit to control the Church. But the Legislature? The Legislature is no protection. The *Excelsior* of 4 January, 1927 gave an editorial description of the 1926 session of the legislature and then made the following comment:

> "The Senate shows a beautiful balance: it has lost ten per cent of its members (killed) which is quite honourable for a fighting body. Saloon brawls, parliamentary disputes, acts of revenge by chieftains and enemies are responsible for these parliamentary disasters."

But how did the religious persecution in Mexico actually originate?

The answer to that question is easy, in fact it consists of one word—greed. As I have already explained in my preface and in chapter III, part I, the so-called "Liberals" had got into the habit of living on the Church, and their present onslaught is the logical outcome of all their previous confiscations; it is an attempt at a complete absorption of the Church by the State—and by such a State!—and would mean the absolute disappearance of the Church, not a continuance of its life in subordination to the State.

To realize that this is the case, we have only got to examine the anti-religious laws which Calles has drawn up and promulgated. According to these laws, the ownership of all churches is vested in the Federal Government, and the Federal Government reserves the right to determine which of them shall continue to be used as churches.

In France this provision would not mean much, as there is no fear of Notre-Dame being turned into a mosque; but in Mexico, where, even under my own eyes, a church serving a busy quarter and always crowded, the church of La Soledad, has been taken from the congregation and is to be turned into a museum, there is real danger of a wholesale alienation of churches from the object for which they were built.

No new place of worship may be dedicated without the permission of the Government. All acts of religion must be performed within the churches. The Mexican State Legislatures determine the maximum number of clergymen, which was fixed at about one priest for every 15,000 Catholics, but one State has decreed that the Catholics are entitled to one priest for every 30,000. Another State has declared that all priests must marry and must be over forty years of age. No clergyman and no religious corporation may establish or conduct primary schools or instructions for scientific research or the diffusion of knowledge. All spiritual exercises or religious instruction in private schools are forbidden. The Church may not establish or conduct institutions for the sick and the poor. Religious corporations are forbidden to own not only churches but clerical residences, schools, orphan asylums, convents or any other building used for religious or educational or charitable purposes. All ministers of religion are forbidden to criticize these and similar provisions of the Constitution or to criticize the Government or the authorities. No religious periodical and no periodical with a marked tendency in favour of religion may comment upon political affairs, or publish anything whatsoever concerning the political authorities. No clergymen may vote or hold public office or take part in any political assemblage.

"But," it is said, "the Mexican Church was tremendously rich. According to the London *Daily Express* of April 10, 1928, President Calles made the following statement to the correspondent of that paper 'Mexicans own only one-third of the wealth of their country, and of that third the Roman Catholic Church owns sixty per cent.'"

This is one of those parrot cries which are repeated hundreds of times, but which are nevertheless false. The Mexican Government which first confiscated the wealth of the Church finished its labours in 1866, and the valuation of that wealth which it gave was, in round numbers, $62,000,000. If to that we add what the Kings of Spain had previously confiscated—for even they did some confiscating on their own account—we get seventy-two million dollars, which sum includes hospitals, schools, lands, houses and hospital funds. Let us add to this twenty-eight million dollars for the vestments, chalices, church buildings, etc., and we get a total of one hundred million dollars at the time of the Church's greatest prosperity, that is, over seventy years ago.

Now, one hundred million dollars was not sixty per cent of the third of Mexico's wealth.

According to the *Baptist Year Book* for the year 1916, the value of the invested funds and property belonging in that year to the Baptist denomination in the United States was given at $98,000,000; the income of the same church was given at $43,000,000; and its church buildings and other unproductive properties were valued at $173,000,000. Finally, it had over 36,000 clergymen against Mexico's 10,000 Catholic priests.

We hear a great deal about "the vast number" of priests in Mexico. One globe-trotter comments on them in his book; other globe-trotters follow suit; and sometimes English and American Catholics admit, weakly, that the proportion of priests is too high. But it is no higher than the proportion in Europe, where it is about one to one thousand. That is the proportion in Ireland.

In Glasgow, it is one to fifteen hundred Catholics, but Archbishop Mackintosh finds that this entails too much work on the priest and is trying to make it one to one thousand.

In England, where the Established Church is always complaining that it is undermanned, there are 20,000 Anglican clergymen for two and a half million communicants. That would work out at one Anglican clergyman for every 125 communicants yet, under the Calles law, the legislature of one State decrees that every 30,000 Catholics must be content with one priest! Moreover, we must bear in mind the fact that a Catholic priest is, as a rule, a busier man than a Protestant clergyman; he has seven sacraments to administer whereas some Protestant clergymen do not seem to have more than one or two. And he is particularly busy in a primitive country like Mexico where, out of a population of fifteen millions, there are only one million whites, all the rest being Indians or *mestizos* (half-castes) who very often expect the priest to give them advice not only about their souls but about their bodies, their ailments, the education of their children, and the sowing of their maize.

Some Americans may disagree with this and say, "Yes, we thought so. Ignorance, dirt and degeneracy always follow in the trail of Rome. Look how different things are in the United States, where every workman has his bath." The average American or British Protestant would be too courteous to hold such language especially to Roman Catholics or to Spaniards; but, if he were to speak with absolute frankness, he would probably put his views on Mexico in words somewhat like these:

"Mexico is a land of perpetual revolution and turmoil. It is a failure, and that for two reasons, first because it was colonized by a decadent race, the Spaniards, and secondly because it was taught by a decadent Church, the Church of Rome. The success of England and of North America shows at once the superiority of the Anglo-Saxon civilization and the Protestant religion. The priests in Mexico tried to keep the people in ignorance, and always showed a preference for a despotic form of Government. The Anglo-Saxons stand for education and democracy: hence it is that they lead the world to-day. The best thing that could happen to Old Mexico would be that she followed New Mexico into the bosom of the United States, which would assure her a good Government, true religion, and compulsory education."

Now, before going further, let us examine this theory. To Anglo-Saxon Protestants it is as interesting and simple and attractive as *Westward Ho* is to an English schoolboy, but unfortunately it will not bear investigation. In the first place Mexico is not Spanish. Out of a population of fifteen millions, there are only about one million whites, not all of them Spanish, and this white colony is decreasing every year. There are about three million pure-blooded Indians, and eleven million *mestizos* or half-castes, but in most of these half-castes the white blood has been entirely absorbed by the native blood, and in all probability this process will continue till Mexico loses all claim to be called a white country, and can no more be called a white country than Japan. The average Mexican is as tawny as a Japanese, his hair is as black, his cheek-bones are as high, and his whole appearance is as un-European. Spain spared the native; this was a biological sin on her part, but a Christian virtue. The pious Pilgrim Fathers on the contrary, placed a price on the head of all Indians, men, women and children, with the result that to-day the United States is inhabited mostly by white people, whereas Mexico is almost altogether Indian, and it is unfair to institute a comparison between the two. It is unfair because, despite the glamour of his past and the mystery which surrounds his origin, the American Indian is apparently a dead weight around the neck of civilization. This is so even in the United States, though the Indians there are so few that one would expect them to be taught at least reading and writing. But though, since 1789, the United States Government has spent on the education of its handful of Indians more than six hundred million dollars, and though numerous religious and charitable organizations have spent hundreds of millions, yet the United States census of 1916 shows that 45 per cent of the American Indians are illiterate.

Naturally, the proportion is higher in Mexico because the Indians are more numerous and the Government less wealthy, but it is unfair to accuse the Church in consequence of encouraging ignorance.

Besides, it must be borne in mind that the control of education was taken from the Church some seventy years ago, and that most of the schools established by the Church and by the old Spaniards were, as I have already pointed out, confiscated by the successive waves of "Liberalism" that swept the country—confiscated, not for the benefit of the poor but for the benefit of the politicians.

Surrender to Calles by the Mexican Episcopate would certainly have meant first the reduction of the Mexican Church to a state of pitiful dependence on the Government, and eventually the disappearance of the Church and of organized Christianity. The state of dependence would be ludicrous as well as pitiful for, according to the law, every chapel which received, say, a candle as a present would have to report this momentous fact to the Government in writing and would have again to report when the candle had been burned. I merely give this as an instance of the minute control that would be exercised.

Under these circumstances, the Mexican Bishops were right in refusing to obey the law, and in withdrawing altogether from the Churches. The laity were also within their rights when they formed the League for the Defence of Religious Liberty, in order to agitate in a constitutional manner for the repeal of this law; and President Calles acted with his usual illegality when he attempted to break up this League by arresting its leaders and shooting them without trial or after trial before a military Court, which is illegal in the case of civilians. At least seventy-five young men connected with the League, and nearly always connected also with the A.C.J.M. (*Asociación Católica de la Juventud Mejicana*, Catholic Association of Mexican Youth) one of the Constituent bodies of the League for the Defence of Religious Liberty were put to death during the first year of the persecution.

PART III

THE MARTYRS

A SUNDAY MORNING IN MEXICO CITY

JUST off the animated Paseo de la Reforma in Mexico City stands a huge skeleton of rusty iron bars, a vast structure which might under certain conditions be described as ghostly, for a belated reveller, seeing the moon shine through it, might well feel as startled as the Ancient Mariner when he saw the moon and the stars shine through the ship of the Dead.

It is the steel framework of the House of Congress, begun by Porfirio Díaz in 1910 and not yet finished, never apparently to be finished, for all work on it ceased long ago. It ceased as soon as the "*Constitutionalistas*" grasped the reins of Government, because of the fact that they also grasped at the same time the funds that had been set aside by the wise old Conservative Dictator for the completion of this great national work. They grasped other funds as well; sixty million dollars which those great "Reformers" found in the Treasury vanished like smoke, and have never been heard of since. And much foreign money disappeared at the same time; the Madero revolution was carried out, in fact, by means of a large sum of money raised by Francisco I. Madero's brother in France, for the construction of a railway. The railway was not, of course, constructed, and the French lenders are still wondering where their money went to.

All work on the new Houses of Parliament ceased as soon as the "Constitutionalists" grasped the reins of power; though one would have expected, on the contrary, that those ardent and eloquent Parliamentarians would have devoted more attention to it than old Porfirio Díaz, the Mexican Mussolini, who was not a great talker himself and had little use for Parliaments. But instead of growing upwards, after the departure of Díaz, the unfinished building began, literally, to grow downwards; it visibly decreased in size on account of the removal from it of old iron by an American company which had entered into a contract with the "revolutionary" Government for the construction of certain roads.

Of the temporary Chamber of Deputies I do not speak, as it is in every way beneath contempt, architecturally as well as politically, and as the deputies are worthy of it. It is situated in what would be called, in Japan, the Red Light district: it meets for only four months of the year, during which time the "legislators" do nothing but talk nonsense and fight duels. During the first ten months of 1927, ten per cent of the M.P.'s had been killed in duels or had met with violent deaths in other ways, but the casualties among the honourable and gallant gentlemen (they are nearly all Generals or Colonels) became so numerous after October the first, when Calles carried out a *coup d'État*, that I lost count. When I first visited Mexico at the beginning of the Calles regime, one deputy proposed that they all leave their revolvers outside the Chamber during discussions, but the proposal was negatived without a division. The legislative power has been practically surrendered to Calles who has been given the right to make new laws when the Chamber is not sitting, in other words Congress gives him a signed, blank cheque on which he can write whatever he likes. The laws against religion were written in this way by Calles or under his personal supervision. Nearly all the congressmen have been nominated by the Dictator, most of them have never seen their Constituencies, and have to sit down and think before they can tell you what the names of their Constituencies are.

Such being the present Congress of Mexico, the reader will understand when I say nothing more about it, and why I return to the derelict skeleton of a Parliament which the Republic owes to Porfirio Díaz.

Leading up to this ruin is the Avenida del Palacio Legislativo and in front of it is the Plaza de la República, an abomination of desolation, grass-grown and deserted, dead as a forum in Pompeii. A workman with a wooden leg was slowly stumping across it on the occasion of my first visit to the place, and his steps echoed hollowly through the silent square. As in Pompeii you are shown the baker's shop and the sculptor's studio, with everything left just as it was when the lava and the ashes came, so in the Plaza de la República you are shown the stonemasons' sheds, the carpenters' benches, the clerks' office and the foreman's room from which life fled when the revolutionary lava rushed down from the mountains and petrified them into eternal immobility.

In the Plaza de la República as in Pompeii, you still see the marks of the chisel on the stone, but in neither place do you see the chisel: in Pompeii it rusted away, in Mexico it was stolen long ago.

At the further entrance to the Avenida del Palacio Legislativo, where that dead street debouches from the lively Plaza de la Reforma, stands a gloomy building in which however there is always great activity, day and night, an activity which is in striking contrast to the sepulchral stillness that broods over the derelict Palacio itself. In front of it there are always motor-cars and groups of people and armed sentries. Motor-cars dash in and out of its iron gates every few moments. There is something peculiar about these motor-cars. They all have drawn blinds. They travel at a quite illegal speed, but they evidently have the right of way, for their chauffeurs *sonan el pito* or blow the policeman's whistle which gives them precedence over all other traffic. The chauffeurs exchange rapid passwords with the sentries before the gates fly open. They are engulfed in the gloom of the umbrageous inner courtyard. The gates close again with an iron clang, which for some inexplicable reason, shakes my very soul with fear. The gates open again for a large hearse-like motor-car on its way out. There are several such cars. Grim and smooth and silent, they remind me horribly of the vans, freighted with death, that used, in the days of the Terror, to issue in the early morning from the Lubyanka at Moscow at a time when I was myself on the wrong side of the Lubyanka's iron bars.

The chill in my soul deepens. I hear the clank of chains, the shooting of prison bars. Peering into the first *patio* or courtyard, I perceive, under the shadow of the trees, women weeping hysterically, soldiers, policemen, officers, jailers. Painted on the adjoining buildings are signs which cannot be described as reassuring—*Museo de Criminologia, Escuela Científica de Policia*. . . . Good God! it is all clear to me now! This is the notorious *Inspección General*, the headquarters of the ordinary and the extraordinary police, of the *Policia Montada* and the *Policia Reservada*. It is the Lubyanka of Mexico. Here, with its windows thrown wide open, is the office of the brutal Roberto Cruz, the Inspector General who so much resembles Dzerzhinsky. Down there beneath my feet are the terrible subterranean dungeons where the Catholics are imprisoned and tortured, *los sótanos de la Inspección General*.

This, then, is the point where the Grand March of the Revolution stopped—at a prison-gate! The heroes and the generals and the silver-tongued orators and the torrential "*Constitutionalistas*" and the fiery *revolutionarios* (all of them with hip-pocket revolvers)—they all halted here. They never reached the Palacio Legislativo, part of which is now used as a garage for the cars of the Secret Police, for the Black Marias and the funeral autos of Liberty. Surely these names should be altered. This should be the Avenida de la Policia, and that the Plaza de la Tirania Callista.

But hark there is a trampling, mixed with loud words of command and the jingle of steel. Surrounded by gendarmes who, with their rifles and bayonets and khaki uniforms, look to me exactly like soldiers, a crowd of prisoners is approaching. Even at a distance I can see that this crowd is composed of two diametrically different elements. There are obvious Convent girls with the white veils and flowers of *la première Communion*, only that the veils are rent, and the flowers torn, and the young eyes red with weeping, and the smooth cheeks crimson with shame. Alongside these pure girls stagger the painted dregs of the Mexican brothels, obscene and drunken harlots who exude an aroma of bad alcohol, cheap scent, and abominable tobacco. Side by side with the daughters of the hidalgos, with the young sons of the Conquistadores, march criminal types, men and women, with vice and degradation stamped on their features. They belong to that class of criminals whose case is heard *in camera*; and they look it: the Mexican criminal generally looks his part. Incest, parricide, knifing, poisoning, rape: these are his usual crimes.

How on earth did such ill-assorted people get together? I turn for enlightenment to a civilian bystander, and he courteously explains. It is Sunday morning; and General Roberto Cruz makes a practice of sending out his myrmidons early every Sunday morning in order to arrest Catholics who go to Mass. Without a warrant and in defiance of the Constitution, these policemen break into private houses where Mass is being said and march the whole congregation off to the *Inspección General*—as these are being marched now.

"But apparently the police also break into brothels," said I, glancing towards the sad señoritas ironically called *filles de joie*.

"No," said the gentleman, "they never do, for that would be a violation of the Constitution."

He smiled ever so faintly and then added: "These women must have been arrested for fighting in the street, or they were probably mixed up in some robbery or murder. There is now a robbery or a murder every night, and on Saturday night there are generally quite a number."

So this explains it. The secret Masses are always said in the grey of the morning, so that the sleuth-hounds of Roberto Cruz generally manage to kill two birds with the one stone; they arrest the señorita who has risen with the lark in order to hear Mass, and at the same time they arrest the murderer staggering home to bed after a night in a gambling den, or the prostitute trying to escape after having cut her lover's throat. And they march them all three together, and treat them exactly alike.

The bedraggled procession comes closer. There are in it diabolical faces and faces which are angelic. The diabolical faces are brazen; the angelic faces are red with humiliation. But not all the female victims of the persecution are young girls; some of them are mature or elderly women; some of them are boys, evidently of pure Castilian descent, with deep-set and brilliant eye, bronzed cheek, and something proud and sumptuous in the modelling of lip and chin. Some are old men with the finely shaped heads and the singular dignity of the Spanish grandee as depicted on the canvas of Velásquez.

The heavy gate slams behind them, and they are brought into the "Identification Bureau" where they are photographed and have their fingerprints taken—the murderer with blood still on his hands, and the young girl fresh from her first Communion.

But among the innocent there are also men and women of pure Indian type, mechanics in their blue overalls, peons wrapt in their ponchos, brown-faced housemaids, hardy old market-women. Their presence proves, what is proved by much other evidence, that Mexico is Catholic to the marrow of its bones, quite as much as Ireland or Belgium. But, as a rule, these poor people are not arrested, partly because of the President's pretence to be the Friend of the Poor and the Downtrodden, but far more because they have no money.

Well may you stare in astonishment, dear reader, but, as a matter of fact, this religious persecution is largely a matter of "graft": it is much less a case of *odium theologicum* than of *aura sacra fames*. Heavy fines are imposed (quite illegally) on persons attending Mass; and General Roberto Cruz has such people arrested every day and large numbers every Sunday, in order that he may screw as much money out of them as possible. Some of that money goes to the Mexican Government, which is desperately "hard up" at the present moment, largely on account of the Catholic rebellion; but more goes into the pockets of Señor Roberto, who is said to make $25,000 monthly in this way since the persecution commenced. This scoundrelly Chief of Police calculates on the natural anxiety of parents to rescue their young sons and daughters from the terrible *sótanos* where they are confined in the same cells as the worst criminals, some of whom suffer from foul contagious diseases, and his calculations are generally right, for he succeeds as a rule in getting a fine of 500 *pesos* or $250 for the release of each prisoner. In the case of priests, his fixed tariff is one thousand *pesos* or $500.

This system of raising money is universal in Mexico at the present moment, and has been since the year 1914 when President Wilson obligingly helped into the saddle the so-called "Constitutionalists" who now misgovern Mexico. Abundant proofs of this are to be found in the records of every American and British Consulate in Mexico. Many proofs will be found in the private letters of Mr. William B. Davis, M.D., who was the American Consul in Guadalajara during the Carranza Revolution, and who is, by the way, a Protestant. Those letters were addressed by Mr. Davis to his married daughter in California, and, though never intended for publication, they were found to be so impartial and so perfectly accurate, that they have been printed for private circulation only, and I am glad to say that they were not "touched up" for publication as is the case with so many letters and even diaries at the present day. They were printed in all their baldness of phraseology and with all their split infinitives and even grammatical slips; and I am grateful for this as I am tired of perusing letters which were not only written for eventual publication but were afterwards so painted and powdered and bewigged and bedecked that their evidence as human documents is greatly impaired. I dwell at this length on these letters of Dr. Davis because I am going to use them again. At present I shall confine myself to one short quotation. It is from page 51 and runs as follows:

"A short time since, a number of people, men, women and children, attended religious services in the chapel of a private residence of the city (all the churches were closed at this particular time). As the worshippers were marching from the building, Carranzist soldiers arrested all the men (twenty-five in number) on the charge of conspiring against the Government. Each 'suspect' had to pay one thousand *pesos* to obtain his liberty, for having attempted to worship God according to the dictates of his conscience. In other words to try to hold religious service in any manner under the then Government was considered as an act of conspiracy. At any rate such has been used in more than one instance as an excuse to extract money from the civilian public."

From this extract it will be seen that the persecution in Mexico is not a desire for the reformation of the Church or for the adoption of another form of Christianity or a case of iconoclastic religious fanaticism; it is simply a case of greed. The curse of Mexico since the time of the Aztecs has been the greed of gold. Gold brought Cortés. Gold inspired the fierce Alvarado to massacre the Aztec nobles. Gold brought the American adventurers who have disorganised the country. Gold is responsible for the plunder of the churches by Juárez, Carranza, Obregón, and Calles. Gold is now responsible for the weekly raids of Roberto Cruz on what the Elizabethans would have called "Masshouses." The annual tribute of gold which now trickles from Mexico to the International Committee of Bankers in New York is partly responsible for the silence of the American Press on the subject of this persecution.

Of Señor Roberto, the Dzerzhinsky of Mexico, I am not going to say any more here, as he deserves a special chapter to himself, and shall get it. But before concluding this chapter I should like to point out that while the *Inspección General* is thus working at full pressure, business is languishing, commercial houses are failing, oil companies are shutting down, and mine after mine is closing. In the fashionable business section of the capital, you might watch the shops for a whole day without seeing a single customer cross the threshold; but you will not have to watch the *Inspección General* very long before you see Catholic prisoners being marched in. And the police are so busy arresting Catholics that they are neglecting the ordinary criminal, whose audacity is therefore increasing every day. Pickpockets swarm to such an extent that it is very unsafe to carry one's money in an outside pocket. I myself was robbed of my purse while buying a postage stamp at the General Post Office, and when I complained of this, I was told that the place is full of pickpockets, who are having a glorious time, thanks to the fact that all the Police are absent on priest-hunts—which pay them better. The hills around the capital are now so infested by bandits, that it is dangerous to go ten miles from the city in some directions. For the same reason all camping expeditions to the hills have been abandoned by the young people of the British and American communities, and golf is no longer played by the elderly diplomatists on the links off the Cuernavaca road. From his office window, Roberto Cruz can see foot-hills where life is unsafe owing to gangs of *banditti*.

But now for Roberto himself.

CHAPTER II

THE DZERZHINSKY OF MEXICO

THE Prefecture of Police in Mexico City was built by a Catholic General of Porfirio Díaz, General Don Fernando González, and appropriated afterwards by the Government. As usual, the anti-clericals were unable to build even a Police office or a prison; they had to appropriate some building put up by the Catholics. The upper floors are now used as *bureaux* by the Police agents, and as dormitories for the gendarmes. The cellar in which the old Porfirian General kept his wine has been converted into a series of prison cells. Mexico City has no good cellars, owing to the dampness of the ground, for the city once stood on a marshy island surrounded by the waters of a lake; these subterranean cells, therefore, or *sótanos*, are quite unfit for human habitation owing to their excessive humidity. The floors are wet, and some of the Catholic prisoners who have been confined in them, have suffered ever since from rheumatism. These dungeons are narrow, dark, and badly ventilated, and, owing to the fact that the lavatory is actually inside each cell, and is seldom cleaned out, the stench is almost insupportable. As many as fifteen persons have been imprisoned together in one cell; and, unless their friends were able to provide them with mattresses, they were obliged to sleep in their clothes on the damp floor, which was generally drenched with the overflow of the lavatory.

This incredible state of things is well known in Mexico City and Bishop Ignacio Valdespino of Aguascalientes, who was imprisoned there in 1927, wrote on the subject a little pamphlet of which typewritten copies have been circulated. (I might add that, probably as a result of his prison experiences, this Bishop died in San Antonio, Texas, in May, 1928.) But no American newspaper will print anything on this subject, though these foul dungeons can be reached in four days from New York, and though a great American newspaper will think nothing of sending a correspondent to Siberia, at the cost of thousands of dollars, in order to investigate prison conditions there. In the same way, American philanthropic societies which protest loudly in Naples on behalf of superannuated horses and in Constantinople on account of abandoned cats, turn a deaf ear to all the appeals that reach them from the dungeons of Mexico.

Facing the Avenida del Palacio Legislativo, and on the ground-floor of the *Inspección General*, is an ample office with a roll-top desk, and, in the centre, a table supporting a vase of flowers. The windows are generally wide open in summer-time, and tobacco smoke is sometimes seen coming out of them, for the occupant of this room frequently has visitors who are heavy smokers. On such occasions that occupant sits in his swivel-chair in front of his roll-top desk—or strides with jingling spurs up and down the room, flicking his riding-boots with a short, flexible leather whip. The visitors, if they are friends, remain seated, if subordinates or prisoners they stand.

This office is the office of Señor Inspector General Roberto Cruz, whom I shall now proceed to describe minutely, so that people may know him when he finally bolts for New York or for Europe.

He is a tall, heavy, bull-necked man of about forty, handsome in an insolent, indolent, and sensual way, with the tooth-brush moustache so much affected in Mexico by Generals who have never been in real war, and with a blue, well-shaven chin, plentifully bepowdered. Like his master Calles and most of the Callista gang, he is a half-breed; and this probably explains the brutality with which he treats the white women and girls who are brought before him. He is always well-dressed in a tight-fitting military uniform, and invariably wears a revolver in his belt, though one also lies on his desk alongside a riding-whip. Though he generally uses an expensive motor-car (a present from his friend Calles), he affects riding boots with spurs. A curious mixture of virility and femininity, he is scented like a *señorita de la vida galante*; and, though only a policeman, who never met an armed man face to face on equal terms, yet Field-Marshal von Hindenburg in all his glory does not look more bellicose than he.

Cruel by nature and with a good deal of savagery latent in him, not far below the surface, he has as little regard for legality as a mad bull, but it must be admitted that his earlier illegalities were directed against the criminal class which, as the result of a long period of civil war, had grown so audacious even in Mexico City that nobody's life was safe there.

This was before the religious struggle began; and there is no doubt that he inspired panic among the criminal classes, especially by his application to them of the *Ley Fuga*, a "law" which may be summarized in five words: "Shot while attempting to escape." A criminal would be arrested on suspicion, say, of having murdered a rich woman and stolen her jewellery. The next thing heard of him would be that he had confessed and offered to point out the exact spot where the jewellery was buried—generally a lonely spot, some distance from the capital—but that, on being brought to that spot by three policemen he had been shot dead by them while attempting to escape.

This would be the official story sent to the papers, and there would be a remarkable sameness about all these stories. The truth of the matter would generally be that the man did not confess (even under torture, for torture is continually employed now in the prisons of Mexico), and that no evidence could be brought against him with regard to this particular crime. As it was certain, however, that he was a habitual criminal, he was brought out to that lonely spot and murdered. This procedure is so well known that the newspapers joke about *La Ley Fuga* as *la fuga de la Ley* (the flight of the Law).

This method is now being applied all over Mexico to Catholics suspected of belonging to the League for the Defence of Religious Liberty, and sometimes these cases are reported in the Press, though the strict censorship prevents most of them from being noticed. One flagrant case was given in *El Universal* of June 27th. It occurred on June 26th. Señor Eduardo Fernandez de Lara, a Catholic gentleman of Tlaxcala near Apizaco, was arrested, without a warrant, by Bartolo Rodriguez who is chief of the Tlaxcala section of military operations and who most probably calls himself General. There was no trial, no investigation of any kind, and the prisoner who was charged with belonging to the League for the Defence of Religious Liberty, was not allowed to make a statement or to communicate with any of his friends. The next thing heard of him was that he had been "shot while attempting to escape"; and the official statement given out by General Bartolo Rodriguez was as follows: having "confessed his crime," and said that "at Acocotla and other places there were hidden stores of arms which he would be glad to hand over, he was conducted under escort to Acocotla to find these arms, but attempted to escape on the way and was therefore shot."

This has every appearance of being a cold-blooded murder, and when the tyranny of President Calles is overthrown, Bartolo Rodriguez should be among those placed on his trial for murder. In the same dock should be Roberto Cruz, Palomera López, General José Mazcorro, and a number of other police officials.

López has reached a stage which was reached by some of the more sanguinary butchers employed in Russia by the Secret Police of the Bolsheviks, the stage at which killing becomes a necessity, as opium becomes, in time, a necessity for the opium-smoker. Though a General, like Calles, Obregón, Cruz and Mazcorro, and head of the Mounted Police, he likes to murder prisoners with his own hands, and sometimes takes them out manacled, by night, to lonely places in order to do so at his leisure and without interruption. The most hardened criminal turns pale, when he is handed over to Palomera López; but it is not hardened criminals who are handed over to him now, it is gentle, innocent, and well-educated boys, belonging to good families, and brought up, as is the old Spanish custom, and as was the old Greek custom, with a refinement of care which in France is bestowed on girls only, and which in England and America is bestowed neither on boys nor girls.

In 1927 one such young man, a member of one of the oldest and finest families in Colima, was arrested in that State on the vague accusation of having worked against the Calles Government, and was brought to the capital. No definite breach of the law could be brought home to him; but, nevertheless, the Government regarded the case as a serious one and resolved on drastic punishment as an example to the country. The luckless youth was accordingly handed over to General Palomera López, as a fly might be handed over to one of those huge hairy, and repulsive spiders which I have seen in the forests of Brazil; and López conducted his handcuffed victim at midnight in a motor car to the heart of the mountains near Contreras, in the Federal District. Three days later, the Italian manager of a neighbouring ranch discovered a handcuffed corpse, riddled with bullets, and reported the matter to the Press with abundant details, but, naturally enough, the police took no interest in the case.

Still more recently another youth, a member of the Mexican Catholic Young Men's Association, was arrested on the usual vague accusation of being an enemy of the Calles regime. Eight gendarmes conveyed him in an automobile along the Puebla road, and, on reaching a deserted spot, they stopped the car and made him get out. One of the gendarmes then drew his revolver and threatened the lad with death unless he betrayed his companions in the Catholic Association. When the young man refused to speak, they beat him with the butt-ends of their revolvers, twisted his arms, threw him on the ground, and then jumped on him like maniacs. Apparently, they had not had instructions to kill him, for he was brought back to the Prefecture of Police, and thrown into a cell where he died, ten days later, after having been surreptitiously cared for by a humane gendarme.

The third chief of police, and in some ways the most disgusting of all, is Mazcorro, head of the Secret Police, a large swollen, and repulsive man, who works like a vampire in the dark, and whom we shall soon see emerging into the bright sunlight of the *patio* from the dark dungeons of the Prefecture with one hand gripping the arm of Father Pro Juárez.

The treatment of Mexican ladies by this evil trio has been peculiarly gross, and this brings me back again to General Cruz.

On one occasion a number of Catholic ladies went in a deputation to the Home Office with a written petition that the Church of the Holy Family, which had been closed by order of Calles, should be reopened. In making this request, the petitioners were only exercising the right of petition granted them by the Constitution, Article VIII of which says that "Public functionaries and employees shall respect the exercise of the right of petition, provided, always, it be formulated in writing and in a peaceful and respectful manner."

The ladies, who numbered several hundreds, were well-educated and belonged to the best families in the capital. One of them, to whom I owe the description which follows, speaks three European languages fluently and finished her education in a Belgian convent. With them were servant girls, poor market women, shopkeepers' wives, mothers of families, maidens of sixteen, and *jovencitas* of twelve; there were University graduates who knew half-a-dozen languages, and Indian villagers who could not speak Spanish; in short, it was a thoroughly representative delegation. It was also an orderly, respectful, even timid delegation, for Spanish, and consequently Mexican women, have a touch of Oriental humility and self-effacement which may possibly be a legacy left by the Moors. In a country which is so extremely democratic (on paper) as Mexico is, this deputation had certainly the right to call on the Minister of the

Interior, but Tejeda, the Minister, received it with a discourtesy which would never have been shown to a similar deputation by any Russian functionary in Tsarist times. He had sent for the brutal Roberto Cruz, who ordered the municipal firemen to turn the water-hose on the deputation as it entered the gate.

"Keep out that deputation at all costs!" were the orders of Roberto, "Machine-guns if they are men, and the fire-hose if they are women!"

His orders were literally obeyed, and, as the deputation entered the gate a few moments later, it was met by a powerful stream of water which wet everybody to the skin. The bulk of the procession was halted, but a few of the younger women managed to penetrate into the Minister's office and to ask him angrily how he had dared to act in this way. Then the savage in this brutal half-caste awoke, and snatching up his riding-whip from the table, he smote one of the women across the face, leaving a blue weal which was visible for weeks after. The infuriated brute then struck at another lady, leaving on her shoulder and breast a mark which is still visible. So at least I am told by the principal lady of the English colony in Mexico City, to whom she showed it. Her husband knows nothing of it, however. She has not told him what happened, owing to her certainty that if he knew, he would attempt to fight a duel with the Chief of Police, and probably get stabbed or shot by one of that savage's assassins. The first lady, too, managed to conceal the facts of this assault from her relatives, who were, luckily, absent at the time from town, but southern blood is hot, Spanish chivalry still lives, and, if Calles ever falls, I fear for the life of Roberto Cruz.

Not only did that savage lay about him with his whip, he also used obscene language. His policemen lost their heads as well as he, for several more of the dripping women had penetrated into the office. People were hustled out of the room. Women were knocked down. Glass was broken. A man's voice was heard in angry remonstrance. Then there was the sound of a shot, and a civilian fell to the ground wounded in the head, just grazed apparently by a bullet.

There was great confusion after Cruz had struck the two ladies with his whip. No wonder, therefore, that the accounts I have received became confused also after this point. The only thing certain is that some male civilian, perhaps a clerk in the outer office, protested against the conduct of the Inspector General, and that he was fired at either by Cruz himself or else by one of his policemen. One of the ladies bound up his wound, which was not serious; but then the room was cleared and the wounded man was lost sight of.

CHAPTER III

VIVA CRISTO REY!

WHILE in Mexico City I met, one night, in a secret place, a prominent leader of the A.C.J.M. (*Asociación Católica de la Juventud Mejicana*, the Catholic Association of Mexican Youth) and he made a deep impression on me by reason of his personal character and of the information he gave me about his organization and its young martyrs. Señor X, as I shall call him, was a man of pure Spanish descent, about thirty years old, a lawyer by profession, of good family, and excellent education; at the time I met him he was travelling under a false name and with a price on his head. So close was the search for him that although his young wife and children lived in Mexico City, he never dared to visit them. For the sake of his principles he had ruined a brilliant career; but as these principles were thoroughly Christian, I could not help admiring him. By confining himself to his legal work he could have lived in peace and comfort, but he chose to associate himself with a society of austere and earnest young men whose study circles and lectures meant for him only a loss of time, and whose uncompromising Catholicity meant for him danger.

The A.C.J.M. closely resembles *les Cercles de Jeunes Gens*, *l'Action Populaire*, and the other Catholic associations which have done such excellent work in France since the war, and most probably its founders copied those French associations, for Paris has a very great intellectual influence both for good and for evil over all Latin America; in Rio de Janeiro, for example, there is at the present moment a Catholic literary movement, directly inspired by the French Catholic revival associated with the names of Henry Bordeaux, René Bazin, Georges Goyau, and Paul Claudel. Judging by the Constitution of the A.C.J.M. and the work it has done, it seemed to me calculated to benefit not only the rising generation of intellectuals in Mexico but even the politicians and the clergy and the whole nation. Catholicism has a capacity of reforming itself from within, and it would be absurd, of course, to deny that the native clergy in Mexico stand in no need of reformation. But the policy of Calles tends to prevent reformation, as it involves the expulsion of the Bishops, the European priests, and the regular clergy, who have as a rule a much higher standard of spirituality than the Indian and *mestizo* padres. I have heard it whispered that some of these native priests, including of course those who have accepted the *Ley Calles* as well as the still smaller group which has joined "Patriarch" Pérez make no secret of their satisfaction at these expulsions. But those who are thus satisfied with Calles' action are the very lowest, most ignorant, most disreputable and most superstitious of the clergy, while on the other hand, the better and the more spiritual-minded the priest or the layman, the greater his dislike for the Calles Law which would only tend to produce a degraded and superstitious Church like the Church of Abyssinia.

In the A.C.J.M. with its highly educated clerics and laymen, Calles seems to have instinctively recognised an enemy, for he attacked it with a diabolical fury and mercilessness. I never realized how great that fury was, until Señor X gave me instances of it. I then realized, but I could not understand for the A.C.J.M. is in the first place a religious association which had established throughout Mexico a network of branches, each with a library and a study circle; and its object seemed to be the encouragement among the youth of study, industry, purity, charity, and frequent Communion. There are many other Catholic Associations, however, and women are at least as active in them as men; but the A.C.J.M. was in the forefront of the fighting and lost over seventy of its members, none of them above thirty years of age, and several of them under twenty.

Señor X told me many touching stories of capture and death, the victims in all cases being unconnected with any political movement. One of the clerical victims was a young secular priest, Father David Uribe, rector of the church of Iguala, Guerrero, and a man of high educational distinction, who was shot dead by Calles' agents, on the road from Cuernavaca to Mexico City, for the crime of distributing handbills to his flock warning them against the peril of schism. I mention this case because, on leaving Mexico, I was entrusted with the last letter of this priest, and it struck me as the letter of a saint. The Mexican Catholic lady from whom I received this precious document was led to part with it only by the fear that if captured in a police raid on her house, it might not only compromise her but likewise be destroyed.

As the histories of other martyrs were told, I was struck by the fact that, whether they were priests or laymen, all these martyrs were young, of good education, and with high ideals; and I realized the object of Calles in striking so mercilessly at the young Christians, while supporting old, vicious, ignorant and schismatic priests like "Patriarch" Pérez who is certainly a repulsive-looking object, evil-looking as sin itself and partially paralyzed. I once saw Pérez saying Mass in the Church on the Avenida Juárez which Calles has given him (it was once a Catholic Church of course) and a more painful and repulsive sight I have seldom witnessed, for the celebrant had to be supported by an altar "boy" who was nearly as old and villainous-looking as himself, while there was no congregation at all save one aged woman who was asleep and had probably drifted into the place by mistake.

Pérez had been a man of notoriously evil life, and had been so long expelled from the Church that he had had time to forget all the little Latin he ever knew and to make a career for himself in the Mexican army (not a school for virtue), where he rose to the rank of captain. That this aged profligate should allow himself to be used as a cat's-paw by the Dictator is not surprising; but what is surprising is the fact that he should be regarded with hope and satisfaction by most Protestant, Anglo-Saxon theologians in Mexico.

Calles' subordinates pursue the same policy of supporting ignorant, vicious, and incompetent old renegades. One Governor declares that in his State (Tabasco), it will not be enough for a priest to register (and thereby commit the sin of schism): he must also be over forty years of age. In Tabasco, therefore, a priest is too young at forty.

This policy on the part of the State during the last seventy years is responsible for the backwardness of the Mexican Church: even Porfirio Díaz, though he was no persecutor, and though he connived at breaches of the anti-religious laws, prevented the free development of Catholic life: that was one of his two capital errors; the other was his neglect of the poor workers. The second error led to his own downfall, the first (with the subsequent assistance of President Wilson), contributed to the downfall of Mexico. How Catholic missionaries and Catholic associations might have saved the situation may be seen by an examination of the good work done by them in other Latin countries, especially in Buenos Aires, Montevideo, Rio de Janeiro and Paris. Father Pierre Lhande tells in his *Le Christ dans la Banlieue* of the invaluable work done in the poorer quarters of Paris mostly by associations of lay Catholic men and women—*les Hommes Catéchistes*, *les Dames Catéchistes*, *les Jeunes Conférenciers*, *les Conférences de Saint-Vincent de Paul*, *les Secrétariats des Familles*, *les Secrétariats d'Action Sociale*, *l'Union Catholique du Personnel des Services de Santé*, *l'Action Populaire*, *l'Union Syndicale des Ingénieurs Catholiques*, *les Cercles de Jeunes Gens*, and many other Catholic associations.

Most of the martyrs of whom Señor X spoke were young men belonging to his own organization, and there was a note of triumph in his voice as he told how they fell, one after another, with the cry of "*Viva Cristo Rey!*" on their lips. Thus, I reflected, did the Christians huddled together in the Catacombs encourage one another with the stories of martyrs who had smiled at death. The Church has not only an Apostolical succession of priests and pontiffs: it has also an Apostolical succession of martyrs, not always priests and pontiffs, more often, indeed, quite simple men and women. For nearly two thousand years the Church has always had a firing-line somewhere or other. Yesterday it was in Moscow: to-day it is in Mexico; and my experience of that firing-line in both places convinces me that the martyrs of the Coliseum must have been much the same as the martyrs of the Lubyanka or the *Inspección General*. In other words, they were human, and not the idealised figures of Mr. Wilson Barrett's *Sign of the Cross* or Sienkiewicz's *Quo Vadis.*

Probably some of them were poor slaves who did not frequent the public baths often enough, whose manners were not refined, and who were consequently a trial to the sons of Senators and Centurions, who, being Christians, had to associate with them. Some may have had untrained, inaccurate minds, and were always liable, therefore, to exaggerate the number of martyrdoms and to confuse fact with mere supposition. Some may have been dear old ladies with a knack of getting things wrong. Some may have been small shopkeepers, whose business and domestic worries went near to blotting out for them the whole expanse of heaven. Some may have been bishops or priests, constitutionally timid, though essentially brave. Some may have been foolish youths, inclined to swagger and boast. Some were doubtless poor clerks whose piety drew on them the good-humoured contempt of their employers, men doing big business in slaves, skins and wine. All these types I met not only among the Mexican Catholics but even among the martyrs elect, *los heraldos de Cristo Rey*, the heralds of Christ the King. And outside I met the modern representatives of the Roman historians, politicians, rhetoricians, and poets who were too busy to tell us anything about the Christians or even about the Founder of Christianity—the able editors, the suave but reticent diplomatists, the genial business men, the enthusiastic golfers, the smart politicians, the literary ladies (one of them distressed about the ill-treatment of horses in Mexico: "Can't you *write* something about it?" she said, turning to me with soulful eyes). Once when these affable and cultured people had dexterously steered the conversation clear of the religious issue, a terrible and mysterious text of Scripture came into my mind—"The prince of this world is judged"—and I asked myself, in horror, if these pleasant and polyglot circles, including even the soulful ladies, the cautious Ambassadors, the discreet journalists, and the enthusiastic golfers, do not form part and parcel of that "world" against which Christ more than once launched such relentless and appalling condemnation.

I must admit that the martyrs elect were not as perfect as Early Christian martyrs generally are at Drury Lane or the Metropolitan Opera House. Some of them even got on my nerves, especially by their want of frankness and of accuracy. Vague, well-intentioned people like these were probably responsible for those apocryphal stories in the Lives of the Saints which the Bollandists have had such trouble in getting rid of; but if they annoyed me, I probably annoyed them, owing to faults due to my upbringing, my profession, and my nationality.

Of all the histories of Saints which Señor X told me that night in a hiding place close to the Prefecture of Police (and all the more likely, therefore, to escape suspicion), the most touching was about a gentle, innocent, and quite unworldly pair, Joaquín Silva and Manuel Melgarejo, two martyrs whose names are as well known among Mexican Catholics as the name of Edmund Campion was among Elizabethan Catholics. Silva was 27 years of age at the time of his death and Malgarejo 17. On 6 September 1926 both left Mexico City for Zamora on a vague pilgrimage of protest and propaganda against the antireligious legislation of Calles, but without weapons, money, luggage, or military plans. "*Con el intento de trabajar por la santa causa de la Iglesia*" (Something of the good old Spanish style about this). It was just such a pilgrimage as St. Francis of Assisi might have undertaken with a companion as simple, frank, pious, outspoken and unworldly as himself; and Silva, whose whole life had been like that of St. Francis, uttered from time to time remarks filled with strange significance, remarks which might have dropped from the lips of *il Poverello* himself. These remarks are treasured up to-day in the heart of the Mexican people, and the young man who uttered them is revered as a Saint.

Such a simple pair could not well escape detection; and it was not long before an agent of Calles had ingratiated himself with them and wormed out of them the fact that they belonged to the A.C.J.M. This agent was a General, no less, his name was Zepeda. He posed as a pious Catholic, and on the pretence of showing them scars on his breast, he let them see, as if by accident, that he wore a number of religious medals around his neck. Soon afterwards this aged Judas threw off the mask and said: "*Amigos, estan ustedes perdidos: los tenemos presos*" (Friends, you are lost. You are our prisoners). To which Joaquín replied: "As to me, kill me or do what you like with me, but as for this youth who is only seventeen years old, let him go free." But Melgarejo would not have it so. "No, Joaquín," he said, "I wish to die with thee."

General Tranquilino Mendoza, the G.O.C. in Zamora, offered to set them free if only they promised to cease their propaganda work and to leave the A.C.J.M., but they refused and were condemned to death. On hearing sentence passed on him, Silva remarked, quite simply, that on entering the presence of God, he would pray for General Mendoza and General Zepeda.

They were brought from the barrack where they had been imprisoned to the cemetery, for, save in Mexico City, shooting is almost always carried out in the cemetery, beside an open grave.

Silva refused to have his eyes bandaged. "Do not cover my eyes," he said, "I am not a criminal. I myself will give you the signal to fire. When I say '*Viva Cristo Rey! Viva la Virgen de Guadalupe!*' (Hail! Christ the King! Hail! Virgin of Guadalupe!) then you can fire."

In some respects the Mexican Army is very peculiar, for against this extraordinary arrangement the O.C. firing party had nothing to say, and a condemned man is never handcuffed or prevented from talking as much as he likes.

Silva certainly talked a good deal, but every word went home, for he talked like one who sees the true values of things and does not judge life and death by the standards of the ordinary man. When he told the members of the firing party that he forgave them and would pray for them, one of the soldiers was so overcome by emotion, that he threw away his rifle saying "*Yo no tiro joven, yo pienso como usted, yo soy catolico*" (I will not fire, young man. I think as you do. I am a Catholic). This soldier was shot on the following day.

When the last moment of Silva had come nigh, and he could see the muzzles of the five rifles facing him at ten paces distant, he turned suddenly to Melgarejo and said: "*Descúbrete, porque vamos a comparecer delante de Dios*" (Take off your hat, for we are going to appear before God), then, addressing the firing party, he cried "*Viva Cristo Rey! Viva la Virgen de Guadalupe!*" whereupon the soldiers fired, and he fell dead, pierced by all of the five bullets.

On seeing this, Melgarejo tumbled on the ground in a swoon, and the soldiers killed him before he had regained consciousness.

Señor X gave me a list of apparently miraculous cures that have been wrought through the intercession of Joaquín Silva; and Joaquín's brother José Silva, who lives in the United States, says that at the very moment of the execution he distinctly heard his own name called by a voice which he at once recognized as Joaquín's. At that time he did not even know that Joaquín had been arrested.

For several nights in succession I met Señor X and he introduced me to other members of the A.C.J.M. They were all between twenty and thirty years of age, but nearer, as a rule, to twenty than to thirty; and they were the best types of Mexican youth that I had yet met. I even found my way into the circle wherein moved the martyrs whose arrest I shall describe in the next chapter, and I am glad that I did so for I was thus placed in a position to contrast the snow-white innocence, the untiring industry and the Christian charity of these young men with the dark background of crime and hatred and blood against which four of them moved, like angels passing the mouth of Hell, when on the 23rd of November, 1927, they crossed the garden of the Prefecture of Police on their way to death.

As for Señor X, he himself suddenly disappeared one day as completely as if the ground had opened and swallowed him; and taking into consideration all the circumstances that surrounded his disappearance, I came to the conclusion that he had gone to join his young disciples, Silva and Melgarejo.

CHAPTER IV

THE ARREST OF FATHER PRO JUÁREZ AND HIS COMPANIONS

O N 13 November, 1927, two bombs were thrown at President Obregón as he was driving in his motor-car through Chapultepec Park, Mexico City, on his way to a bull-fight at the Plaza de Toros. They were thrown from an Essex car containing four men, but though they exploded with a loud report, they did little damage. The windows of General Obregón's car were broken, and the General himself was cut by a splinter of glass, but the wound was so slight that he was able to continue on his way to the bull-ring where President Calles congratulated him on his escape.

Meanwhile, immediately after the attack, General Otero and Colonel Jaime Ramiro Martinez, who were accompanying Obregón in another car, followed in pursuit of the assailants, who, as was reported at the time, when fired upon, abandoned the car and tried to escape. Two succeeded in the attempt; two others, Nahum Lamberto Ruiz and Francisco Olivero, fell mortally wounded. Another man, Juan Tirado Arias, who was also arrested on the scene of the occurrence, denied firmly any participation in the deed.

Olivero seems to have died soon after he was captured; and Ruiz was so badly wounded that his survival for two days was a surprising circumstance, as a bullet had entered the back of his head and come out through one eye. When he was brought to the hospital, the surgeons removed the other eye, leaving him in complete darkness; why they removed the other eye, I do not know; it is said that they simply wished to give him pain, and such things are possible in Mexico. But in all probability he could hardly feel the additional pain owing to the fact that he was in a state of coma which lasted till his death. Despite this fact, and though he was unable to articulate a single word, he was surrounded day and night by policemen whose object was not, of course, to prevent him from escaping or being carried away, but to get from him the names of his companions.

He never spoke, however, but on the day after his death it was announced by the police that he had been induced by a stratagem to give the desired information. According to this story, his wife had been brought to his bedside, and with her came a policeman who represented himself to be his brother-in-law, and asked the dying man if he had any message to leave. Ruiz then said to his supposed brother-in-law; "Tell Father Miguel Pro Juárez, Señor Humberto Pro Juárez and Señor Luis Segura Vilchis to hide."

So the police statement ran, but it was obviously a childish fabrication, such as one would expect from officials like Roberto Cruz or Mazcorro, who are at one and the same time mendacious, unscrupulous and half-savage. There was certainly something of the naïveté of the savage about this extraordinary concoction; and as to analyse it would almost be an insult to the intelligence of my readers, I shall confine myself to asking the following question: Why should Ruiz have sent a warning to his companions, since the mere fact that he was in the hands of the police must have been warning enough for them? But there is no evidence that Ruiz spoke an intelligible word from the time he was wounded till the time of his death; and as Cruz has been convicted of deliberate falsehood over and over again, it is practically certain that he was responsible for this lie also. To mention only one of his falsehoods, he told the Press, after he had murdered Father Pro Juárez and his three companions, that all four had confessed their guilt, though, as will be seen later, this statement was untrue: they all declared their innocence. If Cruz was capable of lying in this way about men whom he had murdered, he was equally capable of lying about the same men before he had murdered them. In brief, this four-fold murder was a "reprisal" pure and simple. An attempt had been made on Obregón's life; and as the Police were unable to arrest the would-be murderers, Calles told them to arrest three of the most prominent Catholics in the Federal Capital and to shoot them. His object was to inspire terror; and he had had similar shootings carried out in the same way and for the same purpose on hundreds of previous occasions. To give one instance from the State of Nayarit, a Callista deputy, Juan Moreno, had been murdered there in Church by a Catholic congregation maddened by his attempt to interrupt a priest at the most sacred part of the Mass, and by his shooting of this priest on the altar steps. Calles had a punitive expedition sent to the scene of the tragedy, and when the commander of this force found that he could get no evidence from the peons, he selected nine villagers at random and hanged them. This is a common practice in Red Mexico as it was a common practice in Red Russia, during the days of the Terror. It *is* the Terror, and I must admit that without it the small minority which rules in Mexico and the small minority which rules in Russia would both be helpless.

On the strength of the bogus statement attributed to Ruiz, the three men whom I have mentioned were arrested immediately after the death of Ruiz, and, two days after the bomb outrage, Father Pro was arrested on the ground that he was one of "the intellectual directors" (*directores intelectuales*) of the attempt on Obregón's life; and, amazing as it may seem, the engineer Segura Vilchis and the young Humberto Pro were accused of having been in the automobile with the dynamitards, though as two of those dynamitards had been killed, and Tirado was charged with having been one of them, that would make five altogether, whereas there were only four men in the Essex car.

It is worthy of note that not one of the three men mentioned above, was in hiding at the time of his arrest. The two brothers

Pro Juárez, together with a third brother, afterwards released, were apprehended while sleeping in their father's house, at three o'clock in the morning. Father Pro Juárez was taken to prison in his pyjamas; the police would not give him time to dress. Had he been guilty, he would have been sleeping in travelling costume with a revolver under his pillow, and he would not have been sleeping in his father's house. His brothers were also in bed when the police came; and Humberto, the brother who afterwards died with him, had been playing tennis at the time the bombs were thrown at Obregón. The engineer, Segura Vilchis, was arrested in the office of the Light and Power Company where he worked. The young labourer, Juan Tirado Arias, could give no information about the attempted murder for the simple reason that he was innocent, and knew nothing about it. He had been taken in Chapultepec Park at the time of the bomb outrage, while he was running away from the scene of the explosion; but in Mexico every law-abiding citizen runs away from a place where bombs are bursting and rifles crackling. No weapons were found on Tirado, and there was not a shred of evidence that he was connected with the bomb outrage: all the evidence pointed the other way. Nevertheless he was eventually shot like the others, without trial. Tirado was a typical young Mexican labourer, with tawny-coloured skin, beardless face, and high cheek bones; in other words he belonged to the race formed by the mixture of Spanish and Indian blood, a race in which the white blood has been absorbed almost entirely by the native blood. In the published accounts of the attack he was first made to appear as one of the assailants, and, later, as the one who gave the information leading to the arrest of the other prisoners. It is surmised that an effort was made to bribe him with the promise of liberty, if he provided a pretext for their execution. If so, it is to his honour that he refused, and he was freed of the charge of being an informer when it was transferred to another, who was dead. Even the official reports do not deny that he consistently declared his innocence. The only evidence about him which the police seem to have found, in addition to his proximity to the place of attack, was the fact that he was a fervent Catholic. We shall not see Tirado again till we see him standing before the firing party in the garden of the *Inspección General.*

I shall now say something of the other prisoners. The authorities knew them to be ardent Catholics, very influential in the Catholic community, and, on that account alone, had cold-bloodedly determined to sacrifice them. Roberto Cruz, Mazcorro the Vampire, and López the Killer must, however, have been perfectly well aware of the fact that the ardour of their prisoners was directed to purely religious work, not to the manufacture of bombs or the organization of murder plots.

The principal prisoner was Father Miguel Augustín Pro Juárez who is generally called Father Pro and, in official documents, Father Pro Juárez, his mother's name being Juárez and the Mexicans, like the Spaniards, being accustomed to give their children the surname of both parents, the mother's surname coming last. I shall call him both Father Pro and Father Pro Juárez, both forms being correct.

Father Pro was, at the time of his death, thirty-seven years of age, but he looked fifteen years younger, and, as will be seen later, he was often taken for a student. In personal appearance, he was of medium height, slim, well formed, well dressed, and with easy, cultured manners. His face was a long oval, his eyes brown, his hair abundant, jet-black and brushed back from his forehead. For a time he wore a slight, black moustache, but when he met his death, he was clean shaven. His complexion was olive coloured, the complexion of an Andalusian. His family had long been settled in Mexico, where it is much respected; his father, Miguel Pro, was in comfortable circumstances and was therefore able to give his sons a good education. Miguel, the younger, was born in Concepción del Oro, in the State of Zacatecas, Mexico, on the 18th of January, 1891, and entered the Company of Jesus on the 10th of August, 1911. He studied at Los Gatos, California, and Granada, Spain, and then spent several years teaching at the Jesuit College in Granada, Nicaragua. In 1922 he went again to Europe, and studied theology, first at Barcelona and then at Enghien in Belgium, where he was ordained in the summer of 1925. Some of the religious poetry he composed at this time both in Spanish and French indicates that he might have won for himself a place in two great literatures, but the Master had more important work for him to do. In July 1926 he returned to Mexico City and threw himself with ardour into religious work there.

In Mexico he did not, of course, wear clerical garb which is forbidden: he had many changes of clothes but they were all of civilian cut. Sometimes he wore a light suit with soft collar and straw hat. At his execution he wore a dark suit with a soft collar and, instead of a waistcoat, a light-coloured cardigan buttoned in front and traversed horizontally by wavy white stripes.

Monsignor Hugh Benson presents us in one of his Elizabethan novels with a picture of another Jesuit, Father Edmund Campion strolling gaily, in civilian costume, into the Tower of London and light-heartedly questioning Topcliffe, the notorious torturer who was soon afterwards to stretch him on the rack. This Mexican Jesuit had extremely little spare time, but he did have some short periods of relaxation, and during one of them he visited Chapultepec Park which is well worth a visit if only for the sake of its gigantic trees, and which is a favourite resort of those living in the Federal Capital. He even strolled on that occasion along the imposing front of Chapultepec Palace, the residence of Calles and the headquarters of the persecution, and while he was doing so, one of his brothers took a snapshot which shows him standing in the strong sunlight, dressed in brown striped clothes with the emblem of a religious association, probably the League of Mexican Catholic Youth—in his buttonhole. The reader might think that it was risky to display such a badge in such a place, but Cruz or Mazcorro would probably mistake it for the rosette of the Legion of Honour. He wore a soft collar, a straw hat, and had a cigarette between his fingers.

On the left is the Palace of the Mexican Nero: on the right is the guard-house and one of Calles' Yaqui soldiers.

To realize how entirely Father Pro devoted himself to religious, charitable, and educational work, we should ascertain how he passed his time, and this it is easy to do, for he made copious and frequent reports which are confirmed by independent testimony. He often heard Confessions from 5:30 a.m. till 11 a.m., and as he was a man of weak health he had on two occasions to leave the confessional in a state of physical collapse. He suffered periodically from his stomach, and the attacks sometimes prostrated him, and obliged him to lie down till they had passed.

He carefully organized his work and arranged secret meeting-places where confessions were heard. He also established "Eucharistic Stations," houses in which Holy Communion would be distributed on certain days; but owing to the pertinacity of the Secret Police of whom there are 10,000 in Mexico City alone, and who are actuated mostly by a desire for money, he had to change these places frequently. He gave Holy Communion to about three hundred persons daily, and on the first Friday of three months, the numbers ran successively to 900, 1,300 and 1,500. In addition to this, he went around every morning on his brother's bicycle, distributing Holy Communion to many people in their own houses; and despite the vigilance of the Secret Police, he was able to perform all his priestly functions. He administered baptism, solemnized marriages, attended the dying, and made many conversions, not from Protestantism, as there are only about 25,000 native Protestants in the country, but from Agnosticism.

He said Mass frequently but in defiance of the unjust law which forbids its celebration in private houses, and he ran great personal risk on every single occasion. In three cases the house where he was to say Mass was surrounded by the police, but he extricated himself from the difficulty with a coolness and ingenuity which was assisted by his youthful appearance. On one of these occasions he opened his coat as if to display a badge of the

Secret Police on his waistcoat. He had no such badge, but his characteristic action in the dim, early morning light, was enough; the police saluted him and allowed him to pass. Having entered, he wished to say Mass but the congregation dissuaded him, though with difficulty. They were so alarmed for his safety that they begged him to escape by the roof, but he insisted on leaving by the way he came, and he received again the salutes of the police as he departed.

Reports of his activities soon came to the ears of the police, and he knew that they were searching for him closely; but fortunately they did not then know him by sight, and did not suspect him when they saw him, for his youthful appearance, his joyous manner, his fashionable costume, and most of all his moustache, threw them completely off the scent. To confuse them still more, he had a disconcerting habit of changing frequently into a differently coloured suit of clothes and a different hat, and of altering the cut of his moustache or even shaving it off altogether.

He frequently gave Retreats to all classes of persons— "Retreats under Fire" he called them; and for the sake of precaution, the place of meeting was changed every day, admission was always by ticket, and a watch was maintained outside the building. Sometimes the lectures were given in the parlours of private houses and sometimes in business offices. Dressed in the blue overalls of a mechanic, he once lectured in the backyard of a private house to fifty taxi-drivers who had asked him to give them a retreat. On another occasion he gave a Retreat to Government employees, but he afterwards lamented humorously that, far from being afraid to come, some of these men were not afraid even of the devil, since they did not believe in his existence. Others of them denied the existence of hell, and were not ready to admit the immortality of the soul; but he had the consolation of seeing all closing the Retreat in good dispositions and going to Holy Communion.

At the end of a Retreat to business men, the closing Mass was said in a house facing the Palace of Justice and close to the offices of the Procurator-General, the very man who, under President Calles, was most conspicuous in hunting down religious services in the capital. But Father Pro seems to have been devoid of fear, for at a time when he was one of the most "wanted" men in Mexico City, he visited the prisons daily, bringing gifts to the Catholic prisoners but also hearing their confessions and giving them Holy Communion if an opportunity offered; and on such occasions he disarmed suspicion by chatting amicably with the warders and the gendarmes.

He had many adventures. On one occasion, as he left the house in which he had just given the first lecture of a Retreat, he noticed two men crossing the street and standing in wait for him at the corner. He went boldly up to them and asked for a match. They replied that he could get matches in a shop. He moved on and they followed. He turned through various streets, but they always kept close behind him. Seeing a taxi standing idle he stepped into it, but the other two followed in another car. Father Pro spoke to the driver and found that he was a Catholic. He told him his plight and the man promised to help him in any way that he could. Father Pro told him to slow down when turning the next corner; he would slip out and the car was to go on. Having put his hat in his pocket and unbuttoned his coat, Father Pro dropped out of the car, strode to the nearest tree, and leaned casually against it in such a position that he should be clearly visible from the road. A moment later the pursuing car passed by, the mud-guard almost touching him. The two men in it saw him, but gave no indication that they recognized him, and he turned away, limping slightly as a result of his fall from the car, but safe.

But this was not his only adventure. On December 4, 1926 the Catholics sent up six hundred little balloons which showered religious leaflets all over the city. Calles was furious, and in order to placate him, the police arrested many Catholic students, and, along with them Father Pro, who was mistaken for a student. The police tried, as usual, to extort money from him, but, though he refused to pay anything, he was finally released with the others.

On another occasion he so won over a police agent who had arrested him, that, instead of conducting him to prison, the man brought him to his own house with a request that he might offer spiritual comfort to his dying mother.

After giving a Mission at Toluca, about fifty miles from the capital, a few weeks before his death, he fell into the hands of the gendarmes, but succeeded in escaping. This was not the only occasion in which he carried on religious work outside Mexico City.

Distressed at the lack of religious instruction which he perceived, he selected from the ranks of the A.C.J.M. 145 young men to give religious conferences and he nominated a directive Committee whose business it was to send speakers to any part of the city where they were wanted. He himself was President of this Committee; his brother Humberto was one of its principal members; and the engineer Luis Segura Vilchis was one of its best orators.

As the number of the poor had been greatly increased by the new Poor, victims of the exactions of Cruz, a Catholic Relief organization was started, and in this organization also Father Pro played a prominent part by receiving and distributing alms. In May 1927 he was able to support thirty-nine families; by October the number had increased to ninety-six.

This work brought Father Pro in contact with a great number of people, and this circumstance was both good and bad. It was bad, for it made him known by sight to some of Calles' detectives, and it was good for it enabled a great many of the people with whom he worked to declare, after his arrest, that his connection with any political plot was unthinkable. One of the leaders of the League for the Defence of Religious Liberty published the following statement:

> "We have made independent investigations and, as a result of them, can affirm on oath that Father Pro and his

brother Humberto had no connection with the attack made on General Obregón on Sunday, November 13th."

Father Pro's Jesuit Superior, who was in close contact with him during the last months of his life, wrote with equal assurance on November 27th:

"I can testify, and I do so under oath, that it is absolutely false that Father Pro attended any meeting in which the attack was planned, or had any part in it, or that he was the actual author of the plot."

Father Pro supported these declarations by his own testimony. A reporter of one of the leading newspapers of Mexico City, the *Excelsior*, interviewed the two brothers in prison, and in his account of the conversation gives Father Pro's statement:

"I am entirely free of any connection with this affair, for I am a man of peace. I am quite tranquil and hope that justice will be done. I deny absolutely, without restriction, that I had any part in the plot."

With regard to the charge that cartridges intended for the rebel forces of Jalisco were found at Father Pro's house, not the slightest evidence in support of this was ever adduced.

However, the strongest evidence of the absolute falsity of the charge against Father Pro is found in the following testimony of Benita Guerra-Leal, the secretary to General Cruz, the chief of police in Mexico City. At the express command of General Obregón, Arturo H. Orci, the General's personal lawyer who was with Obregón in the automobile at the time of the bomb-throwing, went to interview the chief of police who was in entire charge of the prisoners. Orci speaking for Obregón recommended an immediate public trial because Obregón did not believe the prisoners guilty. Guerra-Leal, secretary to the chief of police, informed Orci that General Cruz could not be seen or interviewed at any time or in any place. Asked for the official report concerning the prisoners who were not allowed to see anybody, the secretary showed Orci a paper. After he had read the document carefully, the lawyer, Orci, exclaimed:

"This is no indictment; it is simply your police report."

"But it is all we have," replied the secretary.

"And what does the chief of police think concerning the guilt of the prisoners?" insisted Orci.

Very significantly the secretary answered:

"The brothers Pro, Father Miguel and Humberto have not confessed any complicity in the plot, nor can any such complicity ever be proved against them."

Then the secretary, hearing of General Obregón's recommendations, assured Orci that the public trial was to be held the next day. "What was my surprise," said Orci afterwards, "to learn on the following day that the prisoners had been shot at eleven o'clock that morning! I immediately telephoned to General Cruz to ask him what had occurred, reminded him of my visit to his office the previous night, that the investigation into the prisoners' guilt at that time was far from complete, and that General Obregón had strongly recommended a public investigation. To all this General Cruz replied:

"'True, sir, but even before you had spoken in my office and in spite of the recommendations of General Obregón, I had already received orders to do what I did.'"

The universal opinion in Mexico City is that some friends of Calles were behind the plot to assassinate Obregón; and the very incredibility of the theory is one point in its favour, for nothing is too incredible in Mexican politics, and the "*Liberales*" have, for the last ten years, been as much occupied in cutting each other's throats as in oppressing the people. All the anti-clerical leaders who died violent deaths during the period in question were murdered by other anti-clerical leaders. I need only mention the names of Venustiano Carranza, Jesús Carranza, Francisco Villa, Emiliano Zapata, Manuel Diéguez, Francisco Serrano, Fortunato Maycott, Manuel García Vigil, Salvador Alvarado, and Arnulfo Gómez. There is no doubt that in November 1927, some bad feeling existed between the followers of Calles and those of Obregón, partly because of the new law which gives Obregón six years at Chapultepec; and there was certainly something very suspicious about the furious haste of Calles to have Father Pro and his companions slaughtered, and about the failure of the Police to arrest the man who escaped, or to follow up any clue successfully, though there were many clues—the Essex car, for example, was one.

The case against Cruz and Calles is so strong that it would almost be cruel to show the weakness of it, were it not for the fact that on this occasion Calles and Cruz committed murder. It is so strong that even an American Protestant, Mr. Carleton Beals, the Mexico correspondent of an American Radical weekly, the *New Republic* (New York), asserts in the issue of that periodical published on December 21, 1927, that "every constitutional and humanitarian guarantee was violated in the case of the four civilians, members of the Catholic League of Religious Defence, one of them a priest, who were alleged to have hurled the dynamite bomb at Obregón's auto in Chapultepec Park." For the benefit of non-American readers I should, perhaps, repeat that both Mr. Beals and the *New Republic* are, as a rule, friendly to President Calles and unfriendly to the Mexican Catholics.

Mexican legal authorities point out that seven articles of the Mexican Constitution relating to the arrest, imprisonment, and trial of prisoners were violated by the authorities in the case of Father Pro and his companions. No Constitution that the world ever saw contains so many safeguards for prisoners as the Constitution drawn up at Querétaro in 1917 by Carranza and his friends (without any authority from the nation) and no legal regulations are so favourable to civilians accused of crime as the legal regulations based on this Constitution. Those regulations are not only equitable, they are eloquent, even flamboyant; they are bursting with philanthropy and bubbling over with the milk of human kindness; in short they are just the regulations we would expect from the modern type of sentimental and slightly hysterical Socialist who believes not at all in religion but too much in legislation, who is so enthusiastically on the side of Labour that he reduces the labourer to a state of slavery, so lachrymose with affection for humanity that the jails are crowded, so inexorably opposed to capital punishment that the executioners are working overtime, so intolerant of militarism that he places everybody under the heel of the soldier, so fond of freedom that he abolishes it from off the face of the earth. To give one instance of what I mean, in Mexico there can, in theory, be no such thing as martial law, but the result is that in practice there has been nothing else for the last two years.

On the basis of this ultra-benignant Constitution of Querétaro, Calles drew up his anti-religious laws; and, when any suggestion is made to him that those laws should be modified, the Dictator looks as shocked as a pious Moslem would look if asked to alter the text of the Koran. But, when it is a question of attaining his ends, he violates this Constitution without the slightest compunction and expels or imprisons any journalist who draws attention to such violations. He has committed so many violations of the Constitution that I find it easier to give the cases in which he has acted in accordance with the Constitution: in fact, I think there is only one case, when Ambassador Sheffield asked him to alter his unjust Petroleum Law. On that occasion he pointed reverently to a copy of the Constitution and said that he could not alter a jot or tittle of that sacrosanct document; but when Mr. Dwight W. Morrow came along later and hinted that, unless the alteration were made, Calles would find himself extremely short of money, Calles did make the alteration which the Oil magnates wanted.

I could easily give hundreds of cases where Calles has violated the Constitution, but to do so would involve writing the whole history of the past two years in Mexico, and narrating the painful circumstances of each execution, so that, to avoid wearying the reader, I shall concentrate on the case of Father Pro and his companions, though, as the execution and its preliminaries took place in the Federal Capital and under the eyes of the foreign representatives, less savagery was shown than at the "trials" and executions which were carried out in remote parts of the country. In the same way and for the same reason, I concentrated, in my book on the Bolshevik Persecution of Christianity, on the trial of Archbishop Cieplak and his companions.

According to Mexican law based on the Carranza Constitution, a warrant must be produced when an arrest is made, a civilian prisoner must be brought before a civil magistrate within 48 hours after arrest, and must be put on his trial before a civilian judge within 70 hours after his arrest. He must be allowed to communicate freely with his lawyer. He must be confronted by the witnesses. He must on no account be tried before a military tribunal or prevented from seeing his legal adviser. Now, in the case of the four prisoners whose case we are considering, all these safeguards were violated by Calles who ordered Cruz in violent language to go on with the executions and to ignore all formalities. As in such cases the law holds personally responsible for its violations not only those who order but also those who obey, down even to the gendarmes whose rifles commit the murder, Calles, Cruz, and every member of the firing party are personally responsible for the four assassinations which took place in the garden of the *Inspección General* on the 23rd of November, 1927, but, as the chief murderer probably knows, this state of things operates to his own advantage inasmuch as it binds these men to him as no oath of allegiance could ever bind them. Knowing that they would be tried for murder the instant the Calles regime fell, they take a lively interest in maintaining that regime, just as most Russian Jews take a lively interest in maintaining the Soviet Government owing to their fear of a pan-Russian pogrom the day after the Bolsheviks fell.

The case against Calles is so strong that it would take too much time to give all of it, but one point is particularly strong: it is this—if the guilt of the prisoners was as manifest as Cruz declared it to be, and was even admitted by the prisoners themselves, why, then, was there no public trial and no trial of any kind? Surely, under these circumstances a public trial would terrify the enemies of Calles.

But there is no need to pick out one illegality where there are a hundred illegalities. Father Pro was kept in prison without any legal order; no formal charge was made against him; he was brought before no tribunal; he was given no opportunity of replying to the alleged statement which led to his arrest; he was not allowed to summon witnesses on his behalf or to nominate a counsel for his defence—although, in accordance with the law, he should have been allowed to do so. He demanded a trial. He was anxious for it, because he believed that it would prove his complete innocence. He was quite cheerful about it, because he did not believe that he was in any danger. He knew that he had run the risk of imprisonment by exercising the duties of his sacred calling, but this was a different matter. In this instance there was a specific charge of complicity in a plot to assassinate, and he welcomed the opportunity of showing that at least one of the charges made against him was false. But there was no trial. Six days after his arrest, he was told that he was to be executed, and a few minutes later he was shot. According to the official report, the sentence was decreed by a summary court, but, since there was no form of trial, all that any tribunal could have done was to sign the order for execution.

On the day after the execution of Father Pro and his companions, a group of Mexican lawyers presented to Mr. Morrow, the United States Ambassador to Mexico, a document entitled: "Brief considerations concerning the execution by the Police of four prisoners." The fact that the statement was not prepared for circulation abroad, where Mexican law or the circumstances of the case might not be easily understood or the truth of the assertions verified, but was submitted to the consideration of one living in the capital itself, lends it considerable weight. Although the English in which it is written is not that of an Englishman, the meaning is perfectly clear. The document reads as follows:

"The death of the following gentlemen: Augustín Pro Juárez, priest; Humberto, his brother; Luis Segura and Juan

Tirado is, legally, murder, both because of the deed itself and because of the following circumstances that contributed to it:

"1. This sentence was decreed and carried out by the head of the executive power and his subordinates, who, according to the law and legal procedure of Mexico, are absolutely unqualified to decree it.

"2. The accused were not given any real trial, since they were not brought before any penal tribunal, as is contemplated when dealing with crimes committed by civilians.

"3. They were not given a counsel for their defence, nor any opportunity of nominating one, as the order for execution was communicated to them only a few minutes before it was carried out, thereby making impossible any appeal which could save them from death.

"4. The necessary formalities of legal procedure were not observed.

"5. The accused were regarded as convicted and confessed criminals, solely on the alleged declaration of a dying man, extracted by deceit, and one that could not be contradicted, as the man was dead. In connection with this it is to be noted that this declaration was published after the death of the supposed accuser, and, secondly, that the doctors who attended him, and the police authorities themselves, declared that this man was in a state of complete unconsciousness.

"6. The ground for regarding the accused as confessed criminals is certainly false in so far as it concerns Father Pro, who, according to the note prepared for the press by the police bureau, protested his innocence and declared his desire to be brought before the court to prove it. As for the declarations attributed to the engineer, Segura, they have all the appearance of being false, because, in the history of crime there is not to be found any instance so absurd as that of a guilty man, who not only confesses openly and entirely his crime, but boasts of it and supplies to his accusers more data than he is asked to give, and takes on himself the responsibility for acts that are not imputed to him; and all that, it should be noted, is said to have been done, with such a display of coolness and cynicism, by one who had not in the past been addicted to evil-doing, but was an honourable and peace-loving professional man.

"7. It is equally incredible that the supposed assailants of General Obregón should have calmly returned home after the attack and there awaited the result. This is simply an absurdity, which weighs still more in favour of the accused, for it is well-known that all criminals, through an instinct of self-preservation, withdraw from the scene of the crime and from all places where they would be within reach of the law.

"8. Lastly, even supposing the President of the Republic and his subordinates, the police authorities, had been competent to try the accused men, that these men had been tried, that in the procedure all the formalities prescribed by law had been complied with, that all the protection and help ordinarily granted to every accused person had been granted to those who were charged with the crime—not even then could the penalty inflicted be justified, because, in accordance with the Penal Code now in force, anyone who is found guilty of attempted murder, which is not effectual, may not be condemned to death, but only to imprisonment for a term of eight to twelve years. (Article 195.)"

Mr. Dwight W. Morrow of the great banking house of Morgan was much too busy to answer this letter, or even to read it; he had to join the Dictator in a joy-ride through the country in the Dictator's million dollar train (made in Chicago). Had Father Pro been an anti-clerical, it would have been different: we have seen how the American Ambassador Poinsett visited the rabid anti-clerical and brother mason Zavala when he was in prison. When anti-clericals are oppressed by a Conservative Government in Mexico, America intervenes, in the name of

Humanity: when Conservatives are oppressed by an anti-clerical Government, America sees no reason why she should make even the slightest suggestion on their behalf.

But that was the Old America, with the poison of imported prejudice still in her veins; even as I write, the New America is thundering at the gate.

Humberto Pro was a layman, and, like his elder brother, Miguel, a member of the A.C.J.M. (Catholic Association of Mexican Youth). He was also one of the members of the Committee which arranged the Students' Conferences, and these two proofs of his desire to live like a good Christian led eventually to his death, for if he had been a non-practising Catholic, he would never have been interfered with. He was at home with his brothers when the attack took place, and he declared to the representative of the *Excelsior* that he had furnished means of procuring evidence to testify that he was not guilty of the charge. He held the important post of Treasurer in the Bank of Mexico, where he was greatly esteemed for the uprightness of his character and the gentleness of his disposition.

Luis Segura Vilchis was about the same age and if much the same type as Humberto. Belonging to a respectable family of the metropolis, he made his earlier studies in the French College in Mexico, where he was conspicuous by reason of his exceptional mental ability and of his exemplary conduct. While still very young he entered the College of Engineering, where he took his degree; and before his twenty-first year he was practising his profession at the Necaxa Electric Plant. The Mexico Street Car Company, a branch of the Light and Power Co., a Canadian concern with an English manager, placed him in its engineering department, where he was the youngest member and a general favourite. He was a member of the A.C.J.M. and one of the best speakers at Father Pro's conferences for young men. He was also a member of the League for the Defence of Religious Liberty and of the Sodality of the Blessed Virgin Mary. He was always occupied from morning to night in his office. He was there as usual on the day after the attack, and when arrested told his companions that he would be back immediately, as the policeman had told him that he was required at the Police Head-quarters in order to give an explanation of some of his actions. No evidence was published to prove his complicity with the plot, but in official statements it was announced that he admitted and boasted of it and of his connection with other plots. No witnessed statement to this effect was, however, published, and no one believed it. The only one who had an opportunity of speaking to him after his arrest was a newspaper reporter, and to him he declared that he was innocent. Friends who knew him intimately ridiculed the published account of his "confession" stating that there was nothing of the extremist in him and that nothing could be more contrary to his character than that he should boast of his complicity in violent measures in the manner stated in the official statements.

For six days all four prisoners were kept in one of the under-ground cells of the Prefecture, and they were never permitted to see their legal advisers or their relatives, though the latter called frequently and tried every means to get access to the prisoners. The most pertinacious of these visitors was Ana María, Father Pro's sister; but Segura's mother also came frequently.

Only on two occasions were the prisoners brought up from their damp dungeon, on the first occasion to be questioned by newspaper reporters, and on the second occasion to be shot. On the first occasion, it was the day before their execution, though they were unaware of the fact, Father Pro declared to the news-paper men that he was in no way connected with the supposed plot, and that he had not been engaged in any political activity whatsoever. As General Roberto Cruz, who was present on this occasion, had informed these same newspaper men just before the prisoners' appearance, that Father Pro had confessed his guilt, the newspaper men expected Cruz to say something, but he remained silent. How are we to explain this amazing conduct on the part of Cruz? The explanation is simple. Like his master Calles, he is a savage,—debauched, degraded, demoralized, mendacious, and absolutely careless of what he says or of how much he contradicts himself because he knows that the great newspapers of the world will never expose him. On the present occasion all the leading newspapers of Mexico City braved the wrath of Calles by asserting their belief in the priest's innocence, but all the leading newspapers in the United States printed the statement sent out by the Mexican Press Bureau that Father Pro and his companions had admitted their guilt, and none of them troubled to correct that statement when its falsity was pointed out to them.

Next day, the prisoners were taken out again, and shot like dogs. Their execution had probably been hastened by the knowledge that Mr. Luis E. MacGregor, a lawyer employed by their friends, had succeeded in getting the district judge to grant an *amparo* or stay of execution, but when Mr. MacGregor entered the Prefecture of Police with the necessary documents, he was told that the prisoners had already been shot, and that their bodies were lying in the hospital.

Chapter V

THE GARDEN OF DEATH

THE *patio* or interior garden of the Prefecture was planted originally by Don Fernando González, the Catholic General who built the house in the time of Porfirio Díaz, for, as I have already pointed out, the anti-clericals can neither plant nor build anything. It was once a beautiful garden, as many old Spanish gardens in Mexico are; but it is now a horror, terrible to look at, a place of executions, of corpses and of blood: it is a Garden of Death, symbolical of the condition to which Calles and his kind have reduced beautiful Mexico.

As these executions are always by shooting, and as at such short range—twenty to thirty feet—bullets from modern army rifles would easily penetrate the wall, Cruz has had the sense to erect at the end of the garden rifle butts, in other words a mound of earth for stopping the bullets. This work is extraordinarily crude; the Aztecs and the Pre-Aztecs were far more advanced as architects. At a distance of some six feet from the outer wall, four tree trunks were inserted vertically into holes in the ground, and then, on the inner side of them, other tree trunks were laid horizontally, one above the other, to a height of seven or eight feet, the space between these tree trunks and the wall being filled in with earth, now covered with tangled grass and high weeds, amid which bloom a few wild flowers. This contrivance stops such of the bullets as hit it, but many go high as is shown by the pitted condition of the wall above the stockade. The ground close to the stockade is black with congealed blood, and out of it arise three monstrous wooden images, bearing a close resemblance to the human figure, and a remote resemblance to Huitzilopochtli, the Aztec war-god which once stood on the summit of the Great Teocalli on the spot where the Cathedral of Mexico City now stands. To this hideous idol, no fewer than eighty thousand human beings were sacrificed by the Aztecs to solemnize the coronation of Montezuma, but Cortés threw it from its pedestal and the battered remains of it are now in the National Museum. It might almost seem at first sight as if Calles had, in his hatred of Christianity, set up new idols which can only be appeased by Christian blood, but no, these images are merely targets for executioners to practice on. And some of the budding executioners must have been very young or very inexperienced, judging by the pitted condition of the wall to which I have already referred.

This slaughter-house is not hidden away in a remote part of the capital: it is in the centre. Within fifty yards of it is the headquarters of the *Lotería Nacional*, the State Lottery, a great gambling hell from which the Government derives much of its revenue. Within a hundred yards of it stands the American Consulate-General, and probably from his own roof the Consul-General could look into Calles' slaughter-house and see the bloody work that goes on there. The district swarms with American trippers and with American contingents of various kinds come to see Mexico and do homage to its Dictator. There have been contingents from the American Federation of Labour (come to prostrate themselves before "the Labour President"), from various Chambers of Commerce, from Protestant Churches, from the Elks, Kiwanis, Mystic Shriners, and other strange bodies, most of them with a decided taste for alcoholic beverages which they frequently gratify at the Dictator's expense, for presentation to the great man at Chapultepec is generally the finale of the trip.

Within six hundred yards of the Prefecture is the Hotel Regis, from whose open windows there sometimes floats the stately anthem of the Rotarians:

"Hail! hail! the gang's all here."

Or, in feminine voices of course, the wistful query of the Quotarians:

"Am I a real Quotarian,
  Or do I just belong?
Do I feel that service and not self
  Is part of life's sweet song?"

On the 23rd of November 1927 there was an unusual bustle outside the Prefecture of Police. Two companies of mounted gendarmerie were drawn up in front of the building; machine-guns were mounted on the roof; hoarse words of command were heard; and great brass Generals were seen rushing to and fro. Soon the rumour spread that the prisoners detained in connection with the attack on General Obregón were going to be executed, and a great crowd assembled, but was not permitted to come near the Prefecture. Moscow has, by the way, the same system; when executions are being carried out in the cellars of the Lubyanka, agents of the OGPU prevent anyone from walking even on the footpath which skirts that house of blood. But, whereas in Moscow there would be no crowd, there was a great crowd on this occasion in the Mexican capital: soon the Plaza de la Reforma was black with people; several khaki-coloured boys climbed the pedestal of the statue erected to Charles IV of Spain; the crowd overflowed into the deserted Avenida del Palacio Legislativo and the derelict Plaza de la República; and reinforcements of Police had to be sent for. They were motorcyclists and foot police, and they stopped all traffic through the square during the thirty-odd minutes that the human sacrifices lasted. So great was the desire of some spectators to see the butchery that a score of young men belonging to the Bolshevik organisation CROM risked their lives by scaling to a height of twenty or thirty feet the rusty steel skeleton of the Congress building. Even so, in the good old days of Montezuma, did the inhabitants of Tenochtitlan crowd on the roof-terraces, towers, and embattled parapets of their houses in order to witness the human sacrifices offered up at daybreak in sight of all the city, on the lofty *Techcatl* or altar of green jasper. They watched the slow march of the victims up the narrow path that wound around the Teocalli with the same palpitating interest as a few of their descendants, in the year 1927, watched the progress of Father Pro and his companions down that fatal garden. When they saw the victims suddenly thrown backwards on the jasper altar by the *quacuilli*, they felt the same delicious thrill as some of their children felt on this occasion when they saw the prisoners turn to face the firing party; and when the obsidian knife of the High Priest buried itself in the upturned breast of the captive, they raised the same shout as was raised by one or two Aztecs in the Plaza de la Reforma when the five rifles spoke.

This refers of course, only to a small de-Christianised section of the natives, for, as will be seen later, the great majority of the Mexicans are sincere Catholics who regarded these executions with horror; but man tends towards evil rather than towards good, and, under the influence of Calles' anti-Christian legislation, this small, demoralised minority may grow.

Every nation, like every individual, has its predominant temptation. In some cases it is drink, in others concupiscence, in others it is gold; in Mexico it is blood; and Calles has done a great deal to rebarbarize the young and neglected section of the Mexican people by the butcheries he has had carried out so frequently in public during the last year and by his system of exposing dead bodies, sometimes prone in the market place, sometimes suspended by the neck from trees, sometimes propped up against walls or houses. Thousands of such scenes have been photographed and there are thousands of such photographs in existence: I have a collection myself but all of them are too horrible to be published in a civilized country.

I have already told in chapter III, part II, of Calles' personal lust for blood, and of how in Agua Prieta he once got up at five o'clock in the morning in order to gloat in solitude over the limp body of a victim swinging from a gibbet in front of his police station. All that was needed on the present occasion to bring the scene into harmony with the best Montezumian traditions was the presence of Calles himself seated in a chair of State like one of those Aztec Emperors from whom he claims descent on the mother's side; but his Generals did their best to supply the deficiency, for there was quite a throng of them on a raised platform at the safe end of the garden where their brilliant uniforms were set off by the black dresses of the journalists, photographers, and high functionaries. General Antonio Gómez Velasco, chief of the Traffic Department, was seen chatting affably with Colonel Cornejo, chief of the General Staff, whose duty it was "to be present at the shootings and to take official cognizance of the act." Another war lord, name unknown, was gracefully accepting a cigarette from Señor Guerra Leal, the Secretary of the Chief of Police.

Resplendent among the Generals was the bulky form of Roberto Cruz, the host of the occasion, in khaki, Sam Brown belt, riding breeches, riding boots, spurs, sword, revolver and (to crown all) peaked military cap. The General had his right hand inside the breast of his tunic and his left hand in his trousers pocket. Probably his right hand grasped the butt-end of a revolver, for Cruz fears assassination, and his left hand grasped a powder-puff, for he powders himself like a *demi-mondaine*, and uses scent as well. To give himself a martial, devil-may-care appearance, he had stuck a cigarette between his lips, but had forgotten to light it.

On his left was a man of slighter build wearing a long, military cloak. This was General Jesús Palomera López, better known as "López the Killer," because he is as addicted to murder as a dope-fiend is to dope. López also had his left hand in his trousers pocket though, like Cruz, he had a heavy Colt automatic strapped to his belt.

On Cruz's right slouched an equally sinister figure, the bloated and indescribably repulsive figure of José Mazcorro, the vampire, the ghoul, the head of the Secret Police, the hangman who bears the ironical title of *el Jefe de las Comisiones de Seguridad* (the Chief of the Commissions of Safety).

Mazcorro affects civilian dress because it conceals better than a military uniform would, his protuberant abdomen and his swollen figure, and also because he poses as being a super-detective. His conduct of the case with which I am now dealing shows the kind of detective he is, not the kind Sir Conan Doyle would write about. He is a detective whose ingenuity is more in evidence after an execution than before, for having detected the wrong man and sent him before a firing party, he then devotes all the little brain power that he has to the hopeless task of proving that, after all, the man was just as well out of the way. Mazcorro's insolence is almost equal to his ignorance; and both are proverbial in Mexico City. On the present occasion, he wore a shabby civilian dress set off by a soft, wide-awake hat with an extensive brim which was pulled down low over his thick black eyebrows and his bloodshot eyes, leaving clearly visible only the lower part of the yellow face—the triple chin, the black moustaches with their ends waxed, the thick protruding under-lip and the heavy jaw covered with the grey stubble of slovenly middle age.

Over his civilian dress he wore a large, soiled, and shapeless overcoat, tight and without a wrinkle around the waist-line, like the water on the edge of Niagara, but falling below into a mass of folds, wrinkles, and ripples. The left side of the collar was turned up and the right side down, and a greasy, coloured handkerchief was wound around the thick neck. His left hand was in his overcoat pocket, and remained there during all the subsequent proceedings. With his right hand he clawed from time to time the arm of the young victims whom he conducted, one by one, to their doom; and after the touch of that unclean hand, even the rude blows of the bullets must have seemed pleasant.

Scattered among the military were other "detectives," also in civilian dress, and looking as villainous a gang as the occupants of Madame Tussaud's Chamber of Horrors. All wore slouched hats and overcoats whose turned-up collars made their heads seem sunken between their shoulders. Their manners were furtive; and no policeman in a civilized country would have hesitated a moment to arrest them on suspicion. One detective, clean-shaven and insolent, standing with his legs far apart, wore a damaged and ill-fitting Burberry which he had probably stripped from the corpse of some victim; and for some reason or other he had turned up the collar of this garment, possibly because he wanted to conceal some of his singularly ill-favoured visage, but more probably because his chief had the collar of his overcoat turned up. The pockets of the Burberry were large, strongly marked, and sewed on outside; and the ends of the sleeves were permanently turned up. This was Mazcorro's second in command. I do not know his name, but I shall call him in future "the man in the Burberry."

Mazcorro's third in command also wore civilian dress under a loose, thin, and very dirty overcoat, thrown wide open. He wore Kaiseresque turned-up moustaches, very black, and, like the others, kept his left hand in his trousers pocket. Presumably all these people grasped small automatics with their left hands. But why not with the right hand? Possibly because constant practice with the revolver had made them ambidextrous. Evidently they expected that some Catholic fanatic would make an attempt on their lives, but during all the history of this persecution there is not a single case of assassination by a Catholic. In the opinion of a Chicago journalist who recently visited Mexico, this scrupulousness on the part of the Catholics has handicapped them very heavily in their contest with an opponent who has no scruples.

The background of the dais was taken up by a crowd of subordinate officers, some in khaki, some in blue, some with caps after the style of the French gendarmerie, some with caps after the German style, some with brilliant brass buttons, some with common leather buttons.

The general impression made by these gentlemen on the dais was that they were not gentlemen and not white men. Their faces were too tawny, their cheek-bones too high, there was something indefinably curious about their eyes, "their manners lacked the calm repose that marks the caste of Vere de Vere," and also lacked the higher distinction of the poor, honest, independent man with a good conscience. Some were pure-blooded Indians, and others had a distinct touch of the negro, but the majority were *mestizos*, in other words a mixture, in varying proportions, of Spanish and Indian. Altogether a strange, and disturbing picture, liable to cause a wild stampede among the children in Kensington Gardens or Central Park, N.Y., if suddenly transported thither.

There were many journalists and photographers present, for *el Señor General* Cruz had manifested his desire that the newspaper men should enjoy "the greatest facilities," his impression being that photographs of the executions would strike terror into the Catholics and greatly increase the respect of the outer world for his own resolution and energy. As a matter of fact the outer world is disgusted, and the Catholics are using those photographs as propaganda against both Cruz and Calles.

Ranged against the wall on each side of the dais, stood, in somewhat irregular formation, about forty men belonging to the *Gendarmeria Montada* or Mounted Gendarmerie, most of them apparently pure blooded Indians. In the centre of the garden was an open space which individual gendarmes sometimes crossed, but they all avoided with superstitious care the ominously deserted end of the garden with its three grotesque figures. Suddenly a Major called out words of command: "*Pelotón, firmes! De frente! Marchen!*" and immediately a group of gendarmes detached themselves from the mass, and marched in military order towards the centre of the garden and down the garden, halting at length within about thirty feet of the targets. There they stood in two lines, one behind the other. The first line consisted of four men and the N.C.O.; the second line consisted of four men. According to Mexican practice it is only the first line that fires, the second line remains "at attention." This firing party is called a "*pelotón*" or platoon, though in no other army is a platoon so small. A new firing party was formed after each execution, so that no man had to shoot twice.

All these warriors had evidently brushed and polished and titivated themselves as if for a field-day. They wore their best blue uniforms, of which the numerous brass buttons had been brightly burnished, not only the seven necessary buttons in front but the three unnecessary buttons on the sleeve, and the six still more unnecessary buttons behind. Truly, they were a gorgeous sight, those executioners, for their buckles and badges and all the other metal work which they wore, shone bravely in the rays of the sun, now well up in the heavens, for it was ten o'clock. They were a sight which might make babes and sucklings (Mexican) clap their hands with delight. Their spurs looked like silver, and jangled in a martial way as they shifted their position, for they were standing at ease, and Mexican N.C.O.'s are not martinets. Their high boots had been newly polished, whence it follows of course that their *raison d'être*, the ominous objects from which they take their name, in other words their rifles, had also been polished. Presumably, also, they had used their pull-throughs, though pull-throughs are not used much in the Mexican army.

In charge of these dusky warriors were no less than four N.C.O.'s who were distinguished from the mere rank and file by an ornament of silver cord on the arm, and by a sword on the thigh. In supreme charge of all, *generalissimo* in fact—and looking every inch a *generalissimo* (Mex.)—was a particularly natty young officer, a Major, no less, *Mayor de la Gendarmeria Montada* (Major of the Mounted Gendarmerie) to give him his full title, in well-fitting khaki tunic of English style; Sam Brown belt; very loose, fashionable riding breeches that might have come from the best military tailor in Bond Street; high boots, over the polishing of which his batman must have sweated; the whole "creation," as the milliners would say, being surmounted by a *piquant* French cap with a broad, vivid band and a soft crown, a cap which, together with the chocolate-coloured face beneath it, prevented the *ensemble* from being quite British. The strap of the cap traversed the plump brown cheek and chin of this self-satisfied young savage; who of course wore spurs as do all Mexican officers, whether of land or sea or air. A sword was tucked up high on his left hip, and from the way he fingered the handle occasionally, it could be seen that it had a part to play in the tragedy which followed. It had. He did a great deal of saluting and signalling with it.

It was now ten o'clock, and the hour of doom approached. Who was to descend into the dark lower regions in order to lead forth the victims? Who so suitable as Mazcorro, the vampire, the ghoul that works in the dark? And Mazcorro it was. Cruz nodded to him, and there was an answering gleam of white eyes under the shadow of the broad-brimmed *sombrero*. Mazcorro shambled awkwardly towards the prison, and disappeared inside. Down the dark, narrow steps he went in order to bring Father Pro Juárez forth. But he did not enter the condemned cell himself; he stopped at the threshold and called out in his thick voice the name of his victim, at the same time sending a gendarme into the dark and silent room.

By a refinement of cruelty, the prisoners had never been told that they were to die; none of them ever knew it until he had come to the surface of the ground and seen the garden of death, and the *paredón* or wall at the end of it, and the horrible smile on the face of Cruz—and the rifles of the firing party. But by some instinct Father Pro knew his fate as soon as the gendarme had entered the cell and motioned him to follow. It may have been something in the man's face, for in the event this gendarme proved to be not unsympathetic.

Turning to his fellow-prisoners, Father Pro said: "*Adiós, hermano mío! Adiós, hijos míos!*" (Adieu, my brother! Adieu, my sons!")

He then turned to the gendarme, and the latter huskily asked his pardon, "Not only do I pardon you," said the priest, "but I am extremely grateful to you," and, Latin fashion, he embraced this messenger of death. Why the gendarme asked pardon is not clearly known, but maybe the priest knew. Perhaps he had taken part in the arrest.

The priest then left the cell in order to accompany Mazcorro up the stone steps of the cellar into the outer air.

Thus they emerged into the flower garden, which had been laid out originally by General Don Fernando González, and though the flowers had faded, the touches of colour among the last few autumnal leaves was some compensation. In the distance loomed the great circle of mountains which Cortés had crossed, pre-eminent among them being Popocatepetl with its volcano and Iztaccihuatl with its cap of snow.

There is no more wonderful sight in the world than the environs of Mexico City early on an autumn morning, when the sun shines brightly and there is an exhilaration in the sharp, pure, rarefied atmosphere of the stupendous table-land.

But there is death as well. The bright colour of the leaves comes from decay, not from growth. Popocatepetl is a sleeping demon which has already buried one civilization beneath its boiling lava, and may, at any moment, bury another.

Mazcorro and Miguel emerged, as ill-assorted a pair as ever walked together on this earth, one looking like a bloated Aztec priest, the other like a young Spanish captive destined for the sacrificial altar. In one of the ancient Aztec pictures that are still preserved (and which, by the way, I have seen and copied) there is represented a scene that recalls this last fatal journey of Mazcorro and his victim. There is a group of three figures, all of them remarkably well drawn. One is an Aztec warrior. In his right hand he holds his shield and *maquauitl* or club, and, in the other, he grasps firmly the long hair of a youthful captive whom he is handing over to a priest for torture and sacrifice. The priest wears a loin-cloth and a red cap, and his body is painted black to indicate his terrible profession; and there is something diabolical in the ardour with which he grasps the shrinking hand of his prey, whose body has been smeared with white infusorial earth (*Tizatl*) to indicate that he is doomed to perish under the sacrificial knife.

Bereft of Christianity, the followers of Calles are going back to the Aztecs. But even if they do go back to human sacrifices, it is doubtful if the New York newspapers will pay any attention. They are too much occupied writing about Chinese politics though they do not propose to *do* anything for the good of China; writing about Europe, though they refuse to shoulder any of the burdens of Europe; writing at interminable length about great domestic discoveries such as the discovery that Mrs. Duke McBeaver of Sioux City has the exact physical measurements of the Venus de Milo. The excuse of the *Chicago Tribune* for its silence today will be an equally valid excuse for its silence to-morrow: "Mexico is a long way off, and the people of the United States are not interested anyhow."

CHAPTER VI

THE MURDER OF FATHER PRO JUÁREZ

WHAT Father Pro Juárez saw, on entering the garden, dissipated any hopes that may have remained in his mind. Everything in that place of death confirmed his worst suspicions—the great throng of belted "Generals" all with their eyes fixed on him intently and in deepest silence; the ominously deserted end of the garden with the *paredón*; the bullet-chipped targets that bore a horrible resemblance to the human figure; the white wall above, pitted with bullet holes; the mahogany-faced journalists in loose civilian clothes, looking at him with glittering eyes over their notebooks; the photographers regarding him with quick, professional glances and fussily arranging their tripods and their black curtains so as to get a "snap-shot" of him as he entered the garden with the heavy figure of Mazcorro slouching at his side; the soldiers lining two sides of the garden, and, behind them, near a gate which led into the street, the Red Cross motor ambulance which was to bring the four corpses to the hospital; finally, the firing party.

As soon as Mazcorro appeared, the Major drew his sword, and raised it to a salute—a Mexican salute, for he still stood in a lounging attitude, one leg in advance of the other, his hands joined in front of him and the raised sword leaning on his right shoulder. Looking more like an Aztec priest than ever, Mazcorro moved forward with his young victim, and then, seeing from the frenzied motions of the official photographer that he, Mazcorro, was about to be "snapped," he stopped short, and at the same moment his villainous-looking second-in-command, the Man in the Burberry, slouched clumsily forward so as to be also in the picture, and stood at the other side of the condemned man, but not so close to him as Mazcorro was. A striking contrast to the unwholesome, yellow-faced figures on each side of him, Father Pro also faced the photographer, deadly pale, with serious, refined, undaunted face, his slim body perfectly erect, his small, white hands clasped tightly in front of him. He was holding his rosary beads.

The official photographer having emerged, smiling, from underneath the black screen of his camera, Mazcorro rolled the bloodshot whites of his eyes in the direction of the Major, who instantly straightened himself up and, reading from an official-looking document in his hand—it was the sentence of death—called out "Miguel Augustín Pro Juárez," at the same time motioning the priest, who had bowed his head in sign that it was he, to come forward. The condemned man took a few steps forward, and then, after having read something in a mumbling tone from the paper, the officer conducted him to the other end of the garden, he himself very stiff and self-conscious, his naked sword stuck upwards, in a sort of salute unknown to any civilized army, and touching his shoulder; the priest walking, perfectly self-possessed, still with head slightly bowed, and with his hands clasped in front of him. I should have said that neither he nor any of the other three were handcuffed. All eyes followed the pair with intense interest, and there was deep silence.

Finally they reached the *paredón* and the three wooden targets, and stood on the blood-stained strip of ground out of which the grim targets rose. The officer pointed with his sword to a spot between two of the wooden targets and close to the *paredón*, but instead of taking up the position indicated, the priest, whose back was still turned to the spectators, was seen to say something to the officer, who nodded. What possible request could the condemned man be making at such a time? The interest at the other end of the garden became extreme.

But it was soon clear what Father Pro had asked, for he knelt down on the blood-stained ground at the foot of the central target but not facing it, taking at the same time from his pocket a plain brass crucifix which he pressed to his lips. I was afterwards told that this crucifix had been given to him when he took his vows. A slight rustle among the spectators indicated that their curiosity had been gratified; they saw that the priest had asked permission to say a last prayer. The Major afterwards reported that, in accordance with the usual practice, he had asked the priest if he had any last request to make, and that Father Pro had replied "*Que me permitan rezar*" (that I may be permitted to pray) a request which the officer had granted. The Major also asked the condemned man if he desired that his eyes should be blindfolded, but was answered in the negative.

The young priest knelt bolt upright, his eyes closed, his arms folded on his breast: even in that place of squalor and death, he was a picture of saintly dignity and recollection. Seeing that several photographers were levelling their cameras at short range, the Major straightened himself somewhat, but without throwing back his head, and brought his legs together for the first time since we made his acquaintance.

Father Pro remained only two minutes on his knees. Then he rose, his countenance aglow as if from some mighty inspiration, faced the greedy-eyed throng of Generals, photographers, reporters, gendarmes, detectives and spectators, and, suddenly raising his right hand with the masterful gesture of a prophet, he deliberately made the sign of the cross over them.

"*Dios tenga compasión de vosotros!*" he said, "*Que Dios los bendiga! Señor, Tú sabes que soy inocente. Perdono de todo corazón a mis enemigos.*" (God have mercy on you! May God bless you. Lord! thou knowest that I am innocent. With all my heart, I pardon my enemies.)

"May God have mercy on your soul!" is the petition which an English judge puts up for a criminal whom he condemns to death, but in this case it was the condemned man who begged God to have mercy on his judges.

And it was no pretence, no play-acting: the moment was too serious for that. Judge and prisoner had changed places; the superiority of the victim was as evident as the inferiority of the executioner; the glory of the sacrifice made Miguel Pro Juárez a Saint whose intercession was to be solicited, not a felon for whom the Litany of the Dying was to be chanted, made Cruz an object to be pitied and prayed for, not an object to be hated and punished.

The Major now moved away a dozen yards or so to the left so as to be well out of the line of fire: he had lowered his sword from the salute, and held it projecting in front of him, parallel to the ground: his eyes meantime sought the gendarmes. But the gendarmes have much experience of executions, and everything went well.

The victim was now left alone in the spot which everyone had so far shunned with such superstitious care, but there was no sense of loneliness and abandonment in the last look he gave at the world: on the contrary a strange exultation shone in his face as if he already felt himself shaded by the mighty wings of his patron, San Miguel, the Archangel of Death, as if he saw in the sky towards which his eyes were raised, the figure of Christ the King, crowned, throned, regal, triumphant, omnipotent, as the morning sun shows him when it streams through the richly jewelled glass of the great eastern window in St. Etheldreda's ancient chapel in Holborn, but infinitely more beautiful, powerful, and tremendous.

"*Preparen!*" yelled the Major, raising his outstretched sword to the level of his breast, and, on seeing the gendarmes take aim, the priest opened his arms in the form of a cross: each hand touched one of the wooden targets as closely as if it was nailed to it. At the same time he cried out in a loud voice "*Viva Cristo Rey!*" (Hail! Christ, the King!)

Hardly had he uttered the last syllable, than the Major yelled "*Apunten!*": at the same time bringing his sword down with a sweep as far as the level of his knees. There was a loud, simultaneous report from five rifles, and five bullets went through the priest's breast. In the eighth of a second the victim had fallen, but in half that slight interval of time the official photographer had "snapped" the dead body while it was still upright. There was a look of agony on the face, the eyes were closed, the knees were giving way, and the spine had come in contact with the wall behind so that the body was slightly out of the perpendicular, but the arms were still extended in the form of a cross and were still pressed against the wooden targets as closely as if they had been nailed to them.

In the eighth of a second the dead body had tumbled pitiably on the ground at the foot of the grim wooden target which I have compared to the bloodthirsty Aztec idol Huitzilopochtli, where it lay, motionless, on its back, as limp as a wet cloth, the knees bent, the head thrown far back, but the arms still extended in the form of a cross. Father Pro Juárez never spoke after that fatal volley.

According to custom, the sergeant in charge of the firing party approached to give him the *tiro de gracia* or *coup de grâce*. Bending down, he approached the muzzle of his rifle to within six inches of the dead man's right temple—then, bang! he had made in the temple, between the ear and the eye, a red, gaping hole large enough to put one's fist into, and the black gunpowder had, in addition, tattooed the whole right temple and cheek and especially the area immediately around the wound, with black particles of powder.

At this moment, while General Roberto Cruz was offering a cigarette to López the Killer, while the photographers were changing their plates, and while Mazcorro was selecting another victim, a feminine voice was heard at the gate leading into the garden. It was the voice of Señorita Ana María Pro, the sister of Father Miguel, who desired to see her brothers. The poor girl had called daily at the Prefecture of Police for this purpose, but had always been refused, and she was refused even now.

CHAPTER VII

THE MURDER OF VILCHIS, HUMBERTO AND TIRADO

THE second victim was the engineer, Luis Segura Vilchis; and Mazcorro never looked worse than he did when he halted on this occasion to get his photograph taken by the official photographer, for the youth at his side was remarkably good-looking and bore himself extremely well, while Mazcorro was more bestial than ever; his blood-lust had been aroused by the murder he had just witnessed, and his appearance was not improved by the maniacal glitter in his bloodshot eye, or by the froth on his thick red under-lip and on the grey stubble that stood out like silvery thorns on the yellow chin below.

Yet a large section of people in America is of opinion that Mazcorro represents Young Mexico in all its purity and vigour, while Vilchis stands for an aged and reactionary abomination. Mazcorro really represents a group of middle-aged and selfish men, debauched, diseased, ignorant and cruel, putrid in mind and in body. Their leader, Calles, has to consult an American specialist periodically about an incurable disease from which he suffers. Segura stands, on the contrary, for the cohorts of eternal youth, for spotless purity, for Christian charity, for ideals high and white as the snows of Iztaccihuatl. But it is not the first time in the history of Christianity that this mistake has been made.

As for Vilchis

He nothing little did, nor mean,

Upon that memorable scene.

Before the Vampire came to fetch him, he amazed the guards by saying: "*Estoy seguro que dentro de unos instantes estaré en el Cielo.*" (I am sure that within a few seconds I shall be in Heaven.) It was a tremendous prophecy, but who shall deny that he had the right to make it, who knows what revelation he may have had?

There was an extraordinary serenity in his face and in his movements; and he glanced gently but fearlessly and even pityingly at the photographers occupied with their cameras, the reporters writing in their note-books, the soldiers busy with their rifles, the officers handling their swords. Even at Cruz he glanced with gentleness, forgiveness and compassion, Cruz with his left hand still grasping the powder-puff in his trousers pocket and his right hand still grasping the butt-end of a revolver in the breast pocket of his tunic.

In the light of that pitying look, the Christian spectator suddenly realized that swords, rifles, and revolvers were the playthings of children, and dangerous playthings, that Segura Vilchis alone had done the work of a man and was now going to receive his reward. The chances are ninety-nine in a hundred that within a few years Cruz will be shot in the back by some of his own comrades and be left lying dead in some hovel like Venustiano Carranza, with burnished flies settling fearlessly on his dilated and glassy pupils, and with his trousers pockets turned inside out. Four months later Mazcorro, so powerful on this occasion, was ruined, dismissed, and in deep disgrace.

After that look of pity and forgiveness, the Christians among the spectators felt no longer eager to see Cruz and Calles punished in some dramatic manner: one felt inclined to pray that, being converted, they might live. For their agents, the Major and the gendarmes, one only felt profoundly sorry.

On hearing his name called out, Segura walked with a firm tread to the place where the Major stood with the death warrant in his hand. He then walked unfalteringly to the end of the garden, more like a young athlete who goes to receive his prize or a young king who goes to mount his throne than a condemned man who goes to his death; and after glancing reverently at the dead body of the priest, he took up his position to the right of that ghastly sight, and then turned round, with sweet and gentle gravity and with perfect self-possession, to face the firing-party. His hands were behind him, his chest was thrown out, his head well back; not by the twinkle of an eyelid or the twitch of a muscle or the slightest change of colour did he show that he was afraid; incredible as the fact seemed, it was obvious that he was not afraid.

Even the Major was impressed. He offered a bandage for the eyes and asked if there was any last wish: Vilchis politely refused the bandage and said that he had no last wish to express, but was thankful for the suggestion.

Addressing the firing-party, he said in a quiet, conversational tone: "*Estoy dispuesto, señores*" (I am ready, gentlemen). Then he looked upwards at the bright blue sky, but a second later, he reeled, his left knee bent, his left arm shot out, his eyes closed, and a look of agony passed across his face. Again, the official photographer succeeded in "snapping" the victim after he had received five bullets in his breast, but before the stricken corpse had reached the ground.

Vilchis tumbled helplessly on his right side, parallel to the wall, his knees bent, his right cheek touching the ground and bruised by the fall; and he lay there limp, silent, motionless. He was undoubtedly dead, but the sergeant went through the usual formality of blowing out his brains.

A few moments afterwards his mother, la Señora de Segura, arrived at the Prefecture of Police with some food for her son. She had been kept in ignorance of the fact that he was to be shot that morning.

The third victim was young Humberto Pro, the brother of the priest. He wore a light-coloured sack coat ("*Americana*" the Mexicans call it), with trousers to match, and, instead of a waistcoat, a fine, white, woollen "pull-over." Mazcorro accompanied him also, and the contrast between him and his victim was as great as it had been on the last occasion, for Humberto was superbly cool and self-possessed. While passing in front of the spectators, he took from the right-hand pocket of his coat a little leather purse, and from it he drew a religious medal. While gazing at this medal, he stumbled against something on the ground; and, on looking down, saw that it was the body of his brother. But he did not even change colour.

"Where shall I stand?" he asked the Major in a gentle tone, whereupon that officer pointed to a spot in front of Vilchis, and there he stood, perfectly upright, head thrown back, legs close together, like a soldier at attention who awaits the coming of a king. The back part of his ankles touched the bent knees of the corpse which lay between him and the wall, and the soles of his boots sunk into the ground, which had been softened by the blood that had poured from Yilchis, but of these trifles he was apparently unaware. He first joined his hands in front of his body, holding the medal in them, then he drew his coat further open as if to let the bullets pass more freely. He politely declined the offer to blindfold him, and, after glancing with a gentle smile at the gendarmes, he turned his eyes heavenwards.

When the bullets struck him, a violent shudder shook his whole frame, his right knee bent, his right arm shot out, and a ghastly look of suffering contorted his handsome face, though probably, by the time the spectators saw that frightful look, Humberto was beyond the reach of suffering. A fraction of a second later he had tumbled full length on his back, legs apart, arms outstretched, and lay there without moan or movement. But, as before, the sergeant approached and blew his brains out.

The last victim was the young Mexican workman Juan Tirado Arias, a tall, lanky youth, twenty years old, with the beardless face of a boy, but with a luxuriant growth of hair on his head. This hair was jet-black and, taken in conjunction with Tirado's coffee-coloured face, brown eyes, and other Indian characteristics, it indicated the almost entire absence of Spanish blood. Tirado had wrapt closely around him a large *manta* or blanket of coarse cotton such as the Indians wear, and was suffering so much from a pulmonary congestion which he had contracted in the underground dungeon, that he was hardly able to walk. He trembled with fear, and was plainly horrified at the sight which met his eyes at the other end of the garden; little wonder that his bearing was far less firm and resolute than that of his three predecessors.

"Where shall I stand?" he asked, and the Major pointed to the fatal *paredón* at the same time asking Tirado the usual question, if he had any last wish to express.

"*Quiero ver a mi madre*," (I wish to see my mother), replied the poor boy, looking up; and he repeated the request a second time; but the Major went away without taking any notice of this prayer, while Tirado, a pathetic figure in his long *manta*, leant, with bent back and knees and with bowed head, against the wooden target at whose base Father Pro was lying. When shot, he tumbled helplessly to the ground like the others, his body from the waist upwards falling on the other side of the ghastly wooden figure which looked more like Huitzilopochtli than ever, now that it had a corpse on each side of it and was splashed with warm blood. Again the sergeant approached and shot the dead man in the head, but, even after this, a medical officer noticed signs of life whereupon the Major ordered another *tiro de gracia* to be fired. This time the sergeant almost touched the head with the muzzle of his Mauser, so that the skull was almost blown to pieces, and the idol of Huitzilopochtli was bespattered with human brains. Huitzilopochtli must have thought that the good old days of Montezuma had come back.

Then the Police ambulance moved forward, and, amid much shouting and confusion, the bodies were thrown into it one by one, with as little reverence as the dead bodies thrown down from the Great Teocalli in Aztec times were dragged to the Tzompatli or ossuary where a horrified soldier of Cortés once counted 136,000 human heads. But now was to be observed the tremendous change that Christianity has made, for it is possible to see through from the street to the place of execution, and the crowd outside showed itself so sympathetic to the martyrs that Cruz feared it would break through and carry the bodies away. He accordingly ordered a strong force of gendarmes to guard the bodies; and to accompany them to the Juárez Hospital, where, in accordance with custom, a post-mortem examination is always made. As the heavily guarded ambulance appeared in the streets the word "martyr" was heard, men raised their hats, and, finally, all the people knelt. Much has been written about the conquest, certainly one of the most dazzling exploits in the history of the world, but, though no popular account of it has ever been published, Spain's complete conversion of this Pagan people to Christianity is a far greater achievement.

At the hospital, when the examination was finished, a white-haired man of seventy-six appeared and asked to see the bodies of his sons. It was Don Miguel Pro, the father of the two martyrs. He was shown to the mortuary by the white aproned attendant, and there, stretched on slabs, were the bodies of his two boys. He went first to the corpse of the priest, and reverently kissed the cold forehead. Then he approached the body of Humberto, and, as he bent over it, he heard a sudden outburst of sobbing behind him. It was his daughter Ana María who had noiselessly entered the mortuary, and had been overcome by the sight of the mutilated bodies. But her father checked her with the words "*Nada de llorar, hija.*" (Daughter, there is nothing to weep for.) Soon after Señora Josefina de Segura arrived.

Meanwhile a very different scene was being enacted in the Garden of Death. General Cruz, López the Killer, Mazcorro, Gómez Velasco, Cornejo, and the other great war lords, (*altos jefes militates*, as the sycophantic newspapers called them) descended from the stoop on which they had been standing and mingled affably with the common herd. They even stood for their photographs, and one official photograph shows us the cultured Roberto, genial, expansive, and with a cigarette in his hand.

In the evening some of General Obregón's friends celebrated the event by giving a banquet in honour of that hero.

Father Pro's other brother, Robert was a witness of the execution from a window of the prison. He expected a similar fate for himself and had already prepared by reciting the Act of Contrition, when the Argentine Ambassador succeeded in having further executions stopped. This intervention is, by the way, of hopeful augury for if the other Latin Republics of the New World take up the question of Mexico, that question may be settled much more effectually than the Government of Washington could ever settle it; and in such intervention it is surely the great States known as the ABC (Argentine, Brazil and Chili), which should take the lead. If they do nothing, they will in a few decades find the United States south of the Panama Canal helping the anti-clerical malcontents of Colombia and Venezuela as they helped Juárez, Carranza, Obregón and Calles.

The official photographs taken on this occasion have had a curious history. President Calles, Roberto Cruz, Mazcorro, and López the Killer were delighted with them; and insisted on their being sent by the Press Bureau to a great number of foreign newspapers with captions indicating that "this is how rebels are dealt with in Mexico," and as "proof conclusive" of the Church's malice. The *P. and A. Photos*, Chicago, released the pictures with the following caption:

> "Five men were taken after a bomb had been hurled at Obregón's car as he rode to Mexico City to a bull fight, and all confessed complicity to a plot on his life. For this reason, no trial was necessary and they were sentenced to die before the firing squad. One of them later died from wounds received in a battle with the police. Among the four left was a priest who prayed before the squad and just before his death, blessed his executioners, asking God to forgive them."

This information came presumably from the Mexican Press Bureau, directly or indirectly, and it is incorrect, for instead of confessing that they were guilty, the condemned men asserted their innocence. But it was reproduced in many American and

European papers. When the truth came out later, the European papers published courteous corrections, but not one of the American papers did so though the true story, which I have given, is confirmed by many authorities, Catholic and non-Catholic. Among the non-Catholic authorities is Mr. Carleton Beals, an American radical and Protestant, resident in Mexico City, who is generally favourable to the Calles Government.

As I have already pointed out on several occasions, Mr. Beals writes for the *New Republic*, a New York weekly of Radical views and a friend of Calles; and on the 21st of December, 1927, he declared in that periodical that Father Miguel Pro Juárez and his three companions had been put to death with the direct approval of Calles; that "every constitutional and humane guarantee was violated" in their case; that they had been given no trial; that no evidence other than mere suspicion was ever advanced against them; that the Press of Mexico City openly professed to believe that the victims were innocent; and that a crowd of twenty thousand people attended the funeral of the martyrs, kneeling in a spirit of reverence.

The *Commonweal* of New York draws attention to the fact that, oddly enough, these gruesome photographs which the Mexican Government itself obtained and sent abroad have become seditious in Mexico itself. On January 24th Roberto Cruz made a raid on the Josefina Convent in Mexico City and arrested twenty nuns. Two days later a similar attack was made upon the Colegio Seminar, where priests and students were taken into custody. In the interim no fewer than half a dozen other raids had been directed against Catholic institutions and groups, so that the number of prisoners taken was reported by the press as being at least three hundred. And what was the charge brought against them? Substantially this: They were found guilty of circulating the illustrations to which I have just referred.

Why did Cruz make these raids? Partly no doubt to get possession of two fine buildings, that of the Josefina Convent and that of the Colegio Seminar, though the Calles law was violated in neither, for the priests and nuns did not wear religious dress. But the principal reason was a sudden discovery on the part of Calles and Cruz that those mangled bodies are mighty yet.

CHAPTER VIII

THE TRIUMPH OF THE MARTYRS

THE remains of Father Pro and his brother were carried to their father's house. During the day the people came in thousands to show reverence to them, so that several traffic constables were required to regulate the crowd. The people treated the bodies, especially that of the priest, as the relics of saints, touching them with rosaries, medals, pieces of cloth, and even begging as precious relics flowers from the wreaths that surrounded them. Parents brought their children to see the remains, and one woman was heard saying to her ten-year-old son: "Look closely, my boy, at these martyrs. I have brought you here to imprint this scene firmly on your mind, so that, when you grow up, you may learn to give your life like them in defence of the Faith of Jesus Christ, and die brave and innocent." The sight of the aged father kneeling beside the bodies of his two sons brought tears to the eyes of many, but he needed no words of consolation.

"The priest was an apostle," he said, "and my boy Humberto lived like an angel all his life. They died for God and are already happy in heaven."

A number of people watched beside the remains all night. Between four and five o'clock two Requiem Masses were celebrated, and all present received Holy Communion. At six the doors were opened, to give the great crowd assembled in the street an opportunity of filing past the remains. They were mostly poor people, who wished to have a last look at "their Father," as they affectionately called Father Pro, before going to their daily work.

On that same day the funeral took place. It was a scene such as had probably never before been witnessed in the city and it resembled rather a triumphal procession. It had been announced that at three in the afternoon the two bodies would be conveyed to the Dolores cemetery. At that hour the neighbourhood of the house and all the surrounding streets were crowded with a great concourse of people and a number of cars. As soon as the coffins appeared in the street, silence fell on all the crowd and everyone knelt. Then, as if inspired by one common thought, all rose together and the air rang with the cries "Hail! Christ the King!" "Hail! Hail! Our martyrs!" From that moment only the presence of the hearses indicated that a funeral was in progress; but even that was hardly enough, for the hearse which bore the remains of the priest was all in white, and the coffin was white. The same colour might be used in the case of all four, as they were all equally martyrs. Flowers were rained on the hearses as they passed through the streets, and at the same time the multitude prayed aloud, sang hymns, and gave exultant cries in honour of Christ the King. All traffic had to be suspended along the route of the procession, which was joined by fresh crowds at every street, until over ten thousand persons took part in it.

It had been difficult to set the funeral in motion, as the people surged around the hearses in their effort to touch the coffins, but after some time it was formed in regular order. A double line of motorcars, over five hundred of which were present, was drawn up on each side of the hearses to keep back the throng. Almost all the people carried flowers to lay on the graves, many recited the Rosary, and, as fresh numbers joined the procession, the cries: "Hail! Christ the King!" "Holy martyrs, obtain for us liberty for the Church!" were renewed.

When the outskirts of the city were reached, at the place where the attack on General Obregón took place, the coffins were taken from the hearses and carried on men's shoulders for the rest of the way. The persons who were in the motor cars also got out and continued the journey on foot. It took three hours to cover the three miles distance.

There were fully twenty thousand people present at the cemetery. Here, amid profound silence, the body of Father Pro was laid to rest in the burial place of the Jesuits, and the cry "Long live the first Jesuit martyr of Christ the King!" was raised. The body of Humberto Pro was brought to the family burial-place. The prayers and hymns were once again interrupted as the priest's coffin was lowered into the grave. Sobs were heard as the aged father of the two victims cast the first shovelful of earth on the coffin, but when the grave was filled, the old man stood up and asked the priests to intone the *Te Deum*. He united his voice to theirs, and the whole multitude joined with him in reciting that prayer of thanksgiving to God. The prayers and hymns continued till nightfall, when the cemetery gates were closed and the people returned to the city.

At the same time as the funeral of the brothers Pro was taking place, similar scenes, though on a smaller scale, were being enacted in another part of the city, while the remains of Luis Segura Vilchis were being carried to the cemetery of Tepeyac, near the Basilica of Our Lady of Guadalupe.

On the following day the burial of the fourth victim, Juan Antonio Tirado, took place in the same cemetery in which the bodies of the brothers Pro were laid. He had been a labouring man, living in extreme poverty with his parents, who were so poor that they could not convey his body from the hospital to the wretched hovel in which they lived; and, moreover, his father was blind. Some Catholics brought the body, however, to the house; and next day the corpse of this poor and unknown man was followed to the grave by a multitude as large as that which had followed the bodies of Miguel and Humberto Pro. It seemed as if the people, by their presence, wished to show their opinion of the attempt to brand him with the charge of being an assassin and a traitor to his companions, and their belief that he suffered simply because of his Faith. His fellow-workingmen carried the coffin the whole way to the graveyard, and the funeral took over two hours. The same prayers and hymns were repeated, and to the cries that were heard on the day before was added that of "Glory to the martyr of the working class." As the procession passed by the United States Embassy, all looked towards it, and probably remembered the appeals for intervention to stop the persecution which had been made to the United States Government.

When poor Tirado was being buried, a lady, knowing the sad plight of his parents now that their bread-winner was dead, collected some money from the people present at the interment, but the police seized this money on the ground that, according to the Calles Law, it belonged to the Government, and only restored it because of the hostile attitude of the crowd.

This incident was characteristic of the usual conduct of the police and their commander, Cruz. It would be difficult, indeed, to find anywhere in recent history (excepting in that of Red Russia) a more perfect example of savage tyranny, complete illegality, and utter contempt for public opinion than we find in this case of Father Pro and his companions.

Roberto, the brother of Father Miguel Pro Juárez, whose life, as we have seen, was saved only by the intercession of the Argentine Ambassador, was ordered to leave Mexico and told that if he returned, he would be shot.

He asked:

"Could you tell me the reason for my exile, in order that I may be able to state it when I am asked?"

The only reply that he received was:

"The orders of General Calles are not to be discussed."

At present Roberto Pro is in Havana. All his property, as well as that of his sister and his father, has been confiscated. Their friends testify to the Christian courage and even joy with which they bear the cross, which they honour as the cross of Christ.

Already there are reports from Mexico of miraculous cures wrought through the intercession of Father Miguel Pro Juárez, among them a case of restored sight.

CHAPTER IX

NON-CATHOLIC EVIDENCE

ONE reason for the silence of the non-Catholic Press on the subject of Mexico, is the appalling nature of the Mexican news. Not that the Press eschews the "dramatic," the "thrilling," the "terrible," and the "astounding"—a glance at the newspaper posters in New York, London, or Paris will show that this is not the case—but the facts of the Mexican persecution are so terrible that they seem exaggerated, and in some cases incredible.

One would have thought that the Great War and the deeds of the Russian Bolsheviks would have made editors see that the twentieth century A.D. is as capable of evil as the first century A.D., but apparently it is not so.

It might therefore be well, before I go further, to show by extracts from the testimony of impartial non-Catholic authorities on Mexico the condition to which that country has been reduced, a condition in which such outrages as the murder of Father Pro and his companions are events no longer extraordinary, but ordinary and inevitable.

My first witness will be Dr. William B. Davis, about whom I have already spoken in chapter I, part III. I may add here to what I said there, that when in Guadalajara in May, 1927, I met some of the people whom Dr. Davis mentions, and formed the impression that this unusual American minimized rather than exaggerated. It will be noticed that he was unable to get any information at all on the religious question.

In one of these letters Dr. Davis tells of a certain Colonel Fierros who "on one occasion, after the surrender of thirty enemy soldiers, mostly boys, personally killed all of them thus: having had a basket filled with loaded pistols, he made the prisoners come up in front of him and kneel; then he put the muzzle of his pistol to the forehead of one after another and shot them in the order as their names were called."

Mr. Thornton, the American manager of the Guadalajara Packing House, made a statement which Dr. Davis gives, after testifying that Mr. Thornton was "an American citizen whom I personally know to be thoroughly reliable." The statement is to the effect that while two of Mr. Thornton's Mexican labourers were going home on one occasion to their dinner, "the Carranzista soldiers fired on them, killing one outright and wounding the other so that he fell to the ground. After waiting some time, a number of employees ventured out in a body to where the victims were. Seeing them, the officer and some soldiers also came to the spot. The labourers explained to the soldiers that the two men in question had long been regular employees of the packing house and had never been known to take part in political affairs, and begged that they might remove the wounded man to the packing house where they could call the physician to dress his wounds. The officer gave them no answer, but, turning to his soldiers, said: 'Finish him with a *tiro de gracia*.' Whereupon one of the soldiers placed the muzzle of his Mauser close against the forehead of the wounded labourer and blew his brains out."

In another place he publishes a letter which tells how a General who was thought to be General Amaro, the present Secretary for War, tried to abduct an American girl, the daughter of Daniel B. Nichols, the writer of the letter, who had a house at Hostotipaquillo. A number of Generals, among them Amaro, had visited this private house and after the fashion of Mexican Generals, ordered dinner as if they were in a restaurant. While devouring the meal, one of these war-lords seems to have caught a glimpse of Nichol's daughter, a beautiful girl of twenty years of age, and, after leaving the house, he sent eight soldiers to abduct her. They shut her up in a room while they were searching the house for gold, but she escaped and took refuge in a neighbouring hut. All the telegraph wires were cut so that Mr. Nichols could not for some time communicate with the American Consul, but he managed to send a letter, which Dr. Davis gives, and thus to save his daughter's honour. Amaro, I might remark, is the man who has so far failed to crush the Jalisco insurrection.

An American miner, Joseph Mulhall, tells how a prominent merchant in Guadalajara once gave a picnic to 150 friends, among them being the best people in that city, including "some 25 or 30 very pretty señoritas." This was a very dangerous thing to do, for during the afternoon, while the guests were dancing, a band of Carranzista soldiers dropped in. These soldiers were, I need hardly explain, followers of Carranza, the notable "patriot" whom President Wilson supported through thick and thin until he became President.

On this occasion, the soldiers robbed these people of their money and jewellery and then held them all for ransom, which they fixed at 10,000 *pesos*, "under threat of making '*soldaderas*' of the young ladies," *i.e.*, of making them their mistresses and slaves.

While the ransom money was being fetched, "one of the five young women whom the soldiers had recently abducted from the surrounding ranches stepped up to the chief of the band and said: 'Señor Jefe, why do you not let us ugly, dark-looking girls go back to our homes and take, in our stead, some of these pretty, white-skinned señoritas?'"

Another case given by Mr. Davis is entitled by him "The case of a young lover," and runs as follows:

An American citizen, Mr. S. S. Gates, whom I have known as a man of truth and veracity, has reported this incident: "On the night of February 6th, between nine and ten o'clock, I saw from my window and heard the following: A young Mexican gentleman aged about 18 years was standing on the pavement of the Jardin Botanico St. (Guadalajara) engaged in talking with his sweetheart through a grated window of her house,—a nightly performance which I had observed had been going on for some time before, when four soldiers, who were standing on the other side of the street, called to him. The young man went over to them at once. They asked him the time of the night. He answered that he did not have a watch. At this juncture a Captain came up and asked what was going on. I could not hear what the soldiers answered, but did hear distinctly the Captain say: 'Take him in and shoot him!'

"The young lover fell on his knees and begged for his life, saying, among other things, 'I am only a clerk in a store, and I have never had anything to do with politics, I come here every night from nine to ten to see my sweetheart, who lives there' (pointing to the house) 'which I had been doing long before you people came to Guadalajara,' etc.

"'The Captain grasped him by the collar of his coat; the soldiers prodded him with their bayonets, and he was thus literally forced and dragged into the nearby *cuartel* (barracks), and in a few moments I heard the discharge of a volley of carbines and felt sure that the young lover had been executed. He has never been seen here since. The next day I went to where this street scene was enacted the night before and could trace the route along which the young fellow had been dragged, all the way to the entrance to the *cuartel* by blood-stains left along the way."

The Consul adds: "I learned from investigations afterwards made that what the young fellow had told the captain was true. . . . I afterwards learned that the assassination of the young lover mentioned above was brought about because his sweetheart had persistently scorned the attentions paid her by the officer in question, and that the officer in this manner avenged his wounded pride on both the lovers.

"Was anything ever done in it? Oh, no; nothing at all. Neither of the families of the lovers would have dared to make a complaint, nor would anyone else. Had any such attempt been made by a Mexican—it would not have mattered what his standing—such accuser would have been turned over to a firing platoon, marched to the cemetery, and shot at the brink of some one of the yawning holes in the ground that had already been prepared for bold meddlers in the affairs of these noble military emancipators of the poor Mexican people!"

Another such statement:

"On the 20th of January on Hidalgo Street, one of the principal streets of Guadalajara, while a labouring man was crossing the said street with some wood on his shoulder, he was accosted by a Carranzista soldier who accused him of being a Villista. The labourer answered that he was not—that he was a working man and was trying to make a living for his family who lived in a little house just round the corner. The soldier replied: 'You look like a Villista anyhow'; and with that remark raised his rifle carbine and shot the man to death."

In another letter, Dr. Davis tells of a soldier being killed by another soldier in front of his hotel, the hotel Fenix, where I myself stopped when I was in Guadalajara. Its position in that city is as central as, say, the position of the Waldorf-Astoria in New York, or the Ritz in London. Hardly had this man been shot than he was stripped of his cap, coat, pantaloons and boots; and the body was left lying naked in the street for twenty-four hours.

Still another statement:

"The clerk of this Consulate, Mr. Charles Carrothers, lives in a suburb of this city, in which there are as yet few houses. One day recently, about 10 a.m., the servants of the house told Mrs. Carrothers that a Carranzista officer was forcibly carrying off a young Mexican girl. Mrs. Carrothers thought that if she went out on the street where this was happening that possibly the officer would desist; so with all the servants of the premises, she went out and watched what was happening. The girl was crying and begging the officer, saying that if he had any reasons to arrest her, that (sic) he would take her through the streets and not, as he was forcing her, to (sic) go into the fields. When the officer noticed that he was being observed by Mrs. Carrothers and her servants, he rode over to where they were and asked them if they had never seen people before. Mrs. Carrothers answered yes, that they had seen many people and were specially observing then what he was doing with that poor girl. The officer immediately rode back towards the girl, who had taken advantage of the interruption to try to make her escape. The last seen of the girl, the officer was forcing her to accompany him through byways."

Dr. Davis says, in conclusion:

"I could continue to relate similar cases *ad infinitum, ad nauseam*, but I have not had the time to procure such witnesses to others, especially now while Mexicans refuse to give testimony, even secret and confidential testimony, on the subject of outrages towards Catholic priests, nuns, and religious institutions.

"In an effort to gather information on the subject of this latter, I put an American lady, a Catholic, well known to be devout to the Church, on the job of collecting data, and she returned to me yesterday with only a few meagre details, saying: 'I don't think you will make use of these notes, for I found it impossible to have the facts substantiated as you require. Actually I cannot get the people most interested to state those facts, for they all seem terrified and afraid even of the echo of their own voices.'"

I may add that I had the same experience. I found that instead of telling about atrocities which never took place, the Catholics concealed from me many outrages which actually occurred; and sometimes victims of Roberto Cruz, the blood-thirsty chief of Police in Mexico City, made me promise not to publish what they told me lest it should lead to some of their male relatives considering themselves obliged to challenge Cruz to a duel and getting killed, before the duel came off, by some of that savage's subordinates.

I have already referred to the American non-Catholic writer, Mr. Carleton Beals, who writes in the *New Republic*, a Radical paper which is friendly to Calles. In the issue of 6 July, 1927, Mr. Beals describes the devastation in Jalisco, and then says:

"For this desolation and exodus, the militarists and irresponsible bandits, not the Catholics, are to blame."

He tells us how people are shot, merely on denunciation and without trial. To quote him textually:

"Throughout the whole country, civil restraints have broken down: human life is not worth the snap of a finger; property belongs to the man with the gun. Every petty militarist has become an absolute tyrant with unrestricted power over the life and happiness of everyone else. He never pays a bill, and takes what he wants from anybody."

It would be unfair to the American Protestant clergymen in Mexico to conclude that they all approve of the persecutions. On the contrary some of them have denounced it. The Rev. Mr. Sydney Sutherland, who lives in the State of Nayarit, described in the *Liberty Magazine* of New York the murder of an aged Parish Priest by a deputy, Juan Morena, who was himself killed by the enraged congregation. A punitive expedition was sent; and as the murderers of Moreno could not be discovered, nine men, taken at random from among the villagers, were hanged. Mr. Sutherland's son photographed their dead bodies as they hung from the boughs of a tree.

Another testimony which can be described as non-Catholic is the *Excelsior* newspaper of Mexico City, an organ that is as free from religious bias as *Le Temps* or *Le Journal* of Paris. On the 13th of January, 1927, this paper published a remarkable editorial on executions which were carried out a short time before at the City of León. The article runs as follows:

"In the official accounts that have been given of the combats that have taken place with groups of rebels, there has been no reference to the 'summary trials' that have taken place, nor to the 'most summary trials,' nor to the immediate executions carried out almost always in the case of civilians who ought not, according to the law, to be punished with the same severity as military men guilty of the same offence. Respect for human life has disappeared completely in this country, and while we involve ourselves in endless disputes with the Yankees on the subject of jurisprudence, in order to justify our legislation, we, Mexicans, ourselves lack the most elementary rights of legal defence, for the rebel who is made prisoner, is not listened to at all.

"Shooting is the order of the day all through the Republic. We could quote numerous cases in proof of this statement, but we shall refer only to one, which took place at León a few days ago, and which was so scandalous, so cruel, so barbarous, so inhuman, and so unjust that it has caused the most profound resentment throughout the whole country.

"A trustworthy person who saw what he describes, writes us from León a most moving letter whose principal paragraphs we reproduce in this article, not only because we wish to show what the public think of this matter, but also because it is necessary that the Federal authorities realize what is happening, and do not, through lack of information or through blindness of passion, lose sight of the national interests and of their own interests as well."

(The *Excelsior* then quotes its correspondent as giving "some details, truly hair-raising, of the shooting of five young men, the eldest of whom was not quite twenty years of age.")

"'The victims (continued the correspondent) were the youths José Valencia Gallardo, Salvador Vargas, Nicolás

Navarro, Ezequiel Gómez, and another young man called Ríos, all of them well known in the district and of very high character. Under some influence or other, they launched into an adventure (the Catholic agitation against the Government on the score of the anti-religious laws), and whatever may have been the degree of their guilt, they never deserved to be assassinated like dogs, and to be tortured before being shot.

"'These young men were arrested on the morning of the attack (made by a band of rebels) at León; and, when first encountered, they were unarmed. A piquet of mounted gendarmes arrested them, conveyed them to the centre of the town, and shot them soon after without any kind of trial and without bringing any witnesses. While the preparations for the execution were being made, one of the youths wept bitterly, whereupon one of his companions in misfortune, Valencia Gallardo, who had exhibited great fortitude throughout, tried to console him, and concluded by proposing to his other companions that they should invoke God in a loud voice; but this proposal made the gendarmes so furious that they cut out his tongue before shooting him.

"'Having executed all the prisoners, the gendarmes exhibited their dead bodies at the door of the Municipal Palace, the sight being truly horrifying (*siendo el espectáculo verdaderaments horripilante*); then, while the bodies lay in great pools of blood, the relatives forced their way with great difficulty through the multitude of spectators, and, when they reached the place where the bodies lay, the outbursts of grief that followed were so painful that they cannot be described.'

"As to the persons responsible for those infamous assassinations, our correspondent writes us as follows: 'The Secretary for War denies that the Federal troops took any part in the shootings; and the municipal authorities, on their side, disclaim all responsibility, and say that they had nothing whatsoever to do with the executions. Public opinion has it that the principal author of the assassinations is the Inspector of Police in León, and there are many circumstances that tell against this official.

"'Our people here are now asking: Will these crimes remain unpunished like those of Colima and Acaponeta? Will they be repeated in other parts of the Republic? Has the State adopted as a definite policy the shooting of prisoners without trial, in absolute contempt of the law and of the canons of civilization? Injustice and barbarity are joined together in these assassinations. Will not such atrocities injure the reputation of the Mexican Government at home and abroad more than the disputes about oil, more than the bands of rebels, more than all the reactionaries taken together?

"'In these assassinations, injustice and barbarity join together to constitute veritable monstrosities of troglodyte bestiality.'"

This ends the quotation from the *Excelsior*, which speaks of five victims, whereas other authorities say there were eleven. Perhaps the *Excelsior*'s correspondent went away after five were shot. I might also remark that the great crowds which surrounded the bodies were not moved by idle curiosity, much less by hostility, for they showed every mark of honour to those martyrs and even knelt and prayed for their intercession. Seeing this unexpected development, the troops attempted to disperse the crowd with fisticuffs and with blows with the butt-ends of their rifles, but all in vain: for ten whole hours lasted that pious pilgrimage of the Leóneses in honour of their young fellow-citizens.

All the foregoing evidence is non-Catholic. Dr. Davis is as absolutely impartial as a man can be, while Mr. Carleton Beals is generally favourable to Calles and opposed to the Catholics.

But the Mexican Catholics keep their records also. I have seen them, and they reminded me of the *Acta Martyrum* of early Christian times, the beginning of that unbroken record of nearly two thousand years. The Mexican record is long, and I cannot give it in detail, for it includes the names of over one hundred priests and many times this number of laymen. Some of the priests were murdered for refusing to register, some for saying Mass, or administering the sacraments. One was murdered for performing the marriage ceremony. One was martyred for refusing to divulge the secrets of the confessional. One had his hands cut off, and afterwards died in the hospital. One became insane, and was shot while in that condition. One was tracked down by the priest-hunters, and identified by means of a photograph in which he was shown in his vestments giving the First Communion to a child. In many cases, these martyrs were tortured before being put to death, and after death they were frequently suspended to trees or posts. There are in existence a whole collection of horrible photographs showing them thus suspended, and I have some in my possession.

The laymen were of all ages, but mostly between twenty and twenty-five. There were boys of seventeen and old men of eighty. There were women and girls. There was even a child, who was beaten by the gendarmes to make him confess where he had received religious propaganda leaflets which he was distributing. As he proved obstinate, his mother was fetched that she might persuade him to confess, but she was a mother worthy of early Christian days: she urged him not to confess, and watched him die under the bludgeons.

One seminarist of Colima, only sixteen years of age, who was put to death on the 5th of August, 1927, bore a name strangely similar to that of the great Englishman who died for his faith under Henry VIII. He was called Thomas de la Mora.

"So you are another of those valiant and boastful rebels, though your mother's milk is still wet on your lips," cried General Rodriguez when the boy was brought before him on the charge of associating with rebels.

"If I was valiant and brave," replied Thomas, "I would have gone with my brothers to fight for God, but as I am a coward, I aid them from here."

The General then ordered the lad to be brutally beaten, and afterwards offered to let him go free if he promised not to communicate any more with "those fanatics," but the boy refused, whereupon the General ordered him to be hanged in his presence by a soldier, and his orders were obeyed.

CHAPTER X

LAS ISLAS MARÍAS

IN Latin-America the Governments seem fond of sending their most dangerous criminals to islands, most of which I have been able to see, not, however, as a *deportado* (convict). French Guiana has its notorious Devil's Island. Brazil has the lonely Fernando Noronha, and the still lonelier Trinidad in the South Atlantic. Ecuador has Chatham Island, one of the Galapagos group. Chile has Juan Fernandez. Mexico has, off its west coast, the Islas Marías (the Mary Islands), an archipelago of four islands, María Madre, María Magdalena, María Cleofás, and the islet of San Juanico. They lie at a distance of 137 kilometres from the nearest point on the mainland and María Madre, the largest of the group, has an area of 14,178 hectares, is ten miles long by four broad, and is covered with dense forests rich in valuable woods like ebony. Like the Galapagos islands further south, the Islas Marías were a resort for the buccaneers of the seventeenth and eighteenth centuries and, as in the Galapagos, those fierce visitors have left no trace behind them.

María Madre is called after the Madonna, but it might with much greater propriety be called after the Prince of Darkness, for only the worst criminals are supposed to be sent to it—and Mexico's worst is pretty bad. When it was explained to me that María Madre is a place only for *los indomables, los asesinos más feroces, los salteadores más sanguinarios* (the untameable, the more ferocious murderers, the most sanguinary highwaymen) I said, "Just the place for Calles, Cruz and Co." whereupon I was informed that those gentlemen were using it as a place of exile and punishment for the Catholics. This interested me greatly, and I resolved to make investigations; but I shall refrain from giving names or entering into personal details as the people I met on the West Coast are in Mexico still.

I did not travel as a journalist, for on my presenting myself as such at the Mexican frontier post in Nogales early in May, 1927, I was summarily ejected from the country, but finally managed to enter under the aegis of the powerful Pacific Railway, an American Company whose line runs almost as far south as Mexico City. In casual conversations I always steered clear of religious and political questions, but manifested a keen interest in the raising of winter tomatoes. In Mazatlán, the port from which convict ships sail for the Islas Marías, I was greatly helped by a paragraph which appeared in *El Correo de la Tarde* on the 29th of May, 1927. It was headed "*Comerciante Americano*," and ran as follows:

El Señor Francis McCulagh, comerciante norteamericano que desde hace tiempo se encuentra establecido en el Puerto de Guaymas, vino a esta ciudad en viaje de negocios.

El Señor McCulagh se hospeda en el hotel Belmar; dentro de breves días y después de que trate los asuntos que le trajeron, regresará al lugar de su residencia.

(American Merchant. Mr. Francis McCullagh, a North American merchant who has for some time past been established in the Port of Guaymas, has come to this city on business. Mr. McCullagh is staying at the Belmar Hotel. In a few days, and after he has settled the business which brought him here, he will return to his place of residence.)

Who gave this interesting information to the *Correo de la Tarde* I do not know; I did not. Anyhow, it helped me very much, and probably saved me from arrest and expulsion. Even in Mazatlán it was so warm at that time that the lightest clothing seemed too warm; but on María Madre the thermometer rose as high as 37° centigrade; and the climate is, as a rule, so moist and debilitating that the hardiest criminals cannot stand it for more than two or three years. Generally speaking, the tropical heat of the New World is far more tolerable than that of India, Persia, Arabia and Africa, but María Madre is as hot as the Persian Gulf. It contains at present 1,700 convicts, and as there are only 120 soldiers or *celadores* (warders), the discipline has to be strict. Even "useless conversations" among the convicts are forbidden lest in these conversations some mutiny or some method of escape might be planned.

To send political prisoners to these islands, especially without trial, is against the law; but it has been done repeatedly by General Roberto Cruz in the case of Catholic political prisoners. The brutal illegality of these proceedings caused an application to the Supreme Court of Justice to be made on the sixteenth of June, 1927, by the "Civic Association for the Defence of Liberty," an organization comprising some of the ablest lawyers and most distinguished citizens of Mexico.

This application of which I possess a copy, points out a few pertinent facts, among others the following: (1) According to Articles 14 and 16 of the Constitution the Inspector-General of Police lacks the constitutional competency to judge persons and to punish them with deportation. (2) Article 13 prohibits the existence of special tribunals of the kind constituted by the Inspector-General. (3) Article 19 says that prisoners must be placed on trial before three days. In the same way, Articles 20, 21 and 29 of this Constitution are also cited to show that in deporting prisoners to the Islas Marías, in detaining them in the Inspectorate-General, and in judging them, General Roberto Cruz is violating the law.

"Our only object," say the signatories of the memorial, "is that the persons detained have the benefit of the guarantees which our Constitution extends to all prisoners, and even to the most atrocious criminals."

About two months later, it was announced in the American Press that President Calles had ordered the release of all the

Catholic prisoners detained in the islands "owing to the fact that the Catholic rebellion had now been suppressed and that perfect tranquillity had been restored."

Some months later, Cruz again began sending Catholics to these islands, and in much greater numbers than before; so that María Madre is now full of Catholic prisoners, many of whom are women and girls; but this resumption of the illegal practice was not noticed in any of the English or American papers which had given prominence, some months earlier, to the announcement that the deportations had ceased.

Some thirty years ago Mr. George Kennan touched the great heart of "God's own country" with his story of Siberian prisons, and he followed up the success of his book on the subject by lecturing throughout America in convict dress and in chains, which, from time to time, he clanked dismally in order to emphasize his points. After him came Mr. Turner with his *Barbarous Mexico*, and his harrowing story of Porfirio Díaz's transportation of the Yaqui Indians to the *henequén* fields of Yucatán, though, as I have already pointed out, Díaz had no other object than to give those Indians something to do.

I do not say that Mr. George Kennan was wrong in trying to excite sympathy for the Siberian convicts. Some years later, when I was a newspaper correspondent in the St. Petersburg of Nicholas II, I tried to excite sympathy for them myself, but I think that, even at the risk of being regarded as out of the fashion, we journalists should plead the cause not only of anti-Christian revolutionaries who are treated with inhumanity by a Christian government, but even of Christian revolutionaries who are treated with inhumanity by an anti-Christian Government.

That we do not always follow this rule could easily be proved from the files of any radical newspaper or review in America or Europe. Take, for example, the New York *Nation*. When, in 1927, the Russian Bolsheviks stood twenty men against a wall and, without even the semblance of what civilized men call a trial, shot them dead, the *Nation* found the executioners guilty of nothing more serious than "nerves apparently frayed." "Twenty Russians accused of various counterrevolutionary movements," it says, "were executed"—and that is all there was to it. Whether they were guilty or not, does not apparently make much difference. The important point is that they were accused of being guilty.

Yet the same review is furious with Sir Austen Chamberlain, the leader of "the dogs of intolerance," as it calls him, because about the same time he permitted a policeman to box the ears of a Bolshevik clerk in the Arcos when the famous raid was carried out on that institution. "The holier-than-thou men of Britain," remarks the *Nation*, "lie and spy," and Sir Austen, when interrogated by Commander Kenworthy, has no resource except in a "weasel answer." And of course it is the solemn duty, apparently, of the *Nation* to denounce week after week, "the obscene brutalities of Mussolini's terrorism."

As nothing has been published, even in Catholic papers, about the transportation of political prisoners and suspects to the Islas Marías, I shall therefore devote several of the following chapters to that subject.

CHAPTER XI

TO PENAL SERVITUDE

To begin with the departure from Mexico City, the unhappy beings destined for transportation are first collected together in the Penitentiary or Prison of the Federal District. In the dark days of monkish rule, this prison was a Convent school and its ample *patio* resounded with the songs and the laughter of children; in these enlightened times of ours, it resounds with the clank of chains, the crack of the whip, and the shrieks of captives. Early in the morning the *presidiarios* or convicts selected for banishment are marshalled in the great central square which was formerly the *patio* of the nuns. Such a band of convicts is known in Mexico as a "*cuerda*," from the Spanish word for rope, which term was formerly applied to batches of galley slaves roped together. To change from the general to the particular, I shall now proceed to give the history of one "*cuerda*" from the moment it was marshalled in the central square of the Penitentiary till it reached the Islas Marías.

Most of the unfortunates who composed it were habitual criminals, and of them I shall say nothing more than this, that I would not like to meet any one of them in a blind alley after nightfall. Some of them were Catholic political prisoners, doctors, lawyers, professors, young students. The names of those students—Ignacio, Calixto, Antonio,—I afterwards heard called out by their mothers, and they reminded me of names I had seen on tombs in the Roman catacombs.

Judging by their appearance, none of the prisoners had had a good night's sleep and none of them had been able to wash or to tidy himself, for they were all red-eyed and dishevelled, their clothes were disarranged, and there was a stubbly growth of beard on the faces of all save three smooth-cheeked young students. These students and most of the other Catholics were, by the way, the only members of the party who could be described as of pure white descent, the others being *mestizos* (half-castes) or natives, and some of them being obviously more negro than anything else.

Calles, I may say, goes one better than his master, Lenin, who only encouraged class hatred, for he encourages colour hatred also, though, under the Spaniards, there was no such thing as a "colour line" in Mexico. Nay, he goes two, three better than Lenin, for he is trying to inculcate also religious hate and xenophobia.

Most of the convicts carried their little belongings in dirty jute bags, but some had battered leather suit-cases. Behind them stood a company of soldiers, armed and in full marching order, the majority of them full-blooded Indians. One of those soldiers seemed to be drunk, and no two of them wore the same kind of uniform; in fact they looked less like a platoon of soldiers than a gang of brigands. The only person in authority who was visible at this stage was a *mestizo* sergeant with a tooth-brush moustache, a cavalry sword, spurs, and a Sam Brown belt.

After a long wait, the Governor of the Prison appeared on the scene in company with Mazcorro, head of the Secret Police, and López the Killer, who was to command the escort as far as the Pacific, and whose presence alone was an additional punishment.

Nearly an hour passed in the examination of documents and the calling out of names. Then the prisoners were made to form twos and the soldiers lined up on each side of them. Finally the prison gates were thrown open, and the order to march was given.

Outside was collected the most depressed-looking crowd of human beings it is possible to imagine. Old women with shawls over their heads, barefooted children, aged men in rags, young painted women, nearly all in tears, and all shivering with cold, for they had passed the whole night waiting. Needless to say they were the relatives of the prisoners, the mothers, fathers, wives, sisters or children. There were also many well-dressed ladies present, among them the mothers of the three young students, the wives of the Catholic *presidarios*, and several *Damas Católicas*, ladies belonging to a splendid association whose members attend all these sad ceremonies in order to encourage the prisoners. Sometimes they even get permission to talk with the prisoners and give them religious medals; and though I have never seen any mention made of these brave and pious ladies in American or European newspapers, I regard them as worthier of notice than those strenuous and much-advertized dames of the Anglo-Saxon race who have ascended the Amazon as far as Manaos, visited the masked Tuareg in his desert, bearded the hairy Aino in his den, and performed other great feats of exploration (thanks to the invaluable assistance of Cook).

There was a wild burst of sobbing as the melancholy procession emerged. Some women tried to pass the file of soldiers but were rudely repulsed.

Other women fainted. The men tried to keep up a bold front. One man said: "*Adiós, no te desanimes, que ya nos volveremos a ver!*" (Adieu! Don't be disheartened! We shall soon see each other again!)

Another man said sadly: "*Adiós, adiós acaso por última!*" (Goodbye! Goodbye! Perhaps for ever.)

But there were also cries of a different kind. "*Santa María de Guadalupe, esperenza nuestra, salvad a nuestra Patria!*" (Holy Mary of Guadalupe, our hope, save our country!); "*Virgen de Guadalupe, Reina de México, salvadnos!*" (Virgin of Guadalupe, Queen of Mexico, save us!); and, finally, in the clear treble of a boy, the words, "*Viva Cristo Rey!*" (Hail! Christ the King!).

This last cry excited Mazcorro as though he were possessed of a devil which hated and feared with diabolical intensity the name that is above all names. He stormed and raved like a maniac at the three students, and made the soldiers drive off the melancholy black fringe of women which had formed on both sides of the column, and was moving with it towards the railway station.

But even the students blushed and hung their heads in shame when, farther on, they passed through more respectable streets, and well-dressed people stared at them in astonishment from the footpaths. There are very few people who can walk through a crowded street handcuffed to a criminal without feeling a sense of degradation, no matter how innocent they may be. The moral suffering of the first *via crucis* was assuredly greater than the physical suffering. Even for me, to whom the three students and the other Catholic "politicals" were unknown, the sight of their humiliation was unendurable, and I had literally to turn away my face. But what an ordeal for their wives, their children, their mothers!

The three mothers who were present concealed their grief, however, as only mothers can, and apparently there was naught but joy and encouragement in their cries to Ignacio, Calixto and Antonio. Along with them went *las damas católicas*, true descendants of those "women of Jerusalem" who are commemorated in the stations of the Cross, and, thanks to their presence, the shout "*Católicas!*" "*Católicas!*" travelled rapidly down the street, with the result that men raised their hats and women crossed themselves as the bedraggled procession of convicts passed.

An order had previously been sent to the Ferrocarriles Nacionales (the National Railways) to form a train for them, and a train consisting of goods waggons and cattle trucks had been formed. Into this train the prisoners were driven like cattle. All the cars were much overcrowded. Political prisoners and criminals were mixed together, and in each car there were armed soldiers. I made most of the same journey in another train, but though I passed the heat of the day in the comfortable special car of a Chief Engineer (American), I was almost stifled with the heat and the dust. The conditions in the closed and windowless waggons can more easily be imagined than described. The disgusting filth and the shameful promiscuity in the train, and afterwards on the boat, were nothing less than bestial.

Like cattle were the convicts driven into the carriages, but they were not treated as well as cattle are treated when being conveyed by railway. A supply of *tortas de pan* or lard cakes was thrown into each waggon before the train started, but the heat was so great, the general conditions so bad, and this food so unappetizing, that hardly any of it was eaten *en route*. And no wonder, for the floors of the cars were covered with excrement, and the air was thick with loathsome flies. The whole scene was a nightmare in which I saw men confined in the cages of wild beasts, and the wild beasts outside guarding them. But with the men there were wild beasts too.

But what a nightmare this journey must have been to the political prisoners! It lasted three days and they must have been unable to sleep all the time, for no beds of any kind had been provided and, owing to the overcrowding, it was impossible to lie down on the floor. Besides, the temperature became higher and higher as the train descended into the dreadful *tierra caliente*, until finally a suffocating heat like a blast from a furnace announced the vicinity of the coast. At last the train came to a halt at the dusty, sun-scorched station of Mazatlán, and the doors were opened, liberating a stench almost strong enough to knock one down, and disclosing masses of human beings piled together like negroes in the hold of a slaver, the perspiration making channels down their dusty faces. At the same instant the gay bugles sounded as if in derision, loud orders were shouted, and the prisoners hastily tumbled out and staggered along the platform, stupefied, blinking, dazed, half-asleep. Some of them yawned. Some rubbed their eyes; some stretched their arms; most of them, suffering acutely from thirst, tried to get some water. In that horrible mass vomited on the station platform, I tried to discover the young students, but succeeded, only after a long time, in discovering one of them. He had gone deadly pale, had evidently been sick, and looked so dirty and woebegone that I could hardly recognize him. He had apparently lost all the contents of his little suit-case; probably the soldiers of the escort had stolen them. But he seemed more concerned about getting a wash than about recovering his property, and in this concern I found a new reason for sympathy. The discomfort suffered by a man of personal cleanliness who is prevented from keeping himself clean is not the least of the discomforts which Calles inflicts on his victims.

My mind suddenly travelled back to the Dictator's million dollar train, and to the joy-ride which Mr. Dwight W. Morrow had in it soon after Father Pro's murder. Does the American Ambassador ever examine convict trains?

Suddenly the voice of the O.C. escort broke in on my meditations, and at the same time made all the convicts spring to attention. "*Los deportados a formar!*" (Prisoners! Fall in!) he shouted.

Once more the production of documents, the verification of names and persons. When that ceremony was over, the prisoners were watered like cattle, drinking greedily from buckets that were passed round, and spilling most of the water on their clothes. Then they were marched to the pier; and as the railway station is at a distance from the town, they had to walk over miles of blindingly white road from which, at every footfall, the fine dust rose like clouds of smoke, enveloping them, stifling them, giving them the air of men walking in a fog.

From the pier they were conveyed in a wheezy steam launch to a *barco de guerra*, with a name which I would translate as "Floating Coffin." It was lying several miles from the shore.

CHAPTER XII

"THE FLOATING COFFIN"

"THE Floating Coffin" was, once upon a time, a pilot-boat, and is now the sole survivor of a mercantile marine Fleet which, in a sudden burst of patriotism, the Mexican Government proceeded to constitute some years ago, with the object of freeing itself from dependence on foreign shipping. But a governmental system which cannot build houses on land is unlikely to build ships on sea. The utter corruption which marks the whole Calles system was too much for the "Fleet," with the result that probably no other Government in the world permits such an unsafe contrivance as the "Floating Coffin" to drift to and fro upon the face of the waters. In some ways, no doubt, the system has its advantages. On one voyage a sister-ship of the "Floating Coffin," freighted with a "*cuerda*" of real, undiluted criminals, sent into penal servitude by Roberto Cruz, sank mysteriously without leaving a trace. The "Floating Coffin" continued, however, to float; and, having become too disreputable for words, it was added to the Navy List. General Joaquín Amaro, the Secretary for War, is, by the way, the ultimate and supreme commander of this disastrous tub, for among the numerous titles appertaining to his office is that of "Secretary for the Navy."

The "Floating Coffin" makes a monthly voyage from Mazatlán to the Islas Marías with mails, provisions, prisoners and employees of the penal colony or of the radio station there.

Sometimes, but very rarely, civilians who have some mysterious business in the islands (seeking, perhaps, for treasure hidden by the buccaneers), get permission to cross by this ill-omened boat; but on such occasions the Captain of the Port of Mazatlán always requires them to sign a declaration promising "to run all the risks of the voyage without right of indemnity in case of accident (*a sufrir todos los riesgos de la travesía sin derecho a indemnización*)."

The prisoners were counted again as they descended one by one into the foul and stifling hold, after which the soldiers took up strategic positions, warning the convicts at the same time that "at the first attempt of insubordination or unruly behaviour they would be fired into *en masse*, mercilessly, indiscriminately" (*al primer intento de insubordinación o de escándalo, serán fusilados sin remedio en masa*).

López the Killer had remained behind and the party was evidently commanded by the half-caste sergeant with the tooth-brush moustache, now on sea with his spurs and his cavalry sword.

On the voyage the asthmatic engine suddenly stopped during the night when the boat was halfway across to the islands, and there was a panic among the prisoners and their guards. The agitated Captain assured them incoherently, however, that nothing had happened. "*Nada, no ha pasado nada*," he said, "*se ha descompuesto parte de la maquinaria*." (Nothing has happened. Part of the machinery has got out of order.) An explanation which sounded like "Yes, we have no bananas." No wonder the Captain was himself "*descompuesto*," for he knew better than anyone else what a death-trap the "Floating Coffin" was. Meanwhile this ship of the dead drifted helplessly, for the anchors were useless, as the ocean at this point is fathomless.

Finally, days afterwards, a cry was heard at dawn from the look-out. "*Las Islas Marías a la vista!*" ("The Islas Marías in sight"), and, rushing on deck, the soldiers saw a number of dots on the horizon. Some hours later, the steamer anchored in the little harbour of El Valleto, a town which was founded by pirates, burned, and then partially rebuilt by concessionaires of wood and salt. It consists of about a dozen wretched houses, almost smothered by the luxuriant forests which cover the island; nevertheless, it is the capital of María Madre, the residence of *el gobernador de la colonia*, the governor of the colony, General Agapito Barranco, and the centre of such "administration" as there is. The governor's house, near the primitive wooden jetty, is the largest in the island. There is an electric light plant, an ice plant, a small radio station, and, further inland, the offices and houses of the employees. All these are built on flatter ground than is to be found elsewhere save on the dreary salt-pans, and all form a single street of square, white, one-storied huts looking like the army huts of the Great War, but constructed of stone and mortar, so as to resist the tremendous cyclones which, travelling from the China coast about the middle of the year, lash into foam the waters of these Western seas. In the early autumn of 1927 one of these storms played havoc even with the strong stonework of the Mazatlán bund, tearing up the great blocks of masonry and hurling them about as if they had been corks.

The far end of the little street is composed of wooden huts for the convicts: apparently it does not matter whether the convicts are blown away or not. Very sharply does this white village of the one street stand out against the dense green mass of tropical forest in the background.

The "Floating Coffin" had not been anchored long before there was a sound of drums and bugles from the shore, about a hundred yards distant. It proceeded from a small kiosque in a *plazoleta* or little square in front of the Governor's house; the band was the military band of the garrison. There were other signs of life, for a few *celadores* (warders) appeared, all in white, on the little street; and afterwards a long line of melancholy figures with naked feet and bowed heads, traversed a clearing and disappeared under a heavy guard into the forest. They were *los deportados* (the convicts). They were all bare-headed and wore only shirts and drawers.

CHAPTER XIII

THE FATAL ISLES

FROM fear of a mutiny, having for its object the seizure of the wretched boat, great precautions are always taken whenever a fresh "*cuerda*" of convicts arrives. The *celadores* parade under arms; and there are several weighty conferences between the captain, the half-caste sergeant with the tooth-brush moustache, and the director of the colony (*el director de la colonia*, as he is called). The prisoners are never landed till the day after the boat arrives, and then only in groups of ten, small launches being employed. They are brought to the commandant of the guard, and wait outside his office while the *celadores* close in around them to prevent any communication between them and the convicts already on the island. On the other hand, the soldiers of the escort sprawl carelessly on the dry sand and even permit themselves to fall asleep, for their task is finished.

Once more endless formalities, conferences between the director of the colony, the chief of the guard, and the half-caste sergeant with the spurs.

The newly-arrived convicts are always kept for a few days in El Valleto, where they are employed in carrying stone and wood for building purposes or in agricultural work in the adjacent fields. Then, when more or less acclimatised, they are all distributed among the "encampments" scattered through the island. These "*campamentos*" are: *Las Caleras, El Rehilete, La Ladrillera*,

Los Centenos, El Reventón, El Puerto, Arroyo Hondo, and the terrible *Salinas*.

In some of them, the prisoners cut fire-wood, or timber. In others they make bricks. In others stones are collected for building purposes. In others salt is collected from salt-pans. Finally, agricultural work is carried on by other convicts. Those who carry building material have to pull carts like horses, and those who carry bricks are sometimes made to carry weights of from one hundred to one hundred and twenty kilos on their shoulders. The discipline is very strict, patrols of mounted *celadores* traverse the island frequently and "needless conversations" are prohibited. The work in the salt-pans—*las terribles salinas*—is the hardest of all. Here we see from twenty to thirty men stripped to the waist working for four hours without a break at the great pumps which force the sea-water into the salt-pans. Owing to the reflection of the sun, these convicts soon begin to suffer acutely from headache, so that they are frequently changed.

Boys who have read Robinson Crusoe may see no tragedy in a tropic isle, but, speaking from personal experience, I should say that the torrid sun is as merciless as the Siberian cold, and that the Catholics exiled to the Islas are more to be pitied than those slaughtered in the garden of the Prefecture of Police, Mexico City. If Mexican officialdom is so outrageous even in the Federal Capital under the eyes of the foreign representatives, what must it be on a remote island where there are no foreigners? On María Madre everyone and everything is pitiless, the great sombre forest, particularly rich in serpents, and the inexorable sun, equally with the jailers and the irreclaimable, habitual criminals, many of the latter suffering from incurable diseases, eight or nine of them raving lunatics, all of them having vice stamped on every feature. To send into such a hell delicate women and young men of seventeen or eighteen, none of them criminals, all of them accustomed to an atmosphere of moral purity, is to inflict on them a punishment worse than death.

If religious services by a chaplain were allowed, there would be one source of consolation; but no such service is permitted on the island. Sunday is a day of rest, but it is generally spent by the convicts in washing themselves and their clothes. The Catholic "politicals" meet, however, on that day to say the rosary, and, so far, they have not been prevented from doing so.

"But why does not somebody write about these things in the newspapers?" asked the average sympathetic person.

"These things *are* written about, my good sir or dame, but the newspapers will not publish anything. And how can one expect them to publish what happens in the remote and impenetrable forests of María Madre if they refuse to publish the news sent by their own representatives of butcheries carried out in the garden of the *Inspección General* at Mexico City, a garden overlooked by the roof of the adjoining American Consulate?"

Very often convicts show signs of failing strength. They grow thin, their eyes become sunken, their step feeble, and finally, one day, the *campamento* is told that "*Ya murió el deportado número tantos.*" (Convict number so-and-so is dead.) The body is brought to the hospital or *lazareto* where the M.O. certifies the death, then four men rapidly convey the coffin of white, unpainted pine to the cemetery or *panteón* which consists of white sand so exceedingly fine that one might imagine it to be powdered bone dust.

The first Catholic "*cuerda*" exiled to the mysterious archipelago consisted of fifteen young men who were apprehended in different parts of the Republic and all sent to the subterranean dungeons of the Prefecture of Police in Mexico City. They all belonged to good Mexican families, were members of the Catholic League of Youth, and were opposed to the Calles regime, though no definite crime could be charged against them. After keeping them for some time in the Federal Capital, Roberto Cruz incorporated them in a "*cuerda*" of one hundred and twenty criminals sentenced to the Islas Marías. With them was also sent an old man of seventy, also a Catholic.

Having arrived at the islands, they were stripped of their clothes and forced to put on shorts. They had to work for sixteen hours a day, sometimes in collecting salt on the sea-shore, sometimes in carrying on their shoulders sacks of lime for great distances. After two months of captivity they were released under the amnesty which Calles granted in the autumn of 1927, but they will probably carry to their grave with them the scars of the wounds caused on their shoulders by the friction of the coarse hempen bags, and the marks of the lash which was freely used by their guards.

On leaving Mexico I was entrusted with a number of letters written by men who had been put to death or exiled, and one of them was from a youth of twenty years who had been sentenced to deportation to the María Islands; it was written on the day before his "*cuerda*" left. It begins in the affectionate Spanish style, so difficult to translate into English, "*Muy queridos Papacitos y Hermanos*" (Very dear Parents, Brothers and Sisters), and then continues as follows:

"I write you this letter to say many things that cannot be spoken. My only anxiety is that nothing may happen to you because of me, or rather for the cause of God. Do not have any anxiety for me. What is happening to me is, I assure you, the very best that could have happened to me. I never asked God that they should not send me to the María Islands, because sometimes one asks what is not best for one. I have always asked Him that what was best for me and for my country should happen to me. As I was completely powerless and did not want to remain so when Mexico was going through these difficult times, I offered Him whatever sufferings He wished to send me to bear for Him, and no doubt He accepted, not my sufferings, but yours, Mother, who are a saint, and those of everyone else at home. Do not let them fail to offer those sufferings also, themselves, because God likes best the prayers of those who suffer, and much more the prayers of those who suffer for Him.

"If on one side He is exiled and reviled, at least let there be some place where He is blessed and recognized as King. This will be the way in which we shall help our cause in secret.

"As for us, when we go, it is not three of us who go, but four and the fourth is God; and really it is not four who go, but One alone.

"Take many kisses from your son who expects your blessing and your resignation. Let the motto of our house now be 'For God and country.'

"Many grateful messages to Señora and to the boys of my class, and to everyone who remembers me.

León.

P.S.: Suffering and difficulties are what form a man."

Even without physical punishment, life on María Madre would be hard enough for a soft and innocent lad like the *jovencito* who wrote this letter, for a convict's working hours extend from 4 a.m. to 6 p.m., but there is physical punishment as well, especially scourging, which goes on day after day. The *Relampago*, a prison founded by Governor Luis Huerta, is filled with convicts whose spirits the governor has determined to break by the imposition of endless, heavy work—principally the carrying of stones and adobe—which lasts from dawn till nightfall. There is another method of punishment called *"El Bramadero,"* which consists in tying the convict by his thumbs to a tree and scourging him till he becomes unconscious. The discovery of this form of torture is attributed to Zermeño, a former governor, who lost his position owing to his murder of several prisoners.

One would expect the Calles Government to insist that the Islas Marías are a health resort, that the prison system there is mild and humanitarian, and that the Governor is a philanthropist. But, seeing that the foreign Press will publish no attacks on this system of transportation, the newspapers which speak for the Dictator conceal none of its horrors: on the contrary, they proclaim them from the house-tops. In July last, when several "*cuerdas*" of Catholics were sent to the Isles, Calles' newspaper, *El Sol*, published a number of articles in which it gloated over the terrible hardships of prisoners in the Islas Marías, and on the way thither. None of the horrors were omitted.

There were even drawings of half-naked prisoners working in quarries and salt mines and on the torrid beach. *El Sol* exulted openly at the punishment of the only men in Mexico who dared to stand up for religious liberty. Yet this newspaper, and the party it represents and the head of that party, are highly esteemed by various bodies of "highbrows" and "advanced" thinkers in the United States.

It pointed out in huge and jubilant headlines that "the heat is suffocating and the work most exhausting. The immense white savannahs of the salt-pans reflect the rays of the sun, and cause acute agony to the convicts." Another exultant headline runs as follows: "Forced labour constitutes the worst punishment in the Islas Marías." These savage announcements were flaunted day by day in the eyes of mothers whose young sons had been sent to the islands for no other crime than that of fidelity to their faith, and many were the little stratagems adopted by their families to keep such mothers from passing the places on the street where such newspapers were sold. One spot specially avoided was a corner on the Avenida Juárez where the *Sol* and other Red newspapers were displayed on the pavement, and where one could hardly help seeing the screaming headlines which announced: "*Mas sediciosos capturados*" (More seditious persons captured), or "*La Fatidica Lista de Deportados.*" Such crude announcements would not be calculated to mitigate the anxiety of a mother whose boy was on that "fatidical list" or among those "seditious persons captured."

(How angry, by the way, are the successful conspirators who now rule Russia and Mexico with "seditious persons" who plot against themselves! Formerly these words "seditious persons" sounded sweetly in their ears. How furious is the *Sol* with "*los elementos perturbadores de la paz pública,*" the agitators who disturb the public tranquility!)

Another issue of the *Sol* describes the prisoners on parade at daybreak in the *patio* of the *Penitenciaría*, "more or less brutalized by the thoughts which chased one another through their brains as they lay tossing all night in the black abysses of insomnia."

And, to give further quotations from the same paper: "The train is not comfortable. Why should it be comfortable? It is a cage for wild beasts. And like wild beasts the stupefied convicts enter it, their minds unilluminated by any logical thought.

"Those unfortunates who form the '*cuerda*' give the impression of strange animals in human form. The eyes have become bovine through suffering, the clothes have become disarranged on the journey, the hair is tossed and tangled, the faces are covered with sweat."

Finally, we are told of the slave-ship "disembarking its cargo of human flesh" (*su cargamento de carne humana*).

How Mr. Brailsford and Mr. Massingham and Mr. Wallis and Dr. Moses J. Olgin, and all the Radical writers of London and New York would have protested if, in 1905, the *Novoe Vremya* had described as "cargoes of human flesh," Trotsky and the other Bolsheviks who were then sent to Siberia! Yet the Mexican Reds, who write thus of prisoners, won power owing to their success in playing upon the soft-hearted (and sometimes soft-headed) sentimentalists of the United States. As I have already pointed out, some of these scribes of theirs are certified murderers, "wanted" by the Spanish Police, and imported to Mexico by Calles to conduct his newspapers for him. Yet these scribes, who themselves deserve the gallows, dare to scoff thus at innocent men!

Where, oh where is Sir Arthur Conan Doyle, formerly of the Congo? Where are those doughty knights of the pen who swarmed into Russia in 1905 to see that Bolshevist bomb-throwers got fair play? Where is Sir Philip Gibbs, who once championed the cause of the Portuguese Royalist prisoners? Where is that Bayard of the Press, Mr. H. W. Nevinson?

Their excuse might be that they were not told by the traveller in men's suspenders who was until recently the correspondent of the greatest American paper in Mexico City and the principal source of the world's information with regard to events in the Mexican Republic, but that excuse would indicate, methinks, the existence of a grave defect in our whole system of procuring and distributing news.

One of Calles' newspapers is the *Sol*. Another is *El Mexican-ista*, which once printed with joy a letter which was sent from the Fatal Isles (probably to his mother) by León Ávalos, one of the Presidents of the League for the Defence of Religion, but which must have been intercepted by the authorities.

The letter in question is a cry of agony which fills *El Mexicanista* with joy. "Do all you can," wrote Señor Ávalos, "to get me taken back to Mexico even if I am kept there all my life in a Penitentiary, for if I stay here any longer, I believe that I shall soon die."

Ávalos, an elderly scholar of frail physique, had been made to work in a quarry on the island, and this work under a burning sun, had proved too much for the unfortunate gentleman, in whose physical collapse the cultured editor of *El Mexicanista* exulted with a frank shamelessness and brutality worthy of Calles himself.

CHAPTER XIV

IN PRAISE OF MEXICAN WOMEN

A MBASSADOR Sheffield once informed the state department that among the people thus sent to Penal Servitude in cattle-trucks were two nuns. These were probably the first women to be banished to the islands, but so many are sent now that one frequently sees references in the papers to " *'cuerdas' de Damas Católicas enviadas a las Islas Marías*" (gangs of Catholic ladies sent to the Islas Marías). In some cases these ladies are women of high intellectual distinction, who have studied in Spanish or Belgian convents, yet the English Suffragettes who made such a noise fifteen years ago on the subject of votes for women, regard in perfect silence the spectacle of Mexican ladies being treated like a herd of cattle. Perhaps they do not see this sight, owing to the reticence of the Press; but in any case something is wrong somewhere.

The leaders of England's women are disappointing on this subject. Some of those brilliant ladies spend much of their time and energy writing to the London newspapers on behalf of their sex, now attacking Lord Birkenhead for saying that there have been no women writers of the *status* of Shakespeare, now calling Dean Inge to task for declaring that women are more cruel than men, but betraying in these very letters a want of originality and an incapacity to strike out a line of their own. In other words, they are spoon-fed by what they themselves would call a man-controlled Press; they base all their theories on news sent by male correspondents in Mexico City, and carefully sifted by male editors in New York and London; they watch Lord Birkenhead and the Dean of St. Paul's so that they may be able to pounce on any criticisms these gentlemen may pass on women; but they make no independent investigation, they send no ladies out to Mexico to ascertain how women are treated there, though by doing so they would make good use of their new-found liberty and show all men what an important factor that liberty may be in the future history of the world. From this criticism, however, I must exempt the Women's Catholic Associations of America, which have certainly done their best to bring this Mexican horror before the public in their own country. On the occasion of Colonel Lindbergh's flight to the United States, a Catholic Women's Association sent to the White House a dignified protest, which was not, however, acknowledged.

If the Women's Associations of Great Britain sent a representative to Mexico, she would find that her sisters in Mexico have suffered much and achieved much, and, if that lady had a camera with her, she would be able to take photographs of Catholic ladies sent in *"cuerdas"* to the Islas Marías. Four of the ladies sent in the last *"cuerda"* were arrested in Mexico City, early in April, 1928, on the charge of being connected with a religious school for girls at No. 121, Tenoxtitlán Street in Mexico City; but they were never placed on their trial and their punishment is a case of arbitrary administrative order. Five ladies were arrested about the same time in León on suspicion of having aided the insurgents in Jalisco and other States, but in their case also there has been no trial.

The real offence of these ladies in the eyes of the Government is that they belong to the organization of *las Damas Catolicas*, which, as I have already pointed out, has done magnificent work throughout this persecution. Even the poor market women, laundresses and shop-girls have displayed great activity. On one occasion when a handful of schismatics, supported by the police, tried to wrest one of the churches in Mexico City from the Catholics, the poor Catholic women fought much better than the men, and when Monje, one of the two schismatic priests, emerged afterwards from the sacristy, under police protection, in order to say a sacrilegious Mass, an athletic young woman gave him such a buffet on the face that he had to return to the sacristy and give up his intention of saying Mass that day. Some time later he made his submission to the Church and is now in Rome, doing penance.

On a third occasion a young "woman of the people" perceived an irreverent soldier going towards a sanctuary lamp in order to light his cigarette whereupon she dealt him such a blow on the nose that he changed his mind and left the church.

But on the other hand there are many cases of systematic violation of the young girls of good family who acted as piquets in the boycott organised by the Catholics early in 1927. In the encyclical letter[1] to which I have already referred, the Pope made special mention of this: "Young girls, too, who were imprisoned, were criminally outraged." But the Holy Father says no more on this subject, and I shall likewise refrain from giving details, though appalling information regarding these outrages lies before me as I write.

---

[1] Encyclical *Iniquis afflictisque* of Pope Pius XI (see Appendix II).

CHAPTER XV

THE MASS BEFORE DAWN

THE only time I attended Mass in Mexico during the year 1927 was once in Mexico City; and, in order to attend it, I rose at 3 a.m., long before the dawn, for owing to the persistence of the priest-hunters, Mass has to be said at an early hour.

The place selected for the service is connected with the great name of Hernán Cortés, the Conquistador; I cannot specify it further, as Mass is said there still. As I went along the ill-lighted and ill-guarded streets of the Federal Capital, I wondered at times if I had not been imprudent, for out of the night-clubs some very unpleasant-looking personages were coming into the street, and the few policemen I encountered were still less reassuring. Moreover, in my heated fancy, the clinking of the large quantity of silver money which I carried on my person must, I fancied, have been audible for yards. Nobody trusts the Government's paper money, and the result is that when one takes money from the bank, one takes it in silver, and the bank furnishes little cotton bags wherein to carry it. I had to carry a good deal for I was a newspaper correspondent and might have, at any moment, to send off long telegrams; in fact I had placed little bags of silver not only in my pockets but all over my person. In the silent streets the clinking of this money seemed to me an unmistakable invitation to any prowling cut-throat who was armed with a *machete* (and every cut-throat in Mexico has got a knife of some kind.) I wondered if the silver would act as a protection, but, even so, I did not relish the prospect of rushing through the dark streets with a stream of *pesos* pouring out of me, and a bandit at my heels.

I managed, however, to reach my destination in safety. The precautions which surrounded this celebration were extraordinary, quite worthy of those taken, under similar circumstances, during the Penal Days in England and Ireland. The little congregation was representative, including, as it did, descendants of the Conquistadores and descendants of the Aztecs. The priest, who had come in the blue overalls of a mechanic, was evidently of pure Spanish descent; the little altar boy who served Mass was a pure-blooded Aztec; and among the congregation were Indians, white women, and half-castes. The Indians were closely wrapped in their ample *mantas* (blankets), for the aborigines have a great fear of the matutinal cold, and their huge *sombreros* lay generally on the floor beside them. One of the ladies present was the daughter of a distinguished diplomatist and had been presented to King George. Some of the men were successful administrators.

The service proceeded in the utmost silence. The altar boy even refrained from ringing the bell; the priest read the missal in an almost inaudible voice; and the congregation was so still that it seemed to hold its breath. This fearfulness I could easily understand, for the prospect of extracting ransom from priest and congregation has made the police so active that though the Catholic Legations and Consulates have the right to keep private chaplains, those chaplains have ceased to say Mass. On first coming to Mexico City I had arranged to hear Mass in the Legation of a Catholic country, but learned at the last moment that the service was discontinued on account of the annoyance caused by the Police. Thus, the persecution under Calles is worse than the persecution under Nero or the persecution under Queen Elizabeth, for Nero permitted the Christians to hold religious services in private houses, and Queen Elizabeth permitted the ambassadors of Catholic Powers to have their own chaplains and their own private chapels.

Just before the Consecration, all the watch-dogs that we had on guard, began barking with a fury and a terror that could not have been greater if they had seen demons flying from the house, and a shudder ran through the congregation, for we feared that the priest-hunters had come. But out of the deep darkness which surrounded the lonely mansion no hostile form emerged, and a few moments later, when the solemn words of Consecration had been pronounced, the barking ceased as suddenly as it began, and the first gleam of dawn came from the east. Before the Mass was over, a long beam of sunshine fell on the Masshouse and on the altar.

Part IV

MEXICO AND AMERICA

CHAPTER I

AMERICAN-MEXICAN RELATIONS

THE diplomatic position of the United States in Mexico is extremely strong, owing to a great variety of reasons, among others the following:

Europe has been so weak and impecunious since the Great War, and owes America so much money, that, in things diplomatic, she has quite effaced herself not only in Mexico but throughout all Latin America. The day of the "gunboat policy" is past; gunboats are too expensive. The British Legations in Cuba and Panama seem, for the moment, to be costly anomalies; even in Rio de Janeiro and Buenos Aires, the British Embassies do no diplomatic work; they occupy themselves either in social functions or else in "booming" British goods. Sir Malcolm Robertson, who was British Minister in Argentina in 1926, went in strenuously for the latter line, which, though useful, is, after all, Consular work and might be carried out better and more cheaply by a Commercial *attaché* with the help of a large staff and a permanent local exhibition of British manufactures. The withdrawal of all British diplomatists from Latin America would result in the saving of much money to the British taxpayer; but, of course, British pride would never consent to this; even so staunch a Little Englander as the London *Daily News* rejoiced exceedingly when, in the Spring of the year 1928, £80,000 was appropriated for the building of a new British Embassy in Rio de Janeiro. Personally, I do not see any good in wasting large sums annually on diplomats who are so afraid of Uncle Sam that, in conversing with a newspaperman of their own nationality, they are afraid to venture an opinion even on the weather.

While Europe has sunk thus low, America, on the other hand, has become so enormously strong and wealthy since the Great War that she overshadows not only Mexico but the Caribbean and the Northern Republics of South America. Every European Legation in Mexico City now keeps one eye on Washington and the other on Chapultepec, just as every foreign Legation in Cairo keeps one eye on the Egyptian Foreign Office and the other on London. When the heads of the European Missions in Mexico are questioned on the subject, they say: "The Monroe Doctrine prevents us from taking any action at all. We must follow the lead of the United States."

Most Americans are unaware of how strong is the position which their Government holds in Mexico, but the following true story may enlighten them.

A distinguished Mexican who visited Europe in 1927 in order to see if anything could be done for his native country, was able to meet the highest authorities in France and Spain; but in both these countries he was told that America's "protection" of the Calles Government precluded even the sending of remonstrances to Mexico by any European nation.

The spokesman for Spain said: "We have sent no complaints of any kind to Mexico, and have even prevented any Spanish newspaper from writing about the expulsion of the Spanish ecclesiastics, the murder of Spanish landowners, and the confiscation of Spanish property. We act in this way because we do not wish to offend the United States Government, which is evidently protecting Calles. Our *peseta* depends on the dollar; and, as we have, moreover, domestic difficulties of our own, we cannot afford to quarrel with the United States."

This spokesman might have used much stronger language, for all Spain must have been bitterly humiliated by the expulsion of the Spanish priests from Mexico, and by the indignities that accompanied their ejection, yet no Spanish journalist was permitted to publish a word about these expulsions and indignities.

The answer of the highest authority in France was similar. It was to the effect that as the *franc* depended on the dollar, as the European question was still delicate, and as France herself was confronted by a number of critical problems, it would be madness for her to quarrel on the subject of Mexico with the greatest and richest country in the world, a country which, moreover, "is apparently protecting President Calles."

Even the Roman Curia said that since Washington was supporting President Calles, it could do no more than it had already done. The British Government has been represented in Mexico by a number of particularly able Ministers, one of whom, Sir Lionel Carden, prophesied quite accurately in 1914 what President Wilson's unbalanced enthusiasm would result in; but subsequent events proved otherwise. The disreputable Calles gang, perhaps became too familiar and possibly the British Minister believed and accepted their version of what was happening; and told the Foreign Office that there was no religious persecution, that the Episcopacy had itself to blame for the difficulties in which it was involved, and it could easily extricate itself by the exercise of a little ingenuity and tact. He is, I believe, the only foreign representative who holds these extraordinary views; and he only holds them because he is far below the standard of Sir Lionel Carden.

To understand how it is that America occupies such a predominant diplomatic position in Mexico, it is only necessary to examine the recent diplomatic history of the two countries. It is a curious history, creditable neither to Mexico nor to the United States. First we have the President Wilson of 1913, with his lofty idealism which prevented him from tolerating on the same Continent any President whose hands were stained with blood, and then we have the President Wilson of 1914, embracing Carranza, whose followers were guilty of many murders. At present we have President Coolidge on the best of terms with Calles, who is bespattered with blood from head to foot—first with the blood of the Catholics whom he put to death in 1926, 1927 and 1928, and secondly with the blood of his political opponents whom he slaughtered wholesale all over Mexico in October, 1927.

Excessive idealism yesterday leads, apparently, to undisguised materialism to-morrow. Yesterday the world was to have been made safe for democracy: to-morrow it is to be made safe for High Finance.

In chapter V, part I, of this book, I have spoken of President Wilson's relations with Mexico. Here I can only express my amazement that the obvious contradiction between his words and his acts was not pointed out at the time; but probably the Great War and the unsettled condition of Europe after the War gave Europeans quite enough to think about.

What maddened President Wilson most of all was the fact that "eighty-five per cent of the Mexican people have never been allowed to have any genuine participation in their own Government."

It did not occur to him that he had no right to intervene in Mexico for the purpose of removing this defect, and that his over-flowing charity might have begun at home in an attempt to secure for the negroes of the South the advantages which were won for them in the Civil War and guaranteed by an amendment in the Federal Constitution—advantages which they do not enjoy.

The result of President Wilson's lofty altruism was Carranza who was as little concerned as Porfirio Díaz himself about the votes in ballot-boxes. The peons have, it is true, got the franchise, but it is of as little use to them as it is to the negroes in South Carolina.

This is admitted even by the Mexicans themselves. In July, 1926, the *Universal*, one of the two leading newspapers in Mexico, said: "The people do not vote because they consider it to be useless to take part in a farce . . . rehearsed beforehand. The suffrage has been converted into a public calamity. . . . Instead of

the elections being something of a school for the exercise of cit-
izenship, they have become a scene of immoralities and the theatre of all kinds of violence."

In one word, the Socialists whom Wilson placed in power
have done none of the good things that the Porfiristas certainly
accomplished, and have done all the bad things that the
Porfiristas were ever charged by their worst enemies with having done.

Addressing, in 1918, a deputation of Mexican editors, President Wilson said that he had "sent troops into Mexico . . . to
assist you to get rid of a man who was making the settlement of
your affairs for the time being impossible"—the man in question
being none other than Victoriano Huerta, the constitutionally
elected President of Mexico, whom the Mexicans did not want
to get rid of.

How he reconciled that statement with his repeated
announcements of his fixed resolution not to use physical force
and not to countenance armed intervention in the affairs of
another State, is difficult to understand.

Coming, next, to President Coolidge, we find him taking no
interest in votes for peons and great interest in the commercial
and industrial enterprises of United States citizens in Mexico.
In June, 1925, his Secretary of State issued a public warning to
Mexico, which was, said the Secretary, "on trial before the rest
of the world."

"We will insist," he continued, "that adequate protection
under the recognized rules of international law be afforded
American citizens."

The reference was, of course, to the Agrarian law under
which American citizens were deprived of 470,000 acres without compensation, and the Petroleum law which was regarded
by the State Department as retroactive and confiscatory. The oil
Barons of Tampico, as the American Oil magnates of Mexico
are called, were, naturally, in favour of intervention unless
Calles gave way, but, for reasons which I shall subsequently set
forth, Wall Street was opposed to intervention. In the following

pages I shall describe the progress and result of the duel between these two great Powers.

From November, 1925, to November, 1926, Mexico attempted to justify its policy of confiscation and repudiation; but the State Department said: "Such a policy can have but one result—the destruction on a vast scale of the vested property rights of American citizens, to which the United States will not consent."

At the end of 1926, as I have already pointed out in chapter IV, part II, the Americans in Tampico expected a landing of United States marines to take place there at any moment, but when Uncle Sam was majestically facing the foe, he was suddenly hit over the head from behind by a weird jumble of protestants, pacifists, radicals, and humanitarians. It was exactly a year before he was able to sit up and take notice, and his first acts were calculated to amaze Englishmen accustomed to an Uncle Sam who is an expert tail-twister, for those first acts were (1) to send as Ambassador to Mexico a Mr. Dwight W. Morrow of the financial house of John Pierpont Morgan, whose business it is apparently to talk gently to Calles, and give him "tips" about investments; (2) to send Mr. Will Rogers, America's champion humorist, to act as temporary Court jester to the Dictator; (3) to dispatch Colonel Lindbergh, America's best aviator, to risk his neck performing "stunts" round Chapultepec Palace for the delectation of Calles and the choice collection of Yankee Communists and "crooks" whom he has gathered around him there. It was almost as if Great Britain had sent Sir Robert M. Hodgson back to Moscow with his tail between his legs and a letter of apology in his hand, and had at the same time sent Sir Alan Cobham to perform "stunts" above the Kremlin, and Sir Harry Lauder to amuse Stalin with his kilts, his big walking stick, and his funny songs.

It was worse even than this, for the American Ambassador set out on a long joy-ride with Calles and Will Rogers in the President's million dollar train on the very day that four particularly brutal murders had been carried out by direct orders from

Calles—I refer to the murder of Father Miguel Pro, his brother, and his two companions. And in order to facilitate still more the work of Mr. Dwight W. Morrow, the Arms Embargo on the frontier was lifted in Calles' favour, and a large number of rifles as well as several bombing aeroplanes which had all been detained there, were allowed to enter the country, and were at once used against the Catholic insurgents on the mountains of Jalisco.

At the same time all the attempts of Catholic gun-runners were defeated by the watchfulness of the American frontier authorities. Of this watchfulness I can speak from personal experience for on the two occasions when I passed from United States territory into Mexico during the year 1927, I was searched for arms, and could not have brought even a single cartridge with me, had I been disposed to do so. On suspicion of having been engaged in gun-running, General Adolfo de la Huerta, an enemy of Calles, was arrested, together with several other Mexicans, by the United States authorities, and all had to stand their trial in Los Angeles. Señor Gándara was sentenced to two years in the Tucson penitentiary for having sent arms to the Catholic *insurrectos*. General Enrique Estrada was imprisoned by the Americans for even attempting to cross the frontier into Mexico.

Very different was the treatment of the gun-runners who supplied arms to Juárez, Madero, Carranza, Obregón and Calles.

Can this be the America we all knew, the America which stood up for liberty in all parts of the world; which was moved to the heart by the woes of Dreyfus; which was so indignant with the Turks on the occasion of a reported Armenian massacre that it sent warships in menacing and hostile array to the coast of Asia Minor? Can it be the same Government which took such a sympathetic interest in the Jews of Russia when, under the Imperial regime, they were threatened by pogroms?

In the contest that took place at the White House between Oil and Finance, the latter won; and its victory was not entirely due to the well-organised protests against intervention in Mexico which poured in on the President by every post before he had made up his mind what course to follow; it was due to an even greater extent to the unpopularity of oil. In the year 1927 and in the first half of the year 1928, Oil was certainly in bad odour among the "unco guid," the religious minded, and the merely respectable in the United States. An American novelist, Mr. Joseph Hergesheimer, published about the year 1926 a novel called *Tampico* in which he described, without exaggeration, the state of things some years ago in and around Tampico, the great sinful Oil town which American capitalists have built up in Mexico. The Tampico of this novel resembles in some respects the Johannesburg of thirty years ago; in both cases some of the great local magnates were fabulously wealthy and at the same time utterly unscrupulous; and just as English Liberals were opposed to Great Britain being dragged into war by the Gold Barons of the Rand, so almost all Americans unconnected with Oil, were determined that America should never be dragged into war by the Oil Barons of Tampico.

Tampico has, indeed, a much worse reputation than Johannesburg ever had. Fishing in such troubled waters as those of Mexico is sometimes an extremely profitable occupation for a Yankee "crook" who has been in business, in journalism and in jail, who knows a little Spanish, is an expert liar, a clever forger, an experienced burglar, a suave confidence man, a good shot, in short an all-round rascal. There is plenty of money to be made by such men as secret agents of unscrupulous oil magnates. There are Mexican Generals to be bought; there are American officials to be squared; there are arms to be purchased; and in all these cases, a considerable sum of money may be slipped into the agent's own pocket without risk of detection. Towards the end of 1927 the *Excelsior* of Mexico City gave a case where a secret agent of Oil had appropriated $50,000 on the ground that he had used that sum to bribe a certain Mexican official, who denied having ever received a *centavo* of it.

Such agents are quite prepared to sell their own masters or to work for both sides simultaneously, but the one thing they do not want is a peaceful settlement of Mexican-American difficulties. Their ultimate employers in New York City are generally respectable men with an extraordinary ignorance of Mexico and a curious disinclination to go to Mexico themselves and study the situation. This disinclination to travel South may be due to the bad hotels in Mexico; Americans of the wealthiest class are sometimes spoilt by the luxuries which have become necessities for them in the States. These particular magnates do not object to getting money out of Mexico, but they want to get it without any fuss or any talk of their responsibilities, and they object to being "bothered" on the subject. They are plain business men, they say, and have nothing to do with "uplift" or that sort of thing. In short, their attitude towards Mexico resembles in some respects the attitude maintained by the great English merchants of the eighteenth century towards various territories in the Indies which were being exploited by England, but which had never been officially annexed.

It is easy to understand, therefore, that President Coolidge, a good, canny man, fond of delivering homilies on thrift, should have no desire to get mixed up with a riotous gang of oil men, more especially in view of the great Teapot Dome scandal, which was an attempt of some great oil magnates of America to get hold of national oil lands by the bribery of high Government officials at Washington. This Scandal involved Mr. Fall, formerly a member of President Harding's Cabinet, and an imperialist of the most flamboyant type. Nobody was more anti-Mexican than Mr. Fall, nobody was more anxious to see Old Glory waving over Chapultepec Palace; nobody criticized more severely the Sonora gang, so that now, when the financial corruption of Mr. Fall has been disclosed, anyone who criticizes that gang is regarded by the average American citizen as a propagandist paid by Oil. It is illogical, of course, but it is human nature.

It is not surprising, I say, that, in these circumstances, Mr. Coolidge should avoid this boisterous gang of imperialists, and seek the advice of his old schoolfellow and playmate, Mr. Dwight W. Morrow, of the great banking house of J.P. Morgan & Co.

Having decided not to stand for re-election, the American President was reluctant to interrupt, near the end of his term, the great wave of prosperity which will probably make American grandfathers tell their children, fifty years hence, of the golden days of Calvin Coolidge. Now, in the opinion of Calles' American admirers, a break with Mexico would lead to such an interruption, bring about a war which would unsettle the markets, cause the expenditure of much money for naval and military purposes, and produce acute domestic differences.

It is a pity that, despite all Mr. Coolidge's care there were four million unemployed in the United States in March, 1928. A war with Mexico would, of course, have made matters even worse, but there was no question of a war with Mexico either because of oil or because of religion. Frank and fearless representations to Mexico on both questions would have accorded more with the American character and at the same time proved more effectual than the course which the President finally took; and such representations would, in my opinion, have caused no rupture of Americo-Mexican relations. But the President was shaken by the systematic bombardment to which he had been subjected by the countless pacifist, radical, and protestant societies whose members throughout the country sent at one time over eight hundred letters daily to the State Department demanding the recall of Ambassador Sheffield "because he is not in sympathy with the Mexican Government."

Mr. Dwight W. Morrow has been successful, it is said, in getting the Mexican Government to issue new oil laws which declare in effect that titles to oil concessions valid before 1917 are valid in perpetuity; and it is claimed that this removes one of the main points of contention between Mexico and the United States. This news has been received with enthusiasm by the American Oil Barons as well as by the English holders of shares in Mexican Eagles, but in view of the long list of promises which Mexican Presidents have made and broken, I am afraid that a catch will be discovered somewhere or other in Calles's new Petroleum Law. If so, the wrath of the Oil Barons will be only comparable to that of an oil well which has caught fire; and, in any case, the adjustment of the oil controversy does not finally close the Mexican case. The administration of the agrarian laws, resulting in the virtual confiscation without compensation, under Article 25 of the Constitution of 1917, of an enormous amount of land in Mexico owned by American citizens is yet to be adjusted and the settlement of claims, aggregating hundreds of millions of dollars, presents a formidable task. To these Ambassador Morrow is now turning his attention.

That he will afterwards try to settle the religious question is fairly certain, not because he is a religious man, but because the turmoil produced by the religious persecution and the religious war is reacting most unfavourably on the economic and political life of the country.

CHAPTER II

THE THREE LEVERS

A MERICA can bring pressure to bear on Mexico in three ways, by utilising the financial lever, by utilising the Arms Embargo, or by direct military and naval action. Vera Cruz, as I have already pointed out in chapter IV, part I, is Mexico's wind-pipe; the United States has only to grip it in order to make Mexico give way; but direct military or naval intervention in the interests of *la haute politique* is out of the question owing to the bad effect which it would have on Latin America and on the pacifists in the United States. If carried out, however, in the name of Civilisation and Humanity, even though its real object would be the support of some Mexican politician, unusually corrupt and secretly bound to the United States, such intervention would be possible; but of course the politician in question would have to be carefully whitewashed for the occasion.

The other two methods are so good, however, that they will probably be sufficient. A study of the financial lever and the manner in which it is operated gives us the impression that Mexico has already drifted into that obscure and dangerous position where a country has lost its independence without having come under efficient foreign control.

Wall Street is supposed in some quarters to be forcing America into a Mexican war, but the exact opposite is the case, and the reason can be given in a single sentence—Wall Street is getting out of Mexico certain annual payments, which would cease in case of war. So long as Mexico continues to make those payments, and so long as no other circumstances arise to make a crossing of the Rio Grande financially profitable, Wall Street will protect Mexico and will maintain the present Government of Mexico in all the plenitude of its corruption.

The Mexican Government, according to the Lamont-de la Huerta agreement, as amended by the Lamont-Pani agreement, undertook to pay to the Mexican bond-holders approximately 22,000,000 *pesos* annually, which represents the production and export oil tax. Since this agreement was made the International Committee of Bankers on Mexico have collected approximately 30,000,000 gold dollars from Mexico, and this has been passed on to the European and American bond-holders. Owing to the fact that oil production has steadily fallen off in Mexico since President Calles threatened to seize the oil properties, the tax has steadily dropped. The June payments (1927) could not be made by the Mexican Government owing to the shortage of the oil tax, and also to the fact that some of this tax had been diverted to other purposes.

Early in June, 1927, Mr. T. W. Lamont, of Messrs. Morgan & Co., scoured New York to get money for the Mexican Government, but his requests were turned down on all sides. Finally he discovered that Mexico had a deposit in the United States of a very considerable sum in cash, which, under Mexican law, had to be paid directly into the Treasury at Mexico City or used for Government purposes in America. Mr. Lamont suggested to Señor Arturo Elías, President Calles' brother and Mexican Financial Agent in New York, that this money should be used to meet the bond payments: and finally Lamont, by a process of book-keeping to which he resorted, proposed that the Committee should loan Mexico a sum equivalent to the amount of their cash on deposit in the United States, on a short term note with a certificate of deposit against the cash collateral. Even this sum was not great enough to meet the bond payment, so the Committee proposed to advance the difference on another short term note, under which arrangement future consular fees and other payments due to the Mexican Government in the United States should be used as collateral. Thus, the last payment of something over $700,000 was got by what has been described as "a book-keeping process"; and the rest, amounting to about $2,500,000 was advanced on President Calles's pledging the consular fees.

I merely give this to show how desperate is the condition of Mexico's finances, but the very hopelessness of that condition gave Mr. Dwight W. Morrow his opportunity. He made it clear that he would relax the screw only when Calles conceded all the points insisted on by the American oil men; and Calles who had, a few months before, been firm in his conviction that wealth in petroleum and land must revert to Mexico, regardless of contracts entered into and prices paid, suddenly swallowed his words.

The oil magnates are naturally pleased, but this policy on the part of the United States is rather a decline from the lofty altruism of President Wilson, who once asked an audience at Indianapolis: "Do you suppose that the American people are ever going to count a small amount of material benefit and advantage to people doing business in Mexico against the liberties and the permanent happiness of the Mexican people?"

"It would have been far nobler," says an American weekly, *The Commonweal*, "far more creditable to American integrity and tradition, if this horrible butchery of believing Christians could have been halted by the force of public opinion. If we as a people had wanted to see justice and religious fervour protected south of the Rio Grande, the persecution would have ended months ago. But since this could not be, let us have faith in Morrow and economic common-sense. Let us have faith while asking ourselves if it can really be true that the nation of Lincoln and Lee is growing incapable of thinking clearly in terms of anything except money—that financial power is the only weapon which we now can wield."

In return for his surrender, Calles is to get an extension of time on the present debt, and a new loan of fifty million dollars.

It is rumoured that the new loan will be issued by the Bank of Montreal, one of the banks doing a large business in Mexico, and if this rumour proves true, that Canadian Bank will be acting only as a cover for Wall Street, which is somewhat reluctant about financing openly a man formally and categorically denounced by Pope Pius XI as a worse persecutor of Christianity than Nero or Caligula.

Calles is naturally anxious to get the money as soon as possible, for he intends to spend $2,500,000 of it on aeroplanes, and another $500,000 on cavalry horses, both aeroplanes and horses being intended for the prosecution of the man-hunt which the President is carrying out against all who oppose him with arms. But by all this expenditure, Calles is impoverishing more and more his country, and his exchequer, and making himself more and more helpless *vis-à-vis* of the United States. Unknown to himself, for he is an ignorant man, he is playing the game of the *Gringo*.

But, on the other hand, the diplomacy of the *Gringo* is not beyond reproach. There have been instances in effete Europe of unscrupulous diplomats studying a victim's weaknesses, and, having ascertained that the point to concentrate on was wine or women or money, taking steps to satisfy the predominant passion with a view to gaining some ulterior end. Calles' predominant passion is the killing of Christians, and if Mr. Dwight W. Morrow has not actually thrown Christians to him as one would throw pieces of meat to a caged tiger, he has at all events refrained from protesting against Calles's savagery, and is trying to arrange that Calles shall have more money. Very adroit, certainly, but hardly what we should have expected from the land of "uplift," from the soil sacred to Ella Wheeler Wilcox and Dr. Frank Crane.

Another lever which the United States can use in case of necessity is the Arms Embargo. She can cut off the supply of arms to the Mexican Government as she did during the year 1927, and even in 1928, until Calles gave way on the Oil question. She can raise the embargo on arms in favour of revolution-ists attempting to upset the central Government, and thus make the triumph of those revolutionists certain. She can again impose that embargo and save the Government, if the Government does what she wants it to do. She can make the Government topple over by simply refusing long enough to let it import arms for use against insurgents. In October, 1927, President Calles sent a commission abroad in order to arrange for pur-chases of arms in Europe; but these purchases will not continue if Mexico is unable to pay, and America can make it impossible for her to pay. Moreover, on about a dozen occasions during the last hundred years the United States intercepted arms coming from Europe to Vera Cruz, and she will probably intercept arms again or ask England to do so.

When General Adolfo de la Huerta rebelled against Obregón and Calles in the autumn of 1923, the United States saved Obregón and Calles by selling them an enormous supply of arms and ammunition, without which they could not have maintained their position. She sold them eleven aeroplanes, thirty-three machine guns, fifteen thousand Enfield rifles, five million rounds of ammunition, and other military supplies; but by accepting this assistance they sold the independence of their country. As I pointed out in the preface, Calles has sunk into what is practically a condition of dependence on the United States.

One result is that in any book written about contemporary Mexico, the United States must figure largely, and even in any conversation about Mexico the name America must soon enter, just as in any conversation about the Egypt of to-day, the name England must soon make its appearance. Nominally, Egypt is more dependent on England than Mexico is on America, but in reality it is the other way about, for other European countries have interests in Egypt as well as England and will not be shy about complaining if those interests suffer as a result of English feebleness, whereas though Europe has large interests in Mexico, she carefully refrains from blaming America for the depreciation those interests are suffering, the reason for her silence being that she owes America money. Some American readers may be inclined to declare that Mexico is an independent country, and that America has nothing to do with her, and no responsibility for her behaviour; but this is not quite correct so long as America would object to European warships appearing off Vera Cruz and demanding satisfaction. If England allowed foreigners to be robbed and murdered in Egypt as America allows foreigners to be robbed and murdered in Mexico, the American Press would lose no time in advising England to "get a move on" or else to clear out and leave other nations to settle their accounts direct with Cairo.

The Monroe Doctrine has its obligations as well as its rights; and if it prevents Europeans from keeping Mexico in order, it obliges America to do so. Stay-at-home Americans may refuse to take Mexico to task for the murder of American citizens, but if Mexico goes beyond a certain point in the murder of Europeans, America must either punish Mexico herself or else let the European Powers settle directly with that country. For the moment, as I have already explained, Europe will stand almost anything from anybody; but the Sonora gang may become even more truculent than it is, and Europe may become stronger and more united; and it is not impossible that all the European nations may some day unite in a remonstrance to Washington against the robbery and murder of Europeans in Mexico, and in the presentation to the State Department of a bill, a yard long, for damages sustained by their citizens in Mexico. If America will not let them send warships to collect this bill at Vera Cruz, then she herself must collect it for them. That is strict logic and good law.

CHAPTER III

THE STATE DEPARTMENT AND THE PEOPLE

HAVING now spoken about the Oil Barons and the financiers (the only Americans who really matter in Mexico), I shall say something of the State Department and the Sovereign People. Unlike Downing Street, the American State Department has no permanent officials to carry on a tradition or a policy; and as there is a clean sweep after every Presidential election, there is no fixed foreign policy at all. In the middle of 1927 there was not in the Mexican section of the Department a single international lawyer or a single person with a special knowledge of Mexican affairs. Mr. Robert E. Olds, Assistant Secretary of State, who has had much to do with Mexican business during recent years, has never been to Mexico. He is a respectable country lawyer, was formerly the junior law partner of the Secretary of State, but he has had no international experience and has few qualifications for the important post which he holds. Mr. Franklin Mott Gunther, who is in charge of the Division of Mexican affairs, has never been to Mexico save on one brief visit which lasted three days. These are the people who are in charge of Mexican Affairs in the State Department. I am not trying to poke fun at these gentlemen; I am only trying to explain that the State Department is easy and informal like an American Court of Justice. The system followed in the State Department has much to recommend it, but, unfortunately, it has given Calles many opportunities of stealing a march on the United States.

As for the Sovereign People, they take no interest in Mexico at all. They do not realize the fact that their country occupies a predominant diplomatic position in Mexico. Indeed the average American citizen is irritated rather than flattered by any reference to the influence of the United States between the Rio Grande and Panama, and to the enormous value of American investments throughout that great area, for such references imply responsibilities which may result in the landing of marines, the waging of little wars, the running up of big bills, and an increase of the Income Tax. It is not always the lofty ideals of Pacifism which inspire American fulminations against Mexican intervention; very often it is a narrow selfishness which would endure any humiliation to the national honour rather than encourage vigorous action that might also prove expensive. This selfish element, very often an undigested foreign element, is particularly wroth at any appeal for American insistence on reparation being made for American lives and property. "Why did these people go to Mexico?" they ask. "Why did they invest their money there? They knew the risks they ran. Such people should automatically lose all right to protection as soon as they crossed the Rio Grande."

The great champion of this idea was the late William Jennings Bryan, who was Secretary of State in 1914, and whose anger about the murder and plunder of Americans that went on in Mexico at that time was directed rather against the victims of these outrages than against the Mexican perpetrators of them.

Mr. William Jennings Bryan was an extreme case; but the United States generally does not seem to realize that even if it puts up with the murder of its own citizens in Mexico, it cannot expect Europeans to put up indefinitely with the murder of theirs.

The people of the United States are not to blame for this Mexican muddle. They are not to blame for the editorials, now hot now cold, which appear in the newspapers, or for the voluntary censorship which is exercised by editors over their Mexican news. The American people are above the level of the editors who are supposed to cater for them, and even of the Government which rules them. Nothing touched me more, while engaged on this book, than the letters of encouragement I received from humble people in the Bronx and the Bowery, who had learned from the newspapers that I was writing of the Terror in Mexico, with a view to bringing about its suppression. Enclosed in those letters were specimens of the scanty news on Mexico which is allowed to appear in the Tied Press of America; but though such clippings were useless to me, the intentions of the senders were good, and I take this opportunity of thanking them all.

I find their letters of more hopeful augury for civilization than all the letters which *les grandes dames Américaines* ever wrote from the Riviera to the Paris *Herald* denouncing the cruelty of fishermen to fish and of costers to horses, than all the excuses ever offered by the New York *Nation* and the *New Republic* for the murderers who rule in Mexico and in Moscow, than in all the pompous editorials that were ever penned; and in not one of these letters was there even a hint of armed intervention. A cessation of the torture was all that was asked for.

CHAPTER IV

THE MEXICAN PRESS

COUNT Berchtold, the former Austrian Foreign Minister, once said that "Russia collapsed because of the contradiction between her highly conservative policy at home and her policy of revolutionary agitation abroad"; and there is the same contradiction between America's highly conservative policy at home and her policy of revolutionary agitation in Mexico. As a journalist I naturally paid close attention to the Mexican Press; and the result of my observations was extreme astonishment at three things: the extent to which the Government controls the Press, the hatred for all kinds of religion which the newspapers display, and their violent dislike of America. In all three respects the Mexican Press is very much in the same position as the Russian Press at the present moment, and it is as unrepresentative of the pious Mexican people as the *Bezbozhnik* is of the pious Russian people. There was in Ocotlán when I was there, a paper called *El Rojo* (The Red) which was published at the headquarters of General Joaquín Amaro, the Secretary of War and Commander-in-chief, and which bore an inscription to that effect. It was therefore the official organ of a Cabinet Minister, but it was Bolshevik and anti-Catholic, and while I was in Guadalajara, this Cabinet Minister lent his name to a demonstration in the Degollado Theatre, Guadalajara, at which America, in the person of *Tio Sam* (uncle Sam), was turned into ridicule.

In Guadalajara itself the Red newspaper has a unique title, simply *El 130*, that being the article in the Constitution which has led to the present persecution of the church in Mexico. The editor of *El 130* is a Spanish Socialist and anti-clerical called D. A. Siqueiros who was imported by the Calles government from Barcelona, Spain, where he had committed a murder; and his newspaper must be supported by the Government, for Guadalajara, which is the most Catholic city in Mexico, does not buy ten copies of this indecent and atheistical rag and does not advertise in it.

Siqueiros is a practical and desperate ruffian; far handier with the *machete* than with the pen, and having at his beck and call many bravos as desperate as himself. His paper closely resembles the *Bezbozhnik* of Moscow, especially in its indecency, its jolty style, its caricatures and its slip-shod language. Señor Siqueiros must have studied the Russian Bolshevik press very closely for he has mastered all the jargon and all the tricks, down even to the typography. His typographical tricks I will make no attempt to reproduce in the following quotations, as the broken sentences, and the frequent use, for whole phrases, of italics, small capitals, and even black capitals, would shock any civilized compositor, spoil the appearance of the letterpress, and convey the impression of a handbill announcing a bargain sale or some mad kind of Futurist poetry.

Like the Bolshevik editors, he is fond of extremely violent language. "United Front Against the Reaction." This is the motto in frantic capitals, beneath the title-page, and the phrase is, of course, quite Bolshevik. It might have fallen from the lips of Zinoviev himself.

Then there are indecent attacks on the clergy. "*Los Amores del Padre Iñiguez*" is the title given to a series of articles, advertised by means of flaming posters pasted even on the walls of the venerable Cathedral, which, though at present Government property, is not protected from such indignity. Padre Iñiguez is a local priest of good character, but now outlawed and in hiding, and therefore unable to defend himself against these accusations.

Some of the illustrations are so blasphemous that they cannot be reproduced. In the issue of May 22, 1927, there is, on the front page, a caricature of Christ as bad as anything ever published by the *Bezbozhnik*. An issue which appeared in June, 1927, contained a very indecent article entitled "The Friar," by "Manuel Urbina Castro, Captain of the first Regiment of the Infantry in Guadalajara." But the American people and their economic system is attacked quite as violently as the Catholic Church. There is, for example, a Bolshevist proclamation "against the present capitalistic system" which ends with the famous words of Karl Marx, misquoted, however, "Workmen and peasants of the world, unite!"

In politics this paper is extremely Governmental, and, being Governmental, it therefore supports the candidature of General Obregón. The same can be said of all the Red newspapers in Mexico. The redder they are, the more enthusiastic is their support of Calles and Obregón and the greater is their hatred of the United States. *El 130* declares that "the worst enemy of Mexico is Yankee imperialism."

A Communist poet, Jesús Aguilar Villaseñor, contributes a poem which contains attacks on the United States in every stanza.

"The United States," he says, "demonstrates every moment with deeds, its marked tendency to seek domination—especially over weak peoples. The United States is one of the peoples who boast loudest of the despotism which they wish to impose at all costs.

"The United States systematically throws obstacles in the way of the commercial transactions conducted by our Government in order to increase excitement and discontent.

"The hour of the collapse of the United States is not far distant, not distant is the solemn hour of human freedom.

"In stopping all commercial operations between our Government and the United States, General Calles has only done his duty as an honourable President.

"Yankee imperialism, the most formidable imperialism of all, has seen itself obliged to make a pact with the Catholic clergy in order to stir up a rebellion against the laws of Mexico."

And peppered through it all, are the usual Bolshevik cries: "The experience and the example of the great Russian Revolution and the Soviet Government are a satisfaction for the working class of all the world, towards which (sic), in spite of all marches the universal proletariat."

This may seem foolish, but it must be considered in its effect on the illiterates and semi-illiterates of Mexico, from whom all the steadying and conservative influence of their religion is withdrawn at the moment they need it most, at the moment when this Red propaganda is launched upon them.

Newspapers like *El 130* are the organs of President Calles and are supported by his Government, and, in return, they see good in everything he does and, as I have already remarked, are most enthusiastic supporters of his heir presumptive in the Presidency, General Alvaro Obregón who, to quote *El 130*, "is our candidate for the Presidency of the Republic—because he will be continuer of the grandest work of genius performed by that man of iron will who has given the rallying cry for all Spanish America, that man whose name is Plutarco Elías Calles."

As for the ferocious attacks on America which are a feature of all these Red Mexican newspapers, I have nothing to say, for America is strong enough to look after herself; and lack of space prevents me giving anything more about the Red Press of Mexico. I have collected a great deal of material on this subject, but a far larger collection is to be seen in the State Department at Washington; and it is all of the same type as *El 130*, anti-American, anti-Catholic, Bolshevist and indecent. In these contemptible rags the noble language of Cervantes and Calderon has been mutilated and misused exactly as in Russia the noble language of Gogol and Tolstoy has been mutilated and misused by the Bolshevist propagandists.

"What is to be done about it?"

American Consuls and diplomatists have asked me that question all over Mexico. My answer was always the same. "You have brought this on yourselves by placing in power the Socialist and anti-Christian gang which was represented in 1914 by Carranza, and which is represented to-day by Calles. By encouraging revolutionary agitation in Mexico while pursuing a conservative policy at home, you are preparing for yourselves some awkward surprises."

I might add that in all cases these diplomatists agreed with me. Since the reform of the American diplomatic and Consular Service and the appointment in Mexico of young men who have thoroughly mastered Spanish, it is impossible to find an American representative who approves of the overthrow of Huerta in 1914 by President Wilson, and the installation of the Carranza-Obregón-Calles gang at Chapultepec.

Before taking leave of the Red Press of Mexico, I must admit that one Red Mexican newspaper was particularly useful to me when I was crossing the frontier into the United States. I used it as a wrapper for the last letters of condemned men which I was conveying into safety, and it protruded ostentatiously from a pocket of my overcoat which hung on a hook in the railway carriage while the searchers were examining my baggage at Nuevo Laredo.

Chapter V

THE STRANGE SILENCE OF THE AMERICAN PRESS

ONE of the most disquieting features of the Mexican question is to be seen, not in Mexico but in the United States; it is the strange silence of the American Press on the subject of Mexico. I call this particular feature disquieting because it shakes our whole faith in that system of publicity and free discussion which plays on the whole such a hygienic part in American public life. Once let this system be discarded, and there is no protection for the individual against that tremendous propaganda machine which exists in America, which is growing stronger every year, and which may be suddenly turned some day by its manipulators against liberty and Christianity and in favour of Heaven knows what puritanical, sentimentalist or suicidal folly.

The great American editors of the past had their great faults, but they had one virtue—they were not afraid of any possible kind of discussion. To illustrate what happens at present, I shall give my own case. After leaving Mexico in 1927 I "blew into" the office of a great New York paper where I have many friends, and handed in my Mexican "story," the same "story" practically as I tell here. The Editor was delighted with it, and said that it was confirmed by all the Mexican news he got from other sources. But then the millionaire owner came and, after glancing at the typescript, said curtly, "Don't touch it." Those three words sealed the fate of my articles (and Calles, I may add, showed his gratitude, *more suo*, by immediately afterwards kicking out that paper's correspondent, an inoffensive American who had never once ventured to criticise the Dictator).

There was a similar decision on the part of the two or three other colossal dailies which count. One newspaper outside New York was extremely "keen" on my articles, and had arranged to begin them on a certain day with a tremendous splurge; but unluckily, I wired this paper on the previous day to congratulate it on having more courage than the *New York* ——, with the result that, instead of feeling elated, the editor suddenly became suspicious, and decided at the last moment not to publish. He did not tell me so, however; he simply ceased writing, and the articles never appeared.

Other newspapers, outside New York, got scared when they saw that the Empire City did not start off with my series, and smelt a rat or a libel action, or, at all events, something mysterious. Two great Latin-American agencies which had been very much interested, changed their mind when they saw that New York did not publish. Thus, even the Latin-American Press is controlled from Manhattan, sometimes by journalists who are not themselves Latin, sometimes by Latins who have become completely Americanized. Despite the anti-American feeling which prevails from the Rio Grande to Cape Horn, the United States exercises a great influence over the South American Press by its telegraphic news, its blocks of cheap illustrations, and its cinemas. General Pershing was hanged in effigy in the Tacna-Arica district. A flood of hostile propaganda accused Uncle Sam of dollar diplomacy, of unjust aggression in Nicaragua, and of murdering Sacco and Vanzetti, with the result that the anti-American feeling in Argentina became at one time so strong that the Argentine Ambassador at Washington begged Mr. Kellogg to keep his tariff experts out of Buenos Aires as the Government there could not guarantee their safety. Nevertheless the hated *Gringo* influences the Latin-American Press in the manner indicated.

To return, however, to the panic of which I was speaking, Americans, despite all their hard-headedness, are strangely susceptible at times to these mysterious panics. I remember once an Oklahoma farmer telling how the Ku Klux Klan had planted a cross or some other symbol of terrorism on his land. This farmer was a Protestant but no friend of the K.K.K., so that I expected him to say that he had torn it up, as the average British farmer would have done. "You took it down, of course," said I, whereupon he replied with an air of intense resolution: "No, sir. I did not. I just let it stand there."

From this it will be seen that, despite their individualism, the Americans are developing a curious kind of mob psychology which renders them liable to be stampeded at times like a herd of buffaloes. Their country is full of mysterious taboos which may yet constitute excellent handles for some super-propagandist; and, as I have just pointed out, there is no knowing what kind of mad propaganda may yet sweep those vast plains, where there is nothing to stop it, no particularisms such as we have in Europe, no classes apart and fortified in ancient traditions. The whole subject is, to me, one of mystery, the only clear point being that the Catholic Church in America does not possess the secret word that releases the Propaganda spirit. Why was there always such excitement in America about Jewish pogroms in Tsarist Russia, and why is there no mention made of the Christian pogroms in Mexico, where, since August, 1926, 4,047 people have been executed, among them 16 women? Why was there such an uproar about Germany's use of poison gas in 1917, and nothing published at all about Calles's use, in 1928, of poison gas in aeroplane bombs, although in the latter case whole villages—men, women, and children—were wiped out?

When the Chinese crisis was acute in 1927 one great American newspaper sent half-a-dozen highly paid and very able correspondents to China, in which country America has ultimately no future, whereas in Mexico, which is of vital interest to the United States, the sole representative of that particular paper was a commercial gent who travelled in men's suspenders and had only drifted into journalism by accident. America seems to me to be dissipating her energy very much as England did in the time of the Plantagenets and Yorkists, who wasted all their strength on France whereas, by making a complete conquest of the British Isles and devoting themselves to exploration and trade (obviously the *métier* of an Island Empire), they would have shown much greater foresight. Or I might take the case of Russia, which could have abolished serfdom, put her own house in order, captured Constantinople, and established herself solidly on the Pacific, if she had resisted the inclination to take part in the French Revolutionary Wars which were, after all, no concern of hers. In the same way the Americans are drawn towards Europe and China, where there is nothing for them in the future save bad debts and great disasters, and are neglecting their Latin-American neighbours. I do not mean, of course, that the United States should harbour aggressive designs on her southern sisters. I mean that she should learn to understand them, to speak their languages, and to co-operate with them in the development of the New World. As it is, however, an American newspaper man considers it a hardship to be sent, even for a few days, to Mexico City, while hailing with delight a Paris assignment. This feeling explains to some extent the paucity of Mexican news in the American newspapers.

The European newspapers cannot be blamed to the same extent, for there is not a single European journalist in Mexico; all the news-gathering is in the hands of the Americans; and, for reasons which I have already set forth, no Foreign Office in Europe wants to risk the displeasure of the United States by communicating to the Press any of the official information it gets from Mexico. I have already referred to the action of the London *Daily Express* in breaking this silence, but the very circumstances under which this disclosure took place betrayed the existence of a strange state of affairs in Fleet Street. Mr. Mason, the New York correspondent of the *Daily Express*, went to Mexico and learned from the lips of President Calles himself that about fifty priests had been executed. From personal observation he estimated that there were 50,000 rebels in the field against Calles, and that the whole State of Jalisco was practically independent of the Central Government.

Now, these are amazing facts, which at any previous period of the modern world's history, would have been investigated; but for some mysterious reason they were not investigated for a whole year. Whether the priests were martyrs or criminals, whether the 50,000 insurgents wanted to restore freedom or to restore the Inquisition, in any case they constituted legitimate objects of journalistic curiosity. But the millionaire newspaper owners of New York said "Don't touch it," whereupon Fleet Street meekly bowed its head.

The manner in which the attention of the London *Daily Express* came to be directed to the Mexican question is so curious and so characteristic of the whole business that it must be told. The Hon. Evan Morgan, the son and heir of Viscount Tredegar, was about to be married, and one day a girl reporter from the *Daily Express* called on him to get some details of his *fiancée's trousseau*. Mr. Morgan, who is a sincere Roman Catholic, promised to give her all the information she wanted on condition that she got something into the *Daily Express* about the persecution in Mexico. Finally this London newspaper approached the subject with great trepidation and circumspection, and it has been slapping itself on the back ever since for the extreme courage which it showed on that occasion. Courage? To publish President Calles's admission that he had executed fifty priests? But surely the *Daily Express* is a newspaper, and its business is to give news? Why did it refrain for many months from giving us any news about those fifty executions, or at all events, about the appalling state of things in Mexico? If it was ignorant of that appalling state of things, then it showed incredible journalistic slackness. If it was not ignorant, then it was guilty of suppressing important information. But, after all, it was better than the other London papers, which published hardly anything about the crimes of Calles. Occasionally, of course, they inserted paragraphs about the rounding up of rebels, but their cables about Mexico were very inadequate, especially when compared with their cables about, say, China.

The London *Times* of May 15, 1928, contained a heart-rending letter from Sir Hesketh Bell on the sufferings of the orang-utans captured in Sumatra and furnished with insufficient accommodation on their way to various Zoos in Europe. With deep emotion (to which, in all probability, the somewhat shaky grammar of the following quotation is due) Sir Hesketh Bell told us how "accustomed to roam in spacious liberty, through the huge forests, feeding on the fruits and succulent leaves of their choice, the suffering of these unfortunate captives during their long sea-journey to Europe, cooped up in cages in which they cannot stand upright, needs no description."

All of which is quite right and proper, but the sufferings of the human beings, sent under equally bad conditions to the Islas Marías, should be spoken of too; but, so far as I know, there has not yet been a word about them in *The Times*.

As I have already pointed out, however, the chief blame rests with the American Press, for Mexico is in America's journalistic sphere of influence, and, besides, most newspapers in the Old World are "stony broke" since the War, and would as soon think of sending a special correspondent to the moon as to Mexico. On the other hand the American Press does not know what to do with its money; and, as it has always prided itself on letting the limelight of publicity penetrate into every nook and cranny of public life, its comparative silence at the present moment, on the subject of Mexico, is somewhat startling, especially when we remember that Mexico was never in a worse state of disintegration than it is in to-day.

The American correspondent in Mexico has, like the average journalist elsewhere, a talent for irresponsible writing and a thirst for the sensational, but on the present occasion he is sending his paper a much more restrained and dignified narrative than that which is sent in code by elderly, sedate diplomatists with an ingrained habit of under-statement and a professional hatred of journalistic exaggeration. The journalist is sending narratives dull and monotonous enough to come from the Press Gallery of the House of Lords, whereas the diplomatists are writing secret despatches sensational enough to come from the cellar of the Lubyanka at Moscow. I have seen both the diplomats and the newspaper men; the former gave me the impression that they have sent reports which are far stronger than anything I have published in this book; the latter admitted to me frankly that the situation was as I have described it here, but that their newspapers would not publish a true account of it.

On several occasions a corner of the curtain was lifted, but there was always some unseen but agitated interference, and the corner was hastily dropped again. There was a tussle behind the scenes and vigorous whispering—then silence as before.

To be more explicit, on one occasion an unusually able "special" was despatched to Mexico, and as he has a perfect knowledge of the Spanish language (being himself of Spanish origin), he wirelessed from the American steamer by which he left Vera Cruz the first of a series of articles on Mexico. It was a terrible but perfectly true picture, and by some mishap it appeared exactly as it had been written. A corner of the curtain had thus been lifted; but then there took place the amazing performance which I have already described. There was a mysterious scuffle behind the scenes; and suddenly the corner of the curtain went down with a jerk. Then there was an interval of silence, after which the rest of the articles began to appear. But, alas! how different from the first article! They sounded like Miss Ella Wheeler Wilcox after Homer, like *In the Gloaming* after Tchaikovsky's *1812*.

The journalist in question had two courses before him, to resign his position or to keep quiet and continue drawing the princely salary which he receives. He took the latter course, and is now in another part of the world. I do not blame him, for his resignation would not have enabled him to publish the truth about Mexico, as all the great newspapers would be closed to him. He might, of course, have written a book, and lost money on it, and become a journalistic suspect for the rest of his natural life. ("Impossible person!" his millionaire newspaper owner would say of him, "Never again! I'm through with that guy. You explain to him the sort of dope you want, and dammit if he doesn't send you an entirely different article, which he actually refuses to re-write! Hot stuff, I admit, but on the present occasion it isn't hot stuff that he's paid to deliver.") Finally, it must be remembered that very often "our own special" is a married man, with a wife and motor-car.

Some of the American editors with whom I discussed this matter, said: "We're not going to let the Catholics force us into a war with Mexico." But surely the best thing for a newspaper to do is to open its columns to all comers and to have the battle fought out healthily in the open sunlight, and the worst thing is to close one's eyes and put one's fingers in one's ears. Moreover, this is hardly an American way of meeting a difficulty. It was not in this way that the American people met and overcame all the obstacles which they have surmounted during the last one hundred and thirty years. Undoubtedly there is in some quarters a fear of Catholic propaganda, but this Mexican question has shown the weakness of Catholic propaganda for rousing public opinion in favour of oppressed Catholics. This weakness can be seen when we compare it with the strength and success of the Jewish propaganda in favour of Dreyfus and of the Russian Jews under the Tsardom.

My own failure to get anything about Mexico inserted in the great American newspapers was not unexpected, for how could I succeed where Pope Pius XI and Mr. George Bernard Shaw had failed? At the request of an American Catholic editor, both of these eminent men wrote letters about Mexico for publication in the American Press, and both their letters were "turned down."

It happened in this way. Being on a visit to Rome in the summer of 1927, with a commission to get, if possible, an interview with the Holy Father, Mr. Michael Williams, of New York, a personal friend of mine, and editor of the *Commonweal*, was lucky enough to obtain from Pius XI a very remarkable statement on Mexico which all the great American papers refused on the ground that it was "Catholic propaganda." Mr. Williams therefore wrote to Mr. G. B. Shaw for a letter on the subject which would force the publication of the Papal statement, and Mr. Shaw very kindly sent him such a letter. Among other things he said: "I cannot imagine what the American Press is thinking of in refusing to publish what is practically an interview with the Pope. It is news, and official news, from a person of overwhelming importance. The mere fact that the Pope has at last consented to avail himself of the Press instead of the pulpit as his instrument of publicity would be sensational news even if the message were nothing but a remark on the prospects of the harvest. . . . I have never been able to understand why the subject of the pitched battle between Church and State in Mexico was dropped so suddenly by the British Press after it had been figured with the prominence its importance deserved for several days."

Only one great American paper published the interview and the comment thereupon of Mr. Shaw. This was probably the first occasion on which a letter of G. B. S. was rejected by practically all the American Press.

But that Press is very changeable, or, rather, the forces behind it change their tactics very frequently. In the spring and summer of 1919, the American newspapers which now ignore Mexico, were calling loudly for intervention. The New York *Times* advocated stern measures on the ground that "mere negotiation" could not be expected to "procure satisfaction." The *Knickerbocker Press* declared that it was "the duty of the United States to establish a stable government in Mexico." The Philadelphia *Enquirer* demanded a resort to "drastic measures" in order to suppress this "international nuisance." The *Public Ledger* called upon the administration to "quell the Ishmaelite of the Western hemisphere." The Hartford *Courant* urged the immediate seizure of the Mexican ports. The Washington *Star* declared that conditions were intolerable across the Rio Grande.

The Chicago *Tribune* urged the United States to "perform the same service for Mexico which it [had] performed for Cuba." The Kansas City *Times* asked, very pertinently: "Is the United States to allow a Balkan problem to remain unsolved on the American continent while mixing in at every political flurry . . . in Europe and Asia?" The *Journal*, of the same city, demanded that Mexico be "cleaned up" and that this cleaning process be set in motion at once. Even such southern democratic papers as the Asheville *Times* and the Montgomery *Advertiser* urged that Mexico should be made to feel the wrath of the United States; and the Charleston *News and Courier* said: "Destiny is plain. It cannot be dodged or averted. Sooner or later—and probably soon—we must make an end of the world-nuisance in the only way in which it can be ended."

From this summary, to which I am indebted, by the way, to Mr. J. Fred Rippy's *United States and Mexico*, it will be seen that in the year 1919 the newspapers of the United States were not afraid to talk quite freely of the Mexican question, and that, consequently, their present mysterious silence cannot be due to that *post-bellum* fatigue which has killed the jingoism of most imperialists in Europe.

CHAPTER VI

CONCLUSION

O NE conclusion to be drawn from an examination of the Mexican question and of the way in which the outer world has reacted to that question is that the Press is no longer such a watch-dog in the interests of Humanity (capital H, printer, please) as I once, when very young, believed it to be. If we were to judge newspapers by their editorials, then editors are reckless philanthropists in comparison with whom St. Francis of Assisi was a canny and selfish peasant; their "own correspondents" all over the world have standing orders to report immediately any case of oppression; and the editor himself is always prepared to assist the Downtrodden and the Poor, even though he thereby involves himself in libel actions that will land him in the bankruptcy court. Such was the view I once held, but I am afraid that before an editor attacks any abuse, he asks himself quite a number of questions, to wit (1) if his owner—I mean the proprietor of his newspaper—is involved in the abuse, (2) if any of his big advertisers are involved, (3) if the political party which his paper supports is involved, (4) if the F.O. would be offended and cease supplying further information, (5) if any wealthy religious body would be offended. It does not matter, of course, if a poor and numerically unimportant Church takes offence. In short, the loud declaration of the gigantic modern newspaper that it is always on the side of the oppressed, always the champion of the bottom dog, is quite as false as the similar declaration of the

Soviet Government, or as the ear-splitting advertisements of the great department store that it is selling goods at "an alarming sacrifice," even though it is the customer who is the "alarming sacrifice."

Many people who would refuse to surrender their right of private judgment to the Church are quite ready to surrender it to the editor; although the Press is becoming less and less trustworthy not only as a guide to faith and morals but even as a guide to what is happening in the world around us. Mr. Hilaire Belloc has often pointed out the dishonest manner in which past history is written; and as a historian himself he is entitled to do so. In the same way, I, as a mere journalist, would like to point out the dishonest manner in which current history is written in the newspapers; and this dishonesty may consist in silence as well as in mendacious volubility. The spotlight is thrown on some facts and not on others, with the result that a false impression is produced on the mind of the spectator.

Another conclusion is that there is something not only disappointing and ineffective but unsound and even poisonous in that humanitarianism on which a section of modern society on both sides of the Atlantic prides itself so much. This humanitarianism is the union of a merely emotional mysticism with a science which is only a synonym for materialistic efficiency. It pretends to be more Christian than Christianity, and more compassionate than Christ Himself; it ranks as a sort of religion; but it is, nevertheless, a delusion, a snare, an unhealthy exaggeration far removed from the admirable balance which distinguishes true Christianity. Occasionally it may take up some trifling cause with ardour and impetuosity, but at the same time it will turn a deaf ear to the appeals of real and poignant suffering. It will weep over the hiccough of a superannuated cat while studiously ignoring the wails of children who are dying of hunger and cold. Its patron saint is the Rev. Laurence Sterne who lamented over a dead mule in France while oblivious to the sufferings of men and women in England.

With this kind of humanitarianism, sympathy is only a fad, and the object of that sympathy must be in the lime-light, otherwise there will be "nothing doing."

A concrete instance of its operation was seen in the angry telegrams which deluged the White House, the Navy Department at Washington, and Colonel Charles A. Lindbergh when that idol of the American people chanced to visit a bull-fight on the occasion of his trip to Mexico and Central America towards the end of 1927. The sensitive Puritan Associations of New England, and the Middle West, and the Solid South could not bear to think that their hero should shake hands with Gaone, the killer of bulls, but they made no protest whatsoever when he shook hands with Calles, the murderer of men.

The weakness—half fad, half fanaticism—which I have tried to indicate, is a morbid point in our civilisation, and may ultimately be the ruin of that civilisation, for we must remember that the gang which seized the reins of power both in Mexico and in Russia, prepared the way for itself by playing for a long time on the Anglo-Saxon's tenderness towards the Revolutionist who throws bombs in distant countries. Pitiless, it demanded pity. Merciless, it demanded mercy. Unjust, it demanded a justice which was really weakness. If civilization continues to pay out mercy and to take mercilessness in exchange, it will soon find itself bankrupt.

I do not deny that there are Americans of the highest character who do invaluable work by pointing out instances of oppression in Europe and in European colonies, but even they have a curiously blind side. For example the American Committee on the Rights of Religious Minorities published in May, 1928, a remarkable book on the investigations made by five of their representatives in Rumania; but no attempt has yet been made by this or any other American Committee to investigate the conditions in Mexico which is geographically nearer to the United States than Rumania, and of infinitely more importance. This importance is due to the Monroe doctrine; to the fact that

Washington has created and guaranteed the existence of the present Mexican regime, and underwritten the existing Mexican constitution; and to the tremendous emigration of Mexicans into the United States as a result of the social, economic and financial disintegration of Mexico.

President Coolidge does not seem at first sight to have much in common with either Frederick the Great or Catherine the Great, yet his policy towards Mexico reminds one of the policy pursued by those two unscrupulous potentates towards Poland. He maintains in Mexico a Government which is fast ruining that country, as they maintained in Warsaw a Government which was fast ruining Poland and which did ruin her eventually. They forbade any change in the Polish Constitution which would enable Poland to overcome her internal difficulties. He supplied Obregón with all the arms and ammunition he needed to overawe Adolfo de la Huerta, and to maintain his own iniquitous rule.

In the natural course of things, Mexico would have developed internal forces which would purify her or else the threat of European aggression would have kept her up to the mark, but America allows neither one nor the other. She prevents the free play of internal forces, and so far as pressure by the European Powers is concerned, she is as a wall around Mexico, a wall which makes it impossible for any foreign influence to interfere with the processes of corruption going on within.

It is true that even if there had been no American interference, the course of Mexican history would have been stormy. Even as far back as 1839, Madame Calderón de la Barca commented on the defects of the Mexican Government. I shall quote her remarks in full:

> "It will be impossible for us to leave Mexico without regret. It requires nothing but a settled Government to make it one of the first countries in the world. . . . Everyone has heard of the abuses that produced the first revolution in Mexico—of the great inequality of riches, of the degradation of

the Indians, of the high price of foreign goods, of the Inquisition, of the ignorance of the people, the bad state of the Colleges, the difficulty of obtaining justice, the influence of the clergy, and the ignorance in which the Mexican youth were purposely kept. Which of these evils has been removed? Foreign goods are cheaper, and the Inquisition is *not* . . . but, in the sacred name of liberty, every abuse can be tolerated.

> "O sage regenerators of mankind!
> "Patriots of nimble tongue and systems crude!
> "How many regal tyrannies combined
> "So many fields of massacre have strewed
> "As you and your attendant, cut-throat brood?"

It must be remembered, however, that all the Republics in the New World, not excepting even the United States, experienced the same disillusionment. I have seen manuscript letters of Philadelphia merchants who wrote immediately after the United States had achieved its independence, and, in comparison with their "language" about that memorable achievement, the worst things Lord Carson ever said about the Irish Free State would sound like a benediction. In South America it was the same. The Republic of the River Plate even asked England for God's sake to annex her. But England, then in one of her "weary Titan" phases, sternly rejected the temptation. Things would have righted themselves in Mexico as they have righted themselves on the River Plate, had America only refrained from helping Juárez, Carranza, and other "patriots of nimble tongue and systems crude," together with their "attendant, cut-throat brood."

As I have already pointed out, this attitude on the part of the United States is largely due to the action of those Americans who hope that the downfall of Rome will blaze the way for their own crusades. No such Americans are in the present administration, but they exercise great political power through their control of votes. But even if they have their way and see Catholicity destroyed in Mexico as it was destroyed in Japan by Hideyoshi and his two immediate successors, there is not the ghost of a chance that any other form of Christianity will benefit thereby. On the contrary, it is quite certain that the triumphant Agnostics will then turn on Protestantism, which they regard as a far greater danger than Catholicism because, in their opinion, it is linked up with American propaganda. I have observed this tendency all over South America, but especially in Brazil. Latin-American statesmen, even such of them as are agnostics or Comtists, see that Catholicism is a unifying force and that Protestantism only brings another element of discord into South America, especially as the only forms of Protestantism which seem to get any hold there are those forms which Dean Inge described as "barbarism and belated obscurantism." Those statesmen realize that if ever the day comes when the cathedral of Mexico City will be a Baptist conventicle instead of a Catholic church, on that day Mexican independence and nationality will be things of the past.

So strongly do some South American politicians feel on this point that I foresee on the part of Latin Governments in the New World a tendency to patronize the Catholic Church in order to use it for the secular purposes of nationalism and political unity. In this tendency there lurks the possibility of danger to the Church, but the Church will always be exposed to danger, danger from rulers who are openly hostile, and greater danger sometimes from rulers who pose as friends. The barque of Peter has to fear the doldrums as well as the hurricanes, and whether buffeted by the waves of persecution or menaced by the unhealthy calms of over-confidence, with its tendency towards routine and fossilization, and of State protection, with its tendency towards wealth, wordliness, and bureaucratism, it will never be free from peril till it reaches the haven.

Those American sects which wish to overthrow "Romanism" in Mexico are faced, therefore, by the horns of a dilemma. If Catholicity is wiped out and a persecution of Protestantism is begun, Mexico will certainly be invaded and annexed (or virtually annexed) by the United States, and if the present chaos continues much longer, the result will be the same—intervention and virtual annexation. And in both cases the Catholic Church will benefit, for in every part of Latin America where Uncle Sam has intervened, he has been very favourable to that Church. He has even been accused by *"Liberales"* in Nicaragua and Santo Domingo of having given to Catholic schools the revenues which used to keep up non-sectarian Government schools; and one has only to visit Nicaragua, Panama, Cuba, Haiti, or Santo Domingo in order to see how enormously the Catholic Church has gained by the *Pax Americana.* Moreover, in case Washington imposed peace on Mexico, the Mexican race would increase rapidly in numbers and send many emigrants to the United States, which already contains some three millions of Mexicans, generally very good Catholics; in short, Catholicism in America would benefit as Catholicism in Germany would benefit by Germany's annexation of Austria.

As for the actual situation in Mexico, things are worse as I finish this book, in June, 1928, than they were when I began it two months earlier. All over the Republic there is guerilla fighting, blowing up of railway bridges, burning of houses, killing of men, women and children.

Meanwhile, the chaos is so great that the soldiers are sometimes indistinguishable from the bandits. In April, 1928, a party of American tourists were held up and robbed by highwaymen near Mexico City while the guard of soldiers who had been given them as an escort sat on the side of the road and sang songs.

But while this comic opera business goes on in one part of the country, Government aeroplanes drop bombs on mountain villages in another part; and not all of these aeroplanes were bought in America; twelve of them are Bristol planes bought in England and sent thence to Vera Cruz. As these bombs are charged with poison gas, they sometimes wipe out non-combatants as well as combatants, women and children as well as men. It is said that 4,047 rebels have been executed since August, 1926, among them 16 women, not counting the priests and unarmed prisoners who were put to death. Meanwhile the parochial houses of the clergy are being rapidly converted into barracks by Presidential decree. One such decree, issued on May 4th, handed over to the army three of these houses in different States.

At the same time there are indications of a split among the persecutors, and, as I have already remarked, they may end by exterminating one another. Morones, the Labour leader, has menaced Obregón because he is not going to get enough of the spoils of office from the President-elect; the friendship between Calles and Obregón is cooling; there is discontent in the army; Mazcorro, the notorious head of the Secret Police, has been dismissed; and, on May 30, 1928, General José Álvarez, the President's chief of staff, who was so useful to his master on the occasion of Serrano's murder, was degraded and imprisoned for smuggling large quantities of silk into the country by the use of Calles' name.

Here I conclude this book on "Red Mexico." It has many defects of which no one is more aware than I am myself, but at all events I have endeavoured to treat the religion of an interesting people in what is, I trust, a sympathetic manner. English writers on Mexico and on all Latin America have a tendency to assume a superior tone and lay too much stress on material things, on mineral resources, on industry, on agriculture, on the pearl fisheries of La Paz, the winter tomatoes of Sonora, the fisheries of the Gulf of California, the coffee of Brazil, the copper of Peru, the beef and corn of Argentina. These writers have a tendency to laicize the concept of civilization,—*laicizar el concepto de civilización*, as a South American writer puts it—to reduce the processes of civilization to economic activities, agricultural, industrial, commercial and banking, to the actions of Generals and the indolences of statesmen.

"I think that the religion of a Christian people is a more important matter than all these things put together; and when I speak of religion I do not mean that artistic sentimentality which floods the souls of sensitive and cultured travellers when, guidebook in hand, they walk through ancient churches: the religion

I have in mind is a binding force, a stern discipline, and many things else, but a mere sentimentality it certainly is not. Even from a temporal point of view, Christianity is good for a nation. Misled by anti-Christian theories, mostly Marxian, the present rulers of Mexico are fighting against religion. They may overcome it in Mexico, but they will lose everything else as well. "First seek the Kingdom of God," etc., is as true in the negative as in the positive form. First abandon the Kingdom of God, and you will lose everything else. Mexico is losing everything. With their Christianity, which is almost gone, the Yaquis are losing civilization itself. In the wilder parts of Sonora, at Ónavas, Tecoripa, and Baroyeca, one finds the ruins of beautiful old mission churches which once served Indian congregations whose descendants are in the army (not a school of virtue) or in American mines and factories (not schools for virtue, either). Most of these Indians have practically reverted to paganism.

As for Calles and Co., they cannot lose religion, for they never had it, they cannot lose civilization, for they were never civilized.

The experiences of the persecuted Christians of Mexico must not, apparently, be written about in newspapers with large circulations, though these experiences seem to be a continuation of St. Paul's:

> "bruised, but not beaten; dismayed, yet not despairing; hunted, yet not fainting; stoned, but not slain—ever bearing about in our very body the killing of the Lord Jesus, so that the Life too of Jesus may be revealed in this our dying flesh!"

To me, who witnessed them, they certainly seemed to have that note of petrine Christianity which, according to its enemies, the Catholic Church so conspicuously lacks; and, to put it bluntly, the ministers of the vaguer and more emotional forms of American Protestantism in Mexico do not possess that particular note. Sometimes, after visiting hunted priests on the bleak, volcanic mountains surrounding the great, central table-land, I found such Protestant pastors comfortably installed with their families in the large cities, and listened, not without impatience, as they explained to me that "the law must be obeyed." They had given way to Calles on everything, they had grovelled in the dust before him, with the result that they were permitted to hold services in their churches, to keep their seminaries, to continue issuing their parish magazines and their controversial literature. One hears a good deal about the Anglo-Saxon's love of fair play, but these gentlemen seemed to me little better than ecclesiastical "blacklegs." They saw manifest injustice being done to a brother Christian,—injustice so manifest that it has called forth indignant denunciation from Agnostics both in the New World and in the Old,—but instead of coming to his assistance, they picked his pockets while the common enemy of all Christianity was dragging him on the hurdles to the Mexican Tyburn. Worse still, some of them entered the service of the persecutor. It is against the law for a clergyman of any Church to occupy a Government post, nevertheless several pastors, educated in America, occupy posts in the Calles Government, and frequently do propaganda work in favour of Calles among their co-religionists north of the Rio Grande. One of them is the Very Rev. Moisés Sáenz who was educated and ordained in the United States, and who is now Sub-Secretary of the Mexican Department of Education. In the time of Carranza many such pastors went so far as to accept commissions in the horde of banditti which that "General" described as his army; and a Mr. Warren, who at one time cherished the ambition of being the secretary of President Coolidge, raised two million dollars in the United States with the object of sending into Mexico missionaries who would start an intensive Protestant propaganda and support a schism.

But to confine myself to the comfortable contention of the arm-chair pastors that a Christian must obey the civil power in all things, this theory, if true, would blast the reputation of every martyr in the calendar. If the Christians in Pagan Rome had taken up this position, there would have been no necessity for

any of them to lay down his life; and, at a later period in ecclesiastical history, it was certainly not in these quavering accents
that Athanasius and Chrysostom, Ambrose and Hildebrand
spoke to the civil power.

In the preface to the second edition of my *Bolshevik Persecution of Christianity*, I pointed out that the same phenomenon
occurred in Russia, where several Protestant bodies have publicly swallowed the whole Communist programme without
turning a hair, whereas an inflexible *non possumus* came from
precisely that Christian body which is accused of practising
mental reservation, forgiving sins in advance, and practising all
kinds of trickery. It sometimes occurred to me while witnessing
such things, that the Catholic Church is a great dyke against a
turbulent sea of hate and unbelief, and that all sorts of ramshackle structures have been erected behind it, in shelter of it,
and out of the copious material quarried from its foundations;
and I often felt inclined to ask myself: "Where would all these
ramshackle structures be if, perchance, that dyke gave way?"

I lay down my pen with this persecution still going on, but I
cannot conclude without paying a final tribute to those who are
bearing the brunt of it, and more especially to the members of
the A.C.J.M. They are suffering from every form of discouragement, even from that worst discouragement of all, the knowledge that there are unworthy clerics of their own faith who
work against them, betray them, sell their blood to Calles. But
even that does not make them lose faith, for they know that
there has always been scandal, and that Saint Catherine of Siena
and other great saints described Christ's Body, that is the
Church, as suffering even from leprosies. Despite this supreme
discouragement, they continue their struggle, mindful of the
promise made by the great Apostle of the Gentiles:

> "Therefore play we not the coward; but even though our
> outward man be being worn away, yet from day to day our
> inner self is being renewed; for the trivial anguish of the
> moment works out for us overwhelmingly, overwhelmingly,
> an eternal weight of glory; for we look not on things visible,

but on things unseen. For but an hour the visible endureth: the Unseen is Eternal."

In the light of that great promise, their lesser discouragements are negligible; but one of them, which I try my best to remedy by means of this book, is that they die without a word of sympathy from the world, without drum or trumpet to signalize their going hence, without funeral volley over their graves. The great newspapers do not call them martyrs though that sacred word was used liberally enough and loosely enough ten years ago in a million newspaper articles, and is now to be found engraven on a million tombstones. I do not wish to say a word in disparagement of the young men, my comrades, who fell in the Great War, from which I emerged unscathed, but nobody would have laughed more heartily than they at the word martyr. The Mexican youths who died during the past year have had no eulogies written about them and no tombstones erected to them. The only notices they have had are surreptitiously printed cards like one which lies before me as I write:

On Thursday, the 19th of the present month, the youth, Salvador Gutiérrez Mora, gave his life heroically for our holy religion, at the age of twenty-two years. With great resignation, his mother and his brothers communicate to you this news.

"He that loseth his life for my sake shall find it."—Matthew, x, 39.

Tacubaya, May, 1928.

THE END

APPENDIX I

CRISTEROS IN RED MEXICO

1. The Spanish Heritage

Mexico is a vast Latin American country with great dispari-
ties, from its rough territory with almost all the climates, to its
deep-rooted economic imbalance that has played a key role in
its development. Historically, Mexico stands as the product of
both the formal Spanish Empire and pre-Columbian Cultures,
and to this day these heritages coexist, along with others from
Africa and Asia, creating a rich historical tradition.

Among the most important cultural contributions that Spaniards and others brought to Mexico are the Spanish language,
also known as Castilian, and the Catholic religion. The latter
would become a unifying element for the inhabitants of this
country, regardless of a generalized resistance by natives, who
after centuries of evangelization, adopted the Catholic faith on
their own terms adding elements from their own culture.

Winds of change arrived during the 19th century, welcomed
by some as cooling breezes and others as catastrophic tornados.
Mexico started this century with a revolution, known as the
Independence War, against its former masters, although after
three centuries of occupation local assimilation of the metropolis culture was mostly completed. When the formal New Spain
changed its name to Mexico, becoming a newborn Latin American nation, the country was already predominantly Catholic.

Political independence from the Spanish Crown did not
mean the end of military confrontations, because once freed,
when the future of the newborn nation could not reach general
consensus, Mexicans turned against themselves. During most of

the 19th century, Mexico submerged itself in a series of wars coming from both domestic and foreign fronts, affecting the population in many ways.

The wars brought a general state of bankruptcy and political unrest that divided the country, while at the same time its Catholic religion remained as a common link for the people. This was recognized by Porfirio Díaz, who rose to power in 1876, and occupied the presidential chair with almost no interruption for over thirty-one years, establishing a period of political stability, but at a cost to democracy. Díaz, an army officer who earned his reputation fighting during the French Intervention (1861–1867), was a declared liberal and a notable Freemason, and soon realized that to achieve peace Mexico needed to have economic, social, and religious stability.

During his long presidency he ended confrontation with the Catholic Church, opposing the liberal policies of his predecessors who stubbornly believed that Mexican modernity was only attainable by means of separating Church from State, and enforcing never-before seen anticlerical laws that sought to undermine the clergy's power at all levels. General Díaz was able to reach consensus with liberals, even the most extreme, to stop and in some cases reverse anticlerical measures that divided the country and brought social unrest. With him, the Mexican clergy and Catholics experienced a period of relative peace for some decades, ending with the advent of civil revolution in 1910.

2. The Mexican Revolution

By 1905, Porfirio Díaz's dictatorship showed signs of wear and tear, with high depreciation of the national currency, inflation and a reduction in living standards affecting everyone. As the French Intervention hero completed his seventieth year, collaborators and rivals from his own generation anxiously awaited their turn in power, knowing that Díaz would eventually retire from the presidency. Sensing dramatic changes to come, Díaz granted an interview in 1908 to James Creelman from *Pearson's Magazine*, a British-American publication, in which he reaffirmed his commitment to democracy, and his readiness to step down from the presidential chair if the Mexican people demanded it.

As soon as the declaration was made public, those eager to occupy his position manifested their intentions. However, unsurprisingly and in accordance with dictatorial practice, the experienced general did not endorse his declarations, claiming an absolute triumph over his opponents in the 1910 elections. In spite of this, the longing for democracy had already spread to politicians like Francisco I. Madero who strongly believed that Mexico's problems could be solved with democratic elections, and who eventually became the strongest political rival to Díaz.

When a peaceful transition proved to be impossible, Madero was imprisoned on Díaz's orders, but was still able to organize a national uprising starting on 20 November 1910. His call made such an impact nationwide that it became much more than a political quarrel, it was indeed a revolution. Battles between rebels and pro-government troops began in the northern part of the country and were soon followed in most of the territory, while the entire political regime was shaken at all levels: municipal, state and national. Díaz duly presented his resignation as Mexican president to the National Congress, and went into exile in France, where he died in 1915.

The first phase of the Revolution ended when Francisco I. Madero was designated new president of Mexico after extraordinary elections were held in November of 1911. However, as had happened a century before in 1821 when the war against Spain divided the country, Mexicans were once more unable to unite under a common leader. Just one year and three months after his triumph as president of the republic, a coup d'état ended both Madero's mandate and his life.

Due to the number and length of the battles, the second phase of the Mexican Revolution, after Madero's assassination, involved more combatants and created more casualties than the first. Victoriano Huerta, who organized the coup against

Madero, had more enemies than sympathizers, and those initially hesitant of joining the revolution found a valid cause in fighting the "usurper," as Huerta became to be known.

National unrest against Huerta propelled politicians and non-politicians to organize their armies. This gave the Mexican Revolution one of its main traits, namely that everybody was free to prove their beliefs by fighting in the battlefields. A revolutionary could be a career politician, a civilian with no military training, or a newborn guerrilla leader organizing his own faction or adhering to an existing group. This proved to be both positive and negative, because it created mobility but also demanded no ideological commitment from most of the rebels. Many men stayed together just for a time, changing sides to their liking or convenience, when they saw better chances to win with another leader, or when their formal chief died.

Over time, many initial leaders who survived, together with their troops, joined other rebel forces, which in turn amalgamated into larger factions ultimately becoming the embodiment of the Mexican Revolution. Men like Venustiano Carranza, Pascual Orozco, Emiliano Zapata and Francisco Villa had their own armies with hundreds of men and women following their orders. They all joined the revolution after Madero rebelled against dictator Porfirio Díaz, and were outraged with his assassination in 1913.

The years following the coup d'état were unsettled at all levels. The railroad system, an emblem of the Díaz regime, changed hands constantly from rebels to federal troops who attacked both civilians and non-civilians, and seriously disrupted communications and trade. Roads were as dangerous as railways, and those who risked their lives by leaving their towns often regretted it. Without a settled and peaceful state, the national currency depreciated even more and the whole country sank into a deep financial and social crisis, which took several years to rectify, before achieving favorable diplomatic recognition by the world's major nations.

Venustiano Carranza's official arrival to presidency in 1917, but *de facto* since 1915, seemed to consolidate the revolution, although in reality it prolonged instability. By this time, guerrilla leaders like Emiliano Zapata and Pancho Villa, with thousands of followers in their armies, expressed their animosity to Carranza and his plan for a nation, and continued the war. This was evident when a new Constitution was being voted and factions increased their opposition.

The Constitution became effective on February 5, 1917, legitimizing Carranza and his followers in power. It was a great accomplishment for a leader like Venustiano Carranza, who strongly believed that the real character of the revolution had to be expressed in laws reflecting the political goals of the revolutionaries, and legitimizing the ideals of those who had taken up arms against the dictator Porfirio Díaz.

As a new political class emerged from the Revolution, the country regressed even more into political and economic chaos. Factions claimed their territories, and civilians got caught in-between battles in both rural and urban settings, violence could explode at any moment and it did. Carranza may have won the legal battle, but like Ignacio Madero, was unable to retain power. He was assassinated in 1920 as a result of a coup d'état, three years after becoming the forty-fourth president.

By the time of Carranza's death some of his formal followers had already risen to prominence as members of the Constitutional Army (*Ejército Constitucionalista*), the triumphant faction of the Revolution. At least three key members of this army, Adolfo de la Huerta, Álvaro Obregón, and Plutarco Elías Calles, were born in the northern state of Sonora, bordering the American state of Arizona, which lead to the group's name as the Sonoran Group, characterized by its military efficiency and good weaponry.

In order to claim their triumph, the Sonoran Group had to eliminate the other factions. The two who stood up were Francisco Villa and his Northern Division (*División del Norte*) and Emiliano Zapata with the Liberation Army of the South

(*Ejército Libertador del Sur*). Neither had formal military train-ing, and both came from the working class. Trained military alumni of the Mexican military academy and elite members considered them guerrilla leaders prone to robbery, who lacked ideals and who only joined the revolution for material gain. Their followers saw them as the embodiment of the revolution's ideals and authentic heroes fighting for justice. A series of sig-nificant defeats and perhaps a little bit of luck for their enemies accelerated the fall of Villa and Zapata's contingents. The latter was betrayed and murdered in 1919, while Pancho Villa shared the same fate in 1923.

With the two main opponents out of combat, the Sonoran Group rose to undisputed power. The first of the Sonorans to occupy the presidency was Adolfo de la Huerta, a former mem-ber of Venustiano Carranza's cabinet, whose duty was to pre-pare for the arrival of Álvaro Obregón in December 1920. In return the new president designated him in charge of the Office for the Treasury and Public Credit, a position held for three years after his resignation due to severe disagreements with the new president, which lead him to break ties with his former friends Obregón and Calles, going into exile to California.

Presidential elections were held in 1924 with the triumph of another member of the Sonoran Group, Plutarco Elías Calles, who received the power from Álvaro Obregón. The two politi-cians, equally renowned for their military triumphs as for their corruption, controlled Mexico's destiny for the upcoming years. As prominent members of the winning faction, they successfully adapted to the post-revolution conditions, appointing their cab-inets with unconditional politicians and ex-militaries.

The most tangible example of the Sonoran's corruption was the re-election of Álvaro Obregón for the 1928's presidential term. In order for this to happen they manipulated the Legisla-tive Congress, passing a law that allowed Obregón's new term. His supporters argued that it was "not" a re-election since Elías Calles preceded Obregón whose presidential periods were not consecutive.

Presidential elections were held in July 1928, with the undisputed triumph of Obregón. Sixteen days later while attending a lunch in his honor he was assassinated by José León Toral, a young member of the National League for the Defense of Religious Liberty. Obregón's ambition for power claimed the highest possible price: his life. Obregón has been the only elected president in Mexican history to be gunned down before arriving to office.

With Obregón's death, Plutarco Elías Calles became the only member in power from the Sonoran Group and the path was cleared for his absolute control of the country. This period is known as the *Maximato*, with Calles as the maximum or highest leader in Mexico. He exercised it with no limits, disguising it by imposing his will in all realms including three presidents of the republic, the 48th, 49th and 50th, all unconditional collaborators.

However, his power suffered an irreparable loss in 1934 when one of his collaborators, Lázaro Cárdenas, became the 51st Mexican president and changed what seemed to be a continuation of Calles's power, for a new era free from his control. Taking advantage of his health problems, he proceeded to eliminate Calles's allies in the congress and in political positions, and forced Calles to leave the country and go into exile to California where he remained for five years. Lázaro Cárdenas' daring move ensured no interference from Calles and his supporters. It inaugurated a new era in the political history of Mexico, one with no re-elections and with stability for years to come. Cárdenas sought to solve economic problems, nationalizing mineral resources and the railroad, and his mandate became one of the most important in the post-revolution era.

3. The Cristero War (1926–1929)

This dramatic uprising has deep roots in national history. For years, the official history enforced by the government erased it from books, and it was not mentioned. Even today there are historians who, for various ideological reasons, dismiss the rebellion as unimportant, claiming that it never reached national scale. Now, after a tangible change in the relations between Church and Mexican State, the historical value of the Cristero War has been reconsidered and generally given its real dimension as one of the bloodiest and most unequal ever to exist in national history. The name of this war comes from its self-proclaimed participants "servants of Christ," and maliciously shortened by its enemies as *Cristeros*. Jean Meyer, one of the most eminent authorities of this war, described it as a "David versus Goliath war." It was the last major, armed movement of the 20th century in Mexico. It claimed the lives of thousands, and demonstrated that the revolutionary project did not represent all citizens, as previously claimed.

Tensions between Mexican Catholics and the federal government, the two protagonists of the Cristero War, began once the new Constitution was enforced by the winning faction of the 1910 Revolution. The seeds of rebellion were planted during the years after it became effective on February 5, 1917, and it showed real signs of growth by the beginning of the 1920s. Although military hostilities occurred from 1926 to 1929, the unarmed phase of the war began when the Constitution was being voted on, from December 1916 to January 1917. The historical context of the Cristero War is that of the Sonoran Group's triumph and their intolerance of public criticism at any cost. It lasted during the presidency of Plutarco Elías Calles from 1924 to 1928, ending in 1929 when the interim president Emilio Portes Gil, ironically appointed by Calles himself, signed the official agreements to end the war.

The 1910 Revolution changed the existing dynamic between the Church and the State. Dictator Porfirio Díaz maintained a stable relationship with the Catholic Church during his more than three decades in power, by relaxing and not enforcing the anticlerical laws that his Jacobin friends included in the liberal Constitution of 1857. The Church vehemently opposed the liberal measures, such as expropriation and destruction of their properties, expulsion of several religious orders, closing of cloisters and seminaries, as well as the creation of public schools free from any doctrine, in addition to other government constraints. Some measures were enforced at any cost and others were stopped, but their existence divided the country for several years until Díaz put an end to this soured relationship.

When Díaz was forced to renounce his long presidency and went into exile in France, the new leadership sought to enforce liberalism at all costs, causing tensions with the Church to return. The new Constitution of 1917 turned out to be revolutionary by promising greater equality in labor, ownership and national property. The state believed that the Constitution was the only way to gain stability and to establish social conditions aimed at controlling the people. It was not an easy task and the government faced strong resistance from factions who lost the war, and from new enemies who, on religious grounds, rejected the plans imposed by the new political regime.

These new enemies were the Catholics who felt attacked by the government's anticlericalism enforced by the Constitution, particularly in articles 3, 5, 24, 27 and 130. For them their faith was under attack, their needs neglected, life as they knew it to be dramatically altered, and their life aspirations ignored. They started planning a crusade against the state, angered by the measures to limit the activities and influence of the Church in public life. Resentment grew with the government's intolerance and repression of those who dared to publicly manifest any resistance.

Catholics on one side and government on the other began to increasingly antagonize each other until it became clear that a greater confrontation was soon to follow. The first step taken by the Catholic organizations such as the Catholic Association of Mexican Youth (ACJM) and the National League for the Defense of Religious Liberty (LNDLR) was to organize street protests and to use friendly press to inform others about the way in which the government sought to attack their Catholic way of life. Articles and adverts were printed in newspapers denouncing abuses, while thousands of pamphlets were distributed in major cities like Mexico and Guadalajara asking for solidarity.

When peaceful manifestations resulted only in violent repression, with participants incarcerated, tortured and killed, members and non-members of Catholics organizations planned more active protests. Federal properties were damaged, commercial blockades were launched preventing citizens buying non-essential products, and obstructing the use of government services. In addition, Catholic authorities did their part by, from the pulpit, constantly rallying people against injustice, and what they perceived as a campaign for Mexico's de-Christianization.

At stake were confiscation of the Catholic Church's properties, including churches, convents and schools, banning of several religious orders and religious vows, schools, and a strict limit on the number of priests in the country, expelling from Mexico all those of foreign origin, with no exceptions. Included was the representative of the Vatican, Monsignor Ernesto E. Philippi, who left the country on January 13, 1923. Following his departure, Mexico broke off diplomatic relations with the Vatican, which was extremely troubling for the national clergy loyal to the Pope, as well for Catholic citizens.

Disturbing for the Catholics were articles 3, 5, 24, 27 and 130. The 3rd article of the Constitution, through which secular, non-confessional education was established, while at the same time it did not recognize any academic degrees from Catholic schools (hundreds of which were closed). All of a sudden, citizens educated in schools and universities administrated by the clergy had no recognized qualifications and were considered illiterate by the government. The 5th article outlawed all monastic orders and the seclusion vow, as such things were perceived in direct contradiction to article 1 which guaranteed human rights and forbade slavery. Catholics also fought against article 24, which declared that there was no official religion in Mexico, and that religious ceremonies of a public nature had to be indoors only, forbidding at the same time ancient pilgrimages and any kind of festivities linked to the Catholic faith. Article 27 made all churches national property, which effectively turned government agents into custodians and in numerous cases led to widespread pillaging. Finally, article 130 declared the separation between Church and State, with clergy members prevented from holding public office, while religious associations had to comply with all conditions imposed by the government, which included recognition of only civil marriages, something still effective in Mexico today.

Street protests and other forms of peaceful resistance failed to revoke the desired articles, which coupled with the government's extreme anticlericalism, made civil war inevitable. Violence erupted when President Plutarco Elías Calles announced the *Law for Reforming the Penal Code* (June 14, 1926). Known as Calles's law, this was an attempt by the state to exercise absolute control over the Church by reforming the criminal code of justice in order to increase sanctions for offenders in religious matters. Clergy members faced serious punishment for "crimes" such as wearing clerical garb outside the church, or for voicing any political opinion.

Calles's law was also built upon the 130th article of the Constitution which established that only Mexican citizens could perform religious services. The direct result of such measures was that the number of priests, friars, and nuns in the country dramatically dropped, as hundreds were expelled from Mexico in a very short time. The law ordered all priests who wanted to celebrate mass to obtain a special license from the government, and also required priests to register and report constantly to local authorities. The number of authorized priests diminished so dramatically that in some cases there was only one priest for every 6,000 Catholics. Some governors, particularly Tomás Garrido Canabal in the southern state of Tabasco, went as far as to demand that Catholic priests be married by the state in order to officiate, confiscated all Church properties, and organized campaigns of destruction of religious art and of churches, by brigades of citizens of all ages. Canabal can easily be considered as the most extreme antireligious political figure in Mexican history, as his hate for the Catholic faith knew no limits.

The adoption of the Calles law led to an unprecedented response from the Mexican bishops. On July 31, 1926, the hierarchy ordered the suspension of all religious worship. Although some churches remained open as they had been declared national property, priests refused to celebrate the liturgy or any other sacraments. The tabernacles (locked boxes in which the Eucharist is kept) were displayed empty on altar tables, and many religious sculptures and paintings were covered or hidden. Most parishioners were unaware that such measures had been taken by the hierarchy, and immediately blamed the authorities. Rumors quickly spread that the government wanted to prevent priests from doing their job. Church authorities did nothing to dispel such rumors, and the anger grew rapidly against the government.

The first actions were implemented by the Catholic Association of Mexican Youth (ACJM) and the National League for the Defense of Religious Liberty (LNDLR). They played a fundamental role in channeling the anger of the population to violent actions. When religious worship was suspended by the clergy as a way to protest against the Calles's Law, it inevitably triggered the first physical confrontations. The earliest were in 1926 in the state of Jalisco (western Mexico), where parishioners took up arms and went out to the fields, while others protested in their towns and cities against the government's threats, warnings, and actual repression.

The violence that erupted in 1926 was familiar to most citizens who had experienced more than a decade of war with the Mexican Revolution. Memories of battles, cities under siege, and political chaos, were still alive. The main states in the Cristero rebellion, Jalisco and Michoacán, had already witnessed ravaging for over a decade. The rebellion took the form of a guerrilla warfare and remained largely restricted to central-western Mexico—the states of Jalisco (as the epicenter), Nayarit, Michoacán, Guanajuato, Querétaro, the State of Mexico, Aguascalientes, San Luis Potosi, Guerrero and Colima. While most other states in the south-east, such as Veracruz, Tabasco, Yucatán, Campeche, Quintana Roo, Chiapas and Oaxaca, or in the north (Chihuahua, Nuevo León, Sonora, Sinaloa and Baja California) remained relatively at peace between 1926 and 1929, archival and oral sources provide convincing evidence that most of them experienced some outbreaks of violence during that period. In other words, despite its undeniably regional character, the Cristero War had national importance, for anticlericalism was a federal policy, and so were the strict measures targeting Catholics that lived in the entire nation.

On the other hand, looking at this war at a regional level helps to understand it better, for the violence erupted in the Jalisco-Los Altos region, which to this day remains one of the most profoundly Catholic areas of Mexico. Important religious images worshipped in this land include Our Lady of the Rosary of Talpa, the Virgin of Zapopan and the famous Virgin of San Juan de los Lagos, named after this town and second in the number of pilgrims after the Guadalupe Virgin. The lives of Catholics in Jalisco were, perhaps more than in other parts of Mexico, deeply disturbed by the anticlerical measures.

The severe control of the churches by the government, considered to this day the property of the State, as well as the closing of Catholic schools, seminaries and convents, caused such an outrage that many who were in principle against violence, joined the cause, becoming Cristeros and leaving behind distressing chronicles of modern martyrdom. The regional character of the war also explains the irregular and intermittent battles. At the onset of the rebellion, war funds were scarce and needs far exceeded income. Many clergy and wealthy parishioners donated money, but more was needed. The shortage of money may explain, at least in part, why the rebellion never attained a national scale. Whenever they were short of funds, or defeated by superior forces, the rebels withdrew into the nearby hills and places which were inaccessible to non-locals. In this sense, the geography of Jalisco was favorable for the rebels, although it also made them vulnerable to federal army attacks.

Cristeros fought mainly for what they perceived to be the salvation of their souls. They strongly believed that what Calles and his government wanted was to erase completely the Catholic religion from Mexico. It was not a political fight, since rebels in the years of 1926 to 1929 show no interest in imposing a presidential candidate, or a political party. President Plutarco Elías Calles and many members of his cabinet strongly believed that the future of Mexico and the progress of the nation rested on a strong state and a stable government respected (and feared) by all citizens. The laws they adopted were meant to accelerate that progress, but instead turned the Church and many Catholics into staunch adversaries of what was theoretically meant to be for the benefit of all citizens.

The official position of the hierarchy, cardinals and bishops, was to refuse and condemn violence at all costs. They were ordered to follow the canonical prohibition and the Pope's orders of not showing support to any form of physical violence. When many could no longer express their political opinions and their lives were at risk, they left the country. However, hundreds of others, members of the middle and lower clergy, who had the most contact with people, joined the war and became Cristeros as well. The hierarchy threatened members of the middle and lower clergy with disciplinary measures, including excommunication, for joining the rebellion, especially when they became commandants of their factions. They constantly warned them about the risks of violating both the tenets of Christian doctrine and the Pope's orders. But many simply ignored such warnings, and, like the Jesuit priest Miguel Agustín Pro (1891–1927), chose to fight with all means available to them. Some actually took the weapons, while at the same time hearing confessions, administering the Eucharist and Extreme Unction in the fields, before and after the battles. There are many stories of martyrdoms, the most vivid of which is that of Father Agustín Pro, who was executed without trial after being tortured. He was beatified on September 25, 1988, soon followed by others, such as José María Hurtado (1888–1927), beatified by Pope John Paul II in 1992, and then canonized in 2000. Also canonized at that time was Cristóbal Magallanes Jara (1869–1927), who, like Pro, was executed without trial on trumped-up charges of inciting rebellion, even though he had written and preached against armed rebellion.

The exact number of casualties during the Cristero War remains unknown, but most estimates have around 90,000 people, on both sides. The rebels did not have access to advanced weapons or to standard medical care, but they were driven by the thought that God's plan for them was to triumph over Calles and his army, saving Mexico from becoming a non-religious country. Ironically the leader of the Cristero's army was a non-Catholic career military, Enrique Gorostieta Velarde. His death in 1929 marked the beginning of the end of this war despite some remarkable successes against the federal troops.

The Cristeros could not achieve the triumph over Calles and his army, about which they had initially dreamed. Without any controversy the war ended because of diplomacy, not military victories. Instrumental in bringing the war to an end was a clever Presbyterian, Dwight Whitney Morrow, who in 1927, had been appointed American ambassador to Mexico by President John Calvin Coolidge. Morrow arrived in Mexico at the beginning of the war and befriended President Calles, which allowed him to look for solutions to the conflict. Morrow was greatly assisted by John J. Burke (1875–1936), a Paulist priest, who served at that time as the general secretary of the National Catholic Welfare Council in the United States. Equally helpful proved to be the president who succeeded Calles, Emilio Portes Gil, who was elected in 1928. Portes Gil did not share the radically anticlerical views of his predecessor, and was already looking for means to bring reconciliation. The hierarchy also looked for ways to bring the conflict to an end. Official documents and letters between the Vatican and the Mexican cardinals and bishops show that the latter had constantly sought peace between 1927 and 1929.

By 1928, it was clear that the rebellion had no future, both on economic and moral grounds. The federal position had also sufficiently softened by 1929 for peace negotiations to begin. Such negotiations between President Portes Gil and the leaders of the Church in Mexico took place between June 12 and June 21, 1929, with Ambassador Morrow as mediator. On Sunday, June 30, 1929, churches in Mexico were reopened for worship and the war officially ended on July 21, 1929, with the signing of the agreements known as the *Arreglos*. Leopoldo Ruiz y Flores, Archbishop of Morelia (1900–1941) and Pascual Díaz y Barreto, Archbishop of Mexico City (1929–1936) put their signatures on the document ordering a cease-fire, next to the signature of President Emilio Portes Gil. Priests nominated by hierarchical superiors were required to register with the government, religious instruction would be permitted in the churches (but not in schools), and clergy members could petition the government for reforming the laws. The Church recuperated its properties, even though under the law the Church was still not allowed to own real estate, and several facilities remained federal property. To the great dismay of most Cristeros, the *Arreglos* represented therefore a compromise, which brought little, if any change to the controversial articles of the 1917 Constitution. Some Cristeros continued fighting as outlaws, even when threatened with excommunication by the Church. Ecclesiastical authorities demanded that fighters surrender and hand over their weapons to local authorities. With an agreement signed under what they perceived to be disadvantageous terms, many Catholics felt betrayed by their own clergy. Resentment lasted for decades, and many thought of alternative roads of resistance in the following decades.

Despite its relative brevity, the Cristero War had a long-lasting impact on Mexican political and cultural life, particularly for Catholics. Cristeros, among other Catholic groups, represent a fundamental component of the post-revolutionary religious counterculture of 20th and early 21st century Mexico. Their cause, glorified by many sacrifices, including martyrdom, has gained the Cristeros a special place in Mexican political life. Much of the violence against public school teachers between 1931 and 1940 was perpetrated by disgruntled, former Cristero rebels, although the Calles law was repealed in 1934 under President Lázaro Cárdenas. Much of that violence was caused by the fact that Cárdenas's government continued to apply article 3 of the 1917 Constitution, which was amended in 1934 to promote Socialist ideals in schools. This caused another reaction by Catholics from central and western Mexico, who reorganized under the movement named *Sinarquismo*, founded in 1937 and planned as a civil unarmed resistance, which grew in notoriety until 1940, when President Manuel Ávila Camacho, a self-declared believer, changed some of Cárdenas's anticlerical measures.

The Cristero War has been ignored for several decades by historians and educators, mainly because of the official anticlerical policy of the Institutional Revolutionary Party (PRI), founded by Calles as a social-democrat organization, which held power in Mexico for more than seven decades (1929–1990). The Cristero War is still far from gaining appropriate recognition in modern Mexico. However, under Presidents Vicente Fox (2000–2006) and Felipe Calderón (2006–2012), members of the National Action Party (PAN), a Christian Democrat organization that clearly voices its Catholic faith, the Cristero rebellion has finally begun to be publicly mentioned in both political discourse and history textbooks, a major step towards the recognition of one of the bloodiest and most unequal wars in Mexican history.

María Concepción Márquez Sandoval,
Ph.D. Latin American History, University of Arizona.

Further reading:

• David C. Bailey. *Viva Cristo Rey!: The Cristero Rebellion and the Church-State Conflict in Mexico*. University of Texas Press, 2013.

• Jean Meyer. *The Cristero Rebellion: The Mexican People Between Church and State 1926–1929*. Cambridge University Press, 2013.

• Jim Tuck. *The Holy War in Los Altos: A Regional Analysis of Mexico's Cristero Rebellion*. University of Arizona Press, 1983.

• Alan Knight. *The Mexican Revolution, Volume 2: Counter-revolution and Reconstruction*. Lincoln: University of Nebraska Press, 1990.

APPENDIX II

INIQUIS AFFLICTISQUE

Encyclical of Pope Pius XI on the persecution of the Church in Mexico to the Venerable Brethren, the Patriarchs, Primates, Archbishops, Bishops, and other Ordinaries in Peace and Communion with the Apostolic See.

I N SPEAKING to the Sacred College of Cardinals at the Consistory of last December, We pointed out that there existed no hope or possibility of relief from the sad and unjust conditions under which the Catholic religion exists today in Mexico except it be by a "special act of Divine Mercy." You, Venerable Brothers, did not delay to make your own and approve Our convictions and Our wishes in this regard, made known to you on so many occasions, for by every means within your power you urged all the faithful committed to your pastoral care to implore by instant prayers the Divine Founder of the Church that He bring some relief from the heavy burden of these great evils.

2. We designedly use the words "the heavy burden of these great evils" for certain of Our children, deserters from the army of Jesus Christ and enemies of the Common Father of all, have ordered and are continuing up to the present hour a cruel persecution against their own brethren, Our most beloved children of Mexico. If in the first centuries of our era and at other periods in history Christians were treated in a more barbarous fashion than now, certainly in no place or at no time has it happened before that a small group of men has so outraged the rights of God and of the Church as they are now doing in Mexico, and

this without the slightest regard for the past glories of their country, with no feelings of pity for their fellow-citizens. They have also done away with the liberties of the majority and in such a clever way that they have been able to clothe their lawless actions with the semblance of legality.

3. Naturally, We do not wish that either you or the faithful should fail to receive from Us a solemn testimonial of Our gratitude for the prayers which, according to Our intention were poured forth in private and at public functions. It is most important, too, that these prayers which have been so powerful an aid to Us should be continued, and even increased, with renewed fervor. It is assuredly not in the power of man to control the course of events or of history, nor can he direct them as he may desire to the welfare of society by changing either the minds or hearts of his fellow-men. Such action, however, is well within the power of God, for He without doubt can put an end, if He so desires, to persecutions of this kind. Nor must you conclude, Venerable Brothers, that all your prayers have been in vain simply because the Mexican Government, impelled by its fanatical hatred of religion, continued to enforce more harshly and violently from day to day its unjust laws. The truth is that the clergy and the great majority of the faithful have been so strengthened in their longsuffering resistance to these laws by such an abundant shower of divine grace that they have been enabled thereby to give a glorious example of heroism. They have justly merited, too, that We, in a solemn document executed by Our Apostolic authority, should make known this fortitude to the whole Catholic world.

4. Last month on the occasion of the beatification of many martyrs of the French Revolution, spontaneously the Catholics of Mexico came to Our thoughts, for they, like those martyrs, have remained firm in their resolution to resist in all patience the unreasonable behests and commands of their persecutors rather than cut themselves off from the unity of the Church or

refuse obedience to this Apostolic See. Marvelous indeed is the glory of the Divine Spouse of Christ who, through the course of the centuries, can depend, without fail, upon a brave and generous offspring ever ready to suffer prisons, stripes, and even death itself for the holy liberty of the Church!

5. It is scarcely necessary, Venerable Brothers, to go back very far in order to narrate the sad calamities which have fallen upon the Church of Mexico. It is sufficient to recall that the frequent revolutions of modern times have ended in the majority of cases in trials for the Church and persecutions of religion. Both in 1914 and in 1915 men who seemed veritably inspired by the barbarism of former days persecuted the clergy, both secular and regular, and the sisters. They rose up against holy places and every object used in divine worship and so ferocious were they that no injury, no ignominy, no violence was too great to satisfy their persecuting mania.

6. Referring now to certain notorious facts concerning which We have already raised Our voice in solemn protest and which even the daily press recorded at great length, there is no need to take up much space in telling you of certain deplorable events which occurred even in the very recent past with reference to Our Apostolic Delegates to Mexico. Without the slightest regard for justice, for solemn promises given, or for humanity itself, one of these Apostolic Delegates was driven out of the country; another, who because of illness had left the Republic for a short time, was forbidden to return, and the third was also treated in a most unfriendly manner and forced to leave. Surely there is no one who cannot understand that such acts as these, committed against illustrious personages who were both ready and willing to bring about peace, must be construed as a great affront to their dignity as Archbishops, to the high office which they filled, and particularly to Our authority which they represented.

7. Unquestionably the events just cited are grave and deplorable. But the examples of despotic power which We will now pass in review, Venerable Brothers, are beyond all compare, contrary to the rights of the Church, and most injurious as well to the Catholics of Mexico.

8. In the first place, let us examine the law of 1917, known as the "Political Constitution" of the federated Republic of Mexico. For our present purposes it is sufficient to point out that after declaring the separation of Church and State the Constitution refuses to recognize in the Church, as if she were an individual devoid of any civil status, all her existing rights and interdicts to her the acquisition of any rights whatsoever in the future. The civil authority is given the right to interfere in matters of divine worship and in the external discipline of the Church. Priests are put on the level of professional men and of laborers but with this important difference, that they must be not only Mexicans by birth and cannot exceed a certain number specified by law, but are at the same time deprived of all civil and political rights. They are thus placed in the same class with criminals and the insane. Moreover, priests not only must inform the civil authorities but also a commission of ten citizens whenever they take possession of a church or are transferred to another mission. The vows of religious, religious orders, and religious congregations are outlawed in Mexico. Public divine worship is forbidden unless it take place within the confines of a church and is carried on under the watchful eye of the Government. All church buildings have been declared the property of the state. Episcopal residences, diocesan offices, seminaries, religious houses, hospitals, and all charitable institutions have been taken away from the Church and handed over to the state. As a matter of fact, the Church can no longer own property of any kind. Everything that it possessed at the period when this law was passed has now become the property of the state. Every citizen, moreover, has the right to denounce before the law any person whom he thinks is holding in his own name property for

the Church. All that is required in order to make such action legal is a mere presumption of guilt. Priests are not allowed by law to inherit property of any kind except it be from persons closely related to them by blood. With reference to marriage, the power of the Church is not recognized. Every marriage between Catholics is considered valid if contracted validly according to the prescriptions of the civil code.

9. Education has been declared free, but with these important restrictions: both priests and religious are forbidden to open or to conduct elementary schools. It is not permitted to teach children their religion even in a private school. Diplomas or degrees conferred by private schools under control of the Church possess no legal value and are not recognized by the state. Certainly, Venerable Brothers, the men who originated, approved, and gave their sanction to such a law either are totally ignorant of what rights pertain *jure divino* to the Church as a perfect society, established as the ordinary means of salvation for mankind by Jesus Christ, Our Redeemer and King, to which He gave the full liberty of fulfilling her mission on earth (such ignorance seems incredible today after twenty centuries of Christianity and especially in a Catholic nation and among men who have been baptized, unless in their pride and foolishness they believe themselves able to undermine and destroy the "House of the Lord which has been solidly constructed and strongly built on the living rock") or they have been motivated by an insane hatred to attempt anything within their power in order to harm the Church. How was it possible for the Archbishops and Bishops of Mexico to remain silent in the face of such odious laws?

10. Immediately after their publication the hierarchy of Mexico protested in kind but firm terms against these laws, protests which Our Immediate Predecessor ratified, which were approved as well by the whole hierarchies of other countries, as well as by a great majority of individual bishops from all over

the world, and which finally were confirmed even by Us in a letter of consolation of the date of the second of February, 1926, which We addressed to the Bishops of Mexico. The Bishops hoped that those in charge of the Government, after the first outburst of hatred, would have appreciated the damage and danger which would accrue to the vast majority of the people from the enforcement of those articles of the Constitution restrictive of the liberty of the Church and that, therefore, out of a desire to preserve peace they would not insist on enforcing these articles to the letter, or would enforce them only up to a certain point, thus leaving open the possibility of a *modus vivendi*, at least for the time being.

11. In spite of the extreme patience exhibited in these circumstances by both the clergy and laity, an attitude which was the result of the Bishops' exhorting them to moderation in all things, every hope of a return to peace and tranquility was dissipated, and this as a direct result of the law promulgated by the President of the Republic on the second of July, 1926, by virtue of which practically no liberty at all was left the Church. As a matter of fact, the Church was barely allowed to exist. The exercise of the sacred ministry was hedged about by the severest penalties as if it were a crime worthy of capital punishment. It is difficult, Venerable Brothers, to express in language how such perversion of civil authority grieves Us. For whosoever reveres, as all must, God the Creator and Our Beloved Redeemer, whosoever will obey the laws of Holy Mother Church, such a man, We repeat, such a man is looked on as a malefactor, as guilty of a crime; such a man is considered fit only to be deprived of all civil rights; such a man can be thrown into prison along with other criminals. With what justice can We apply to the authors of these enormities the words which Jesus Christ spoke to the leaders of the Jews: "This is your hour, and the power of darkness." (Luke XXII, 53)

12. The most recent law which has been promulgated as merely an interpretation of the Constitution is as a matter of fact much worse than the original law itself and makes the enforcement of the Constitution much more severe, if not almost intolerable. The President of the Republic and the members of his ministry have insisted with such ferocity on the enforcement of these laws that they do not permit the governors of the different states of the Confederation, the civil authorities, or the military commanders to mitigate in the least the rigors of the persecution of the Catholic Church. Insult, too, is added to persecution. Wicked men have tried to place the Church in a bad light before the people; some, for example, uttering the most brazen lies in public assemblies. But when a Catholic tries to answer them, he is prevented from speaking by catcalls and personal insults hurled at his head. Others use hostile newspapers in order to obscure the truth and to malign "Catholic Action."

13. If, at the beginning of the persecution, Catholics were able to make a defense of their religion in the public press by means of articles which made clear the truth and answered the lies and errors of their enemies, it is now no longer permitted these citizens, who love their country just as much as other citizens do, to raise their voices in protest. As a matter of fact, they are not even allowed to express their sorrow over the injuries done to the Faith of their fathers and to the liberty of divine worship. We, however, moved profoundly as We are by the consciousness of the duties imposed upon Us by our Apostolic office, will cry out to heaven, Venerable Brothers, so that the whole Catholic world may hear from the lips of the Common Father of all the story of the insane tyranny of the enemies of the Church, on the one hand, and on the other that of the heroic virtue and constancy of the bishops, priests, religious congregations, and laity of Mexico.

14. All foreign priests and religious men have been expelled from the country. Schools for the religious education of boys

and girls have been closed, either because they are known publicly under a religious name or because they happen to possess a statue or some other religious object. Many seminaries likewise, schools, insane asylums, convents, institutions connected with churches have been closed. In practically all the states of the Republic the number of priests who may exercise the sacred ministry has been limited and fixed at the barest minimum. Even these latter are not allowed to exercise their sacred office unless they have beforehand registered with the civil authorities and have obtained permission from them so to function. In certain sections of the country restrictions have been placed on the ministry of priests which, if they were not so sad, would be laughable in the extreme. For example, certain regulations demand that priests must be of an age fixed by law, that they must be civilly married, and they are not allowed to baptize except with flowing water. In one of the states of the Confederation it has been decreed that only one bishop is permitted to live within the territory of said state, by reason of which law two other bishops were constrained to exile themselves from their dioceses. Moreover, because of circumstances imposed upon them by law, some bishops have had to leave their diocese, others have been forced to appear before the courts, several were arrested, and practically all the others live from day to day in imminent danger of being arrested.

15. Again, every Mexican citizen who is engaged in the education of children or of youth, or holds any public office whatsoever, has been ordered to make known publicly whether he accepts the policies of the President and approves of the war which is now being waged on the Catholic Church. The majority of these same individuals were forced, under threat of losing their positions, to take part, together with the army and laboring men, in a parade sponsored by the Regional Confederation of the Workingmen of Mexico, a socialist organization. This parade took place in Mexico City and in other towns of the Republic on the same day. It was followed by impious speeches

to the populace. The whole procedure was organized to obtain, by means of these public outcries and the applause of those who took part in it, and by heaping all kinds of abuse on the Church, popular approval of the acts of the President.

16. But the cruel exercise of arbitrary power on the part of the enemies of the Church has not stopped at these acts. Both men and women who defended the rights of the Church and the cause of religion, either in speeches or by distributing leaflets and pamphlets, were hurried before the courts and sent to prison. Again, whole colleges of canons were rushed off to jail, the aged being carried there in their beds. Priests and laymen have been cruelly put to death in the very streets or in the public squares which front the churches. May God grant that the responsible authors of so many grave crimes return soon to their better selves and throw themselves in sorrow and with true contrition on the divine mercy; We are convinced that this is the noble revenge on their murderers which Our children who have been so unjustly put to death are now asking from God.

17. We think it well at this point, Venerable Brothers, to review for you in a few words how the bishops, priests, and faithful of Mexico have organized resistance and "set up a wall for the House of Israel, to stand in battle." (Ezech. XIII, 5)

18. There cannot be the slightest doubt of the fact that the Mexican hierarchy have unitedly used every means within their power to defend the liberty and good name of the Church. In the first place, they indited a joint pastoral letter to their people in which they proved beyond cavil that the clergy had always acted toward the rulers of the Republic motivated by a love for peace, with prudence and in all patience; that they had even suffered, in a spirit of almost too much tolerance, laws which were unjust; they admonished the faithful, outlining the divine constitution of the Church, that they, too, must always persevere in their religion, in such a way that they shall "obey God rather

than men" (Acts v, 19) on every occasion when anyone tries to impose on them laws which are no less contrary to the very idea of law and do not merit the name of law, as they are inimical to the constitution and existence itself of the Church.

19. When the President of the Republic had promulgated his untimely and unjust decree of interpretation of the Constitution, by means of another joint pastoral letter the Bishops protested and pointed out that to accept such a law was nothing less than to desert the Church and hand her over a slave to the civil authorities. Even if this had been done, it was apparent to all that such an act would neither satisfy her persecutors nor stop them in the pursuit of their nefarious intentions. The Bishops in such circumstances preferred to put an end to public religious functions. Therefore, they ordered the complete suspension of every act of public worship which cannot take place without the presence of the clergy, in all the churches of their diocese, beginning the last day of July, on which day the law in question went into effect. Moreover, since the civil authorities had ordered that all the churches must be turned over to the care of laymen, chosen by the mayors of the different municipalities, and could not be held in any manner whatsoever by those who were named or designated for such an office by the bishops or priests, which act transferred the possessions of the churches from the ecclesiastical authority to that of the state, the Bishops practically everywhere interdicted the faithful from accepting a place on such committees bestowed on them by the Government and even from entering a church which was no longer under the control of the Church. In some dioceses, due to difference of time and place, other arrangements were made.

20. In spite of all this, do not think, Venerable Brothers, that the Mexican hierarchy lost any opportunity or occasion by means of which they might do their part in calming popular feelings and bringing about concord despite the fact that they distrusted, or it would be better perhaps to say despaired of, a

happy outcome to all these troubles. It is sufficient to recall in this context that the Bishops of Mexico City, who act in the capacity of procurators for their colleagues, wrote a very courteous and respectful letter to the President of the Republic in the interests of the Bishops of Huejutla, who had been arrested in a most outrageous manner and with a great display of armed force, and had been ordered taken to the city of Pachuca. The President replied to this letter by means of a hateful angry screed, a fact now become notorious. Again, when it happened that certain personages, lovers of peace, had spontaneously intervened so as to bring about a conversation between the President and the Archbishop of Morelia and the Bishop of Tabasco, the parties in question talked together for a long time and on many subjects, but with no results. Again, the Bishops debated whether they should ask the House of Representatives for the abrogation of those laws which were against the rights of the Church or if they should continue, as before, their so-called passive resistance to these laws. As a matter of fact, there existed many good reasons which seemed to them to render useless the presentation of such a petition to Congress. However, they did present the petition, which was written by Catholics quite capable of doing so because of their knowledge of law, every word of which was, moreover, weighed by the Bishops themselves with the utmost care. To this petition of the hierarchy there was added, due to the zealous efforts of the members of the Federation for the Defense of Religious Liberty, about which organization We shall have something to say later on in this letter, a great number of signatures of citizens, both men and women.

21. The Bishops had not been wrong in their anticipations of what would take place. Congress rejected the proposed petition almost unanimously, only one voting in favor of it, and the reason they alleged for this act was that the Bishops had been deprived of juridical personality, since they had already appealed in this matter to the Pope and therefore they had

proven themselves unwilling to acknowledge the laws of Mexico. Such being the facts, what remained for the Bishops to do if not to decide that, until these unjust laws had been repealed, neither they nor the faithful would change in the slightest the policy which they had adopted? The civil authorities of Mexico, abusing both their power and the really remarkable patience of the people, are now in a position to menace the clergy and the Mexican people with even more severe punishments than those already inflicted. But how are we to overcome and conquer men of this type who are committed to the use of every type of infamy, unless we are willing, as they insist, to conclude an agreement with them which cannot but injure the sacred cause of the liberty of the Church?

22. The clergy have imitated the truly wonderful example of constancy given them by the Bishops and have themselves in turn given no less brilliant an example of fortitude through all the tedious changes of the great conflict. This example of extraordinary virtue on their part has been a great comfort to Us. We have made it known to the whole Catholic world and We praise them because "they are worthy." (Apoc. III, 4) And in this special context, when We recall that every imaginable artifice was employed, that all the power and vexatious tactics of our adversaries had but one purpose, to alienate both the clergy and people from their allegiance to the hierarchy and to this Apostolic See, and that despite all this only one or two priests, from among the four thousand, betrayed in a shameful manner their holy office, it certainly seems to Us that there is nothing which We cannot hope for from the Mexican clergy.

23. As a matter of fact, We behold these priests standing shoulder to shoulder, obedient and respectful to the commands of their prelates despite the fact that to obey means in the majority of cases serious dangers for themselves, for they must live from their holy office, and since they are poor and do not themselves possess anything and the Church cannot support

them, they are obliged to live bravely in poverty and in misery; they must say Mass in private; they must do all within their power to provide for the spiritual needs of their flocks, to keep alive and increase the flame of piety in those round about them; moreover, by their example, counsels and exhortations, they must lift the thoughts of their fellow citizens to the highest ideals and strengthen their wills so that they, too, will persevere in their passive resistance. Is it any wonder, then, that the wrath and blind hatred of our enemies are directed principally and before all else against the priesthood? The clergy, on their side, have not hesitated to go to prison when ordered, and even to face death itself with serenity and courage. We have heard recently of something which surpasses anything as yet perpetrated under the guise of these wicked laws, and which, as a matter of fact, sounds the very depths of wickedness, for We have learned that certain priests were suddenly set upon while celebrating Mass in their own homes or in the homes of friends, that the Blessed Eucharist was outraged in the basest manner, and the priests themselves carried off to prison.

24. Nor can We praise enough the courageous faithful of Mexico who have understood only too well how important it is for them that a Catholic nation in matters so serious and holy as the worship of God, the liberty of the Church, and the eternal salvation of souls should not depend upon the arbitrary will and audacious acts of a few men, but should be governed under the mercy of God only by laws which are just, which are conformable to natural, divine, and ecclesiastical law.

25. A word of very special praise is due those Catholic organizations, which during all these trying times have stood like soldiers side to side with the clergy. The members of these organizations, to the limit of their power, not only have made provisions to maintain and assist their clergy financially, they also watch over and take care of the churches, teach catechism to the children, and like sentinels stand guard to warn the clergy

when their ministrations are needed so that no one may be deprived of the help of the priest. What We have just written is true of all these organizations. We wish, however, to say a word in particular about the principal organizations, so that each may know that it is highly approved and even praised by the Vicar of Jesus Christ.

26. First of all We mention the Knights of Columbus, an organization which is found in all the states of the Republic and which fortunately is made up of active and industrious members who, because of their practical lives and open profession of the Faith, as well as by their zeal in assisting the Church, have brought great honor upon themselves. This organization promotes two types of activities which are needed now more than ever. In the first place, the National Sodality of Fathers of Families, the program of which is to give a Catholic education to their own children, to protect the rights of Christian parents with regard to education, and in cases where children attend the public schools to provide for them a sound and complete training in their religion. Secondly, the Federation for the Defense of Religious Liberty, which was recently organized when it became clear as the noonday sun that the Church was menaced by a veritable ocean of troubles. This Federation soon spread to all parts of the Republic. Its members attempted, working in harmony and with assiduity, to organize and instruct Catholics so that they would be able to present a united invincible front to the enemy.

27. No less deserving of the Church and the fatherland as the Knights of Columbus have been and still are, We mention two other organizations, each of which has, following its own program, a special relation to what is known as "Catholic Social Action." One is the Catholic Society of Mexican Youth, and the other, the Union of Catholic Women of Mexico. These two sodalities, over and above the work which is special to each of them, promote and do all they can to have others promote the

activities of the above-mentioned Federation for the Defense of Religious Liberty. Without going into details about their work, with pleasure We desire to call to your attention, Venerable Brothers, but a single fact. Namely, that all the members of these organizations, both men and women, are so brave that, instead of fleeing danger, they go out in search of it, and even rejoice when it falls to their share to suffer persecution from the enemies of the Church. What a beautiful spectacle this, that is thus given to the world, to angels, and to men! How worthy of eternal praise are such deeds! As a matter of fact, as We have pointed out above, many individuals, members either of the Knights of Columbus, or officers of the Federation of the Union of Catholic Women of Mexico, or of the Society of Mexican Youth, have been taken to prison handcuffed, through the public streets, surrounded by armed soldiers, locked up in foul jails, harshly treated, and punished with prison sentences or fines. Moreover, Venerable Brothers, and in narrating this We can scarcely keep back Our tears, some of these young men and boys have gladly met death, the rosary in their hands and the name of Christ King on their lips. Young girls, too, who were imprisoned, were criminally outraged, and these acts were deliberately made public in order to intimidate other young women and to cause them the more easily to fail in their duty toward the Church.

28. No one, surely, Venerable Brothers, can hazard a prediction or foresee in imagination the hour when the good God will bring to an end such calamities. We do know this much: The day will come when the Church of Mexico will have respite from this veritable tempest of hatred, for the reason that, according to the words of God "there is no wisdom, there is no prudence, there is no counsel against the Lord" (Prov. XXI, 30) and "the gates of hell shall not prevail" (Matt. XVI, 18) against the Spotless Bride of Christ.

29. The Church which, from the day of Pentecost, has been destined here below to a never-ending life, which went forth

from the upper chamber into the world endowed with the gifts and inspirations of the Holy Spirit, what has been her mission during the last twenty centuries and in every country of the world if not, after the example of her Divine Founder, "to go about doing good"? (Acts X, 38) Certainly this work of the Church should have gained for her the love of all men; unfortunately the very contrary has happened as her Divine Master Himself predicted (Matt. X, 17, 25) would be the case. At times the barque of Peter, favored by the winds, goes happily forward; at other times it appears to be swallowed up by the waves and on the point of being lost. Has not this ship always aboard the Divine Pilot who knows when to calm the angry waves and the winds? And who is it but Christ Himself Who alone is all-powerful, who brings it about that every persecution which is launched against the faithful should react to the lasting benefit of the Church? As St. Hilary writes, "it is a prerogative of the Church that she is the vanquisher when she is persecuted, that she captures our intellects when her doctrines are questioned, that she conquers all at the very moment when she is abandoned by all." (St. Hilary of Poitiers *De Trinitate*, Bk. VII, No. 4)

30. If those men who now in Mexico persecute their brothers and fellow citizens for no other reason than that these latter are guilty of keeping the laws of God, would only recall to memory and consider dispassionately the vicissitudes of their country as history reveals them to us, they must recognize and publicly confess that whatever there is of progress, of civilization, of the good and the beautiful, in their country is due solely to the Catholic Church. In fact every man knows that after the introduction of Christianity into Mexico, the priests and religious especially, who are now being persecuted with such cruelty by an ungrateful government, worked without rest and despite all the obstacles placed in their way, on the one hand by the colonists who were moved by greed for gold and on the other by the natives who were still barbarians, to promote greatly in those vast regions both the splendor of the worship of God and the benefits

of the Catholic religion, works and institutions of charity, schools and colleges for the education of the people and their instruction in letters, the sciences, both sacred and profane, in the arts and the crafts.

31. One thing more remains for Us to do, Venerable Brothers, namely, to pray and implore Our Lady of Guadalupe, heavenly patroness of the Mexican people, that she pardon all these injuries and especially those which have been committed against her, that she ask of God that peace and concord may return to her people. And if, in the hidden designs of God that day which We so greatly desire is far distant, may she in the meantime console her faithful children of Mexico and strengthen them in their resolve to maintain their liberty by the profession of their Faith.

32. In the meanwhile, as an augury of the grace of God and as proof of Our fatherly love, We bestow from Our heart on you, Venerable Brothers, and especially on those bishops who rule the Church of Mexico, on all your clergy and your people, the Apostolic Blessing.

Given at Rome, at St. Peter's, on the eighteenth day of November, in the year 1926, the fifth of Our Pontificate.

Pius XI

APPENDIX III

FRANCIS MCCULLAGH (1874-1956)

F RANCIS McCullagh, journalist and writer, was born in 1874 in Omagh, Co. Tyrone, in the north of Ireland, the son of a publican. Educated at the Christian Brother's School in Omagh, he planned to become a journalist. His first brief job was in Liverpool, followed by a short spell with a Catholic newspaper in Bradford, after which he decided to return to Ireland, where he attended St Columb's College, Derry, as a seminarian, to determine whether or not he had a vocation for the priesthood. He decided that he didn't, and left to pursue what proved to be a lifetime career in journalism and writing, beginning with an appointment with the *Scottish Catholic Observer* in Glasgow, followed by work in Colombia, Ceylon, and then a move to Bangkok. This was but the beginning of a lifetime pattern of challenging and often dangerous assignments with which McCullagh was to become identified.

McCullagh taught himself Japanese, necessary for his first editorial appointment based in Japan, and Russian for conversing with a Russian acquaintance, and no doubt for its usefulness to him as a journalist. It was not long before he found himself reporting on the Russo-Japanese War for the *New York Herald*. His reputation grew as did the demand for his services, with ongoing assignments covering the Turkish civil war of 1909, the Portuguese revolution of 1910, various Balkan wars, hostilities in Morocco, and the Italian invasion of Tripoli in 1911. On the outbreak of World War I in 1914, he was sent as a journalist to the Eastern front, reporting from the Russian side. After a year he enlisted in the Royal Irish Fusiliers, was posted to Gallipoli and spent most of the war in Military Intelligence. He was then transferred to the British Military Mission in Siberia, concerned with assisting the White Russians in their struggle against the Bolsheviks. In early 1919 he was taken prisoner by the Bolsheviks, but after persuading his captors that he was a British journalist, was released almost immediately, thus legitimising his subsequent travel throughout Russia. However it was only a few months before he found himself again under arrest and this time detained in a Moscow prison. He was subsequently released under the terms of the Brest-Litovsk agreement, and repatriated to Britain.

As well as reporting from the frontline for both American and British national newspapers, McCullagh wrote numerous articles and several books on his experiences. He was a renowned and highly respected 'War Correspondent' and public speaker, whose exploits have been largely forgotten over recent years. He deserves to be remembered as an exceptional journalist, which he was, whose remarkable life and achievements reflect a man of extraordinary physical and moral courage, underpinned at all times by a deep love and respect for his Catholic faith.

His books include:
– *Italy's War for a Desert* (1912), a critical account of Italy's invasion of Tripoli in 1911/12;
– *A Prisoner of the Reds* (1921), relating his experiences as a prisoner of the Bolsheviks from January to April, 1920;
– *The Bolshevik Persecution of Christianity* (1924), revealing the ruthless crushing of the Orthodox Church, and a detailed synopsis of the infamous State trial of Catholic prelates and priests in the early 1920s;
– *Red Mexico* (1928), an account of the persecution of Catholics and the Catholic Church in Mexico in the 1920s, and the critical role of the United States government;

– *In Franco's Spain* (1937), reporting of events in the Spanish Civil War (1936-39), from a Nationalist viewpoint. This was to be the last major conflict covered by McCullagh.

Prior to the outbreak of World War II, McCullagh left his home in Paris and moved to White Plains, New York, where he lived for the remainder of his life. He maintained contact with old friends and the Irish community, but in 1953 was taken to the Bellevue Mental Hospital, White Plains, suffering from dementia, where he was to remain until his death in 1956. Obituaries were published in the *Times*, *New York Times*, and *Irish Independent*, also local Tyrone and Derry newspapers.

Brian Crowe